Fifty Key Thinkers in P

The new edition of *Fifty Key Thinkers in Psychology* introduces the life, thought, work and impact of some of the most influential figures who have shaped and developed modern psychology, considering a more diverse history of the discipline.

The revised text includes new biographies, histories and overviews of the work from scientists and scholars such as Alfred Alder, Isabel Briggs Myers, Katherine Cook Briggs and Karen Horney, as well as major re-writes of the works of Freud, Binet and Jung, and some of the more controversial characters such as Charles Galton and Hans Eysenck. Exploring the often overlooked but significant contributions of black, Jewish and Eastern scholars to the discipline, this new edition looks to address the historically imbalanced focus of particular key thinkers and begins unpicking the impact that race and gender had on the direction and advancement of the field. The book explores contributions to the black psychology movement from George Herman Canady to Mamie Phipps Clark and Kenneth Bancroft Clark, the enormous contribution of Chinese psychologist Jing Qicheng, and some of the many great psychologists whose families were part of the waves of Jewish emigration to the United States escaping oppression, persecution and economic hardship, including Walter Mischel, Cary Cooper and Daniel Kahneman.

This fascinating and informative guide is an invaluable resource for those studying, working in, or who simply want to find out more about psychology, suitable for both students and the lay reader alike.

Alexandra Forsythe is Professor of Applied Psychology at the University of Wolverhampton, UK, Chartered Psychologist and Chair of Europe's largest governing body for business psychologists, the Association for Business Psychology. Alex has been awarded two national awards for outstanding impact on student outcomes: Principal Fellow of the Higher Education Academy and the National Teaching Fellowship.

Fifty Key Thinkers in Psychology

Second Edition

Alexandra Forsythe

Routledge
Taylor & Francis Group
LONDON AND NEW YORK

Cover image: © Getty Images

Second edition published 2023
by Routledge
4 Park Square, Milton Park, Abingdon, Oxon OX14 4RN

and by Routledge
605 Third Avenue, New York, NY 10158

Routledge is an imprint of the Taylor & Francis Group, an informa business

© 2023 Alexandra Forsythe

The right of Alexandra Forsythe to be identified as author of this
work has been asserted in accordance with sections 77 and 78 of the
Copyright, Designs and Patents Act 1988.

First edition published by Routledge 2004

British Library Cataloguing-in-Publication Data
A catalogue record for this book is available from the British Library

Library of Congress Cataloging-in-Publication Data
A catalog record for this book has been requested

ISBN: 978-1-032-13426-0 (hbk)
ISBN: 978-1-032-13428-4 (pbk)
ISBN: 978-1-003-22917-9 (ebk)

DOI: 10.4324/9781003229179

Typeset in Garamond
by Apex CoVantage, LLC

For my mum, for reminding me that anything is possible

Contents

Introduction

Welcome to the 2nd Edition of *Fifty Key Thinkers in Psychology*, where I have complied the biographies, history and an overview of the work of the greats from our discipline. Students of psychology often ask, what is the point of studying the history of our field, and as such, what is the point of a book like this? Why are we still exploring the contribution of controversial characters and research in psychology?

By studying our mistakes, flawed thinking and biases, we can better understand how psychology has emerged and become established as one of the most important scientific, applied, theoretical and academic disciplines. Studying our mistakes clarifies the roles that culture, society, politics, economics, current events and technology play in the development and directions that science takes. Our mistakes teach us much about how to think critically and perform research, which is theoretically, empirically and ethically sound.

Deciding who should be included in a text such as this is always a challenge. If you think of 50 key thinkers as the top 50 in pop music, it is indeed in need of an update. What was number one in 1954 is not necessarily relevant to this week's top 50. However, the classics still live on, and some of the original key thinkers will still be relevant.

The revised text includes new content from scientists and scholars such as Alfred Alder, Kenneth and Mamie Clark, Daniel Berlyne, George Herman Canady, Cary Cooper, Daniel Goleman, Howard Gardner, Henry H. Goddard, Daniel Kahneman, Lewis Goldberg, Starke Hathaway, Karen Horney, George Kelly, Elizabeth Loftus, Walter Mischel, Henry Murray, Isabel Briggs Myers, Katherine Cook Briggs, Jing Qicheng, John Carlyle Ravens, Hermann Rorschach, as well as major re-writes of the works of Freud, Binet and Jung, and also some of the more controversial characters such as Charles Galton and Hans Eysenck. In this new text, we also attempt to address the balance

DOI: 10.4324/9781003229179-1

of the book to honour the impact of female, black, Jewish and Eastern scholars on our discipline and begin unpicking the impact that race and gender had on the direction and advancement of the field.

The inclusion of Elizabeth Loftus, Eleanor Maccoby, Karen Horney, Isabel Briggs Myers and Katherine Cook Briggs represents a breakthrough from other mainstream texts on this subject. Today, women represent the most substantial proportion of the undergraduate curriculum, but as in many areas of psychology, they do not feature heavily in the key-thinker literature. Horney provided feminist leadership to psychology, challenging the ways in which sexist values had been internalised. Briggs Myers and Cook Briggs are so effortlessly criticised within academic psychology that it is almost impossible to understand how they could have developed the world's most popular psychometric test. I hope that by raising the profile of their work and lives, the future students of psychology will be inspired to work in an area that has such an exceptional capacity to improve the lives of others.

Robert L. Williams has profiles of outstanding black psychologists in his text documenting the history of black psychology, including much important biographical and autobiographical content which focuses on founders, presidents and elders of the movement. William's focus is post 1960s and the formation of the Association of Black Psychologists. We now know much more about the lives and contributions of black psychologist's post 1960s; the black psychology movement took great efforts to document significant aspects of their lives and most psychologists, or their families were still alive to provide that information. Although there are some black psychologists that predate the 1960s, they were virtually unheard of and for those who were working as psychologists, not many people took the time to record much about their lives and careers. As such the biographical content may not be as extensive. For this text, I have selected George Herman Canady, Mamie Phipps Clark and Kenneth Bancroft Clark for their significant contributions towards addressing the impact that attitudes and behaviours had on children – Canady for his insights into the impact that race had on the performance of children on psychological tests, and the Clarks for their advocation of the whole child approach to fostering development and learning.

The Chinese psychologist Jing Qicheng has been included for his enormous contribution to the fields of cognition and developmental psychology and for his capacity to be the spokesman for Chinese psychology. He questioned and directed the field towards reform, drawing closer Eastern and Western psychology, and in so doing promoted exchange between China and the rest of the world.

Additionally, psychologists such as Walter Mischel, Cary Cooper and Daniel Kahneman join ranks of the many great psychologists whose families were part of the waves of Jewish emigration to the United States. They or their parents were escaping persecution, restrictive laws and economic hardship. Once deemed a lesser people, these individuals and their children would go on and study how people differed from one another, in many cases making significant advances in educational and societal reform. The sheer impact that the Jewish community has had on the field of individual differences is remarkable; their psychology has helped us all to talk, to be understood and to change.

1 Alfred Alder (February 7, 1870– May 28, 1937)

Founder of the psychology school of individual psychology, and the isolation of the foundations of personality development, particularly ideas around inferiority.

Alfred Alder was born in Rudolfsheim, Austria, near Vienna. Alfred's father was a Jewish grain merchant, a job which provided only a modest income to support his seven children who were sickly. Their diets were poor, and low levels of vitamin D and calcium thwarted normal bone development, resulting in rickets. Alfred could not walk until he was 4 years old and suffered from spasms of the epiglottis, a condition which can be caused by infection or injury. If Alfred became even slightly agitated, he would suffer from acute shortness of breath. At the age of 5, he almost died from pneumonia. His little brother had died the year before, and the experience was so traumatic that he made a decision to become a doctor.

Alfred found academic competition a struggle. He was popular, outgoing and active but was persistently failing in his examinations. His father, by way of 'encouragement', threatened to remove him entirely from school and make him an apprentice to the local shoemaker. Immediately, Alfred's grades improved but never to a level that would enable him to obtain his certification.

Despite his poor grades, Alfred was accepted into the University of Vienna to study medicine in 1888. His ambitions of becoming a doctor were strong. Such a career would bring the much-needed opportunities to his family, but Alfred found the training uninspiring. He was bored by the long hours of study, experimentation and diagnosis. These were distractions from what he really wanted to do – socialise with friends, one of which included the young Leo Trotsky, in the cafes of Vienna. Constantly distracted, Alfred barely passed his examinations. He did, however, manage to graduate in 1895. His first position was as

DOI: 10.4324/9781003229179-2

a volunteer at the Poliklinik, a clinic that focused on supporting impoverished patients suffering from disorders and diseases of the eye. Ophthalmology was an interest he shared with the Sherlock Holmes author Arthur Conan Doyle. Doyle had left Vienna only a few years previously, having spent an unproductive 3 months studying ophthalmology.

Vienna was awash with writers, philosophers, artists and musicians who were encouraging experimentation. As the century drew to a close, the Hapsburg Empire began to fragment; new liberalist demands for rights were emerging. Activists such as Else Jerusalem were prising the lid on Viennese hypocrisy: its poverty, suffering, prostitution and high suicide rates. The archaic ideas of morality and high culture were being broken down, and cafe society was central in shaping ideas about human nature, equality, social relationships and the future of Viennese culture. In this bohemian atmosphere, Alfred met Raissa Epstein, a radical force whose profound thinking impacted on the development of Alfred's thinking. Raissa, a Russian socialist and feminist, came to Vienna because women were not permitted to study topics such as biology and zoology. She helped Alder identify the contradictions that surrounded them and then to embrace socialism as the answer to poverty, oppression and lack of equality. Their political passions linked their hearts and in 1897 Alfred and Raissa married.

By 1898, Alder was formalising his position on the psychology of the human condition, publishing his holistic arguments in *The Health Book for the Tailoring Trade*. Alder argued that disease would be more effectively treated if equal consideration were given to social, economic and psychological factors. Aligning his professionalism with his values, Alder moved his practice to one of the lowliest parts of Vienna, Prater. At the end of the century, the Wiener Prater, a large public park in the Leopoldstadt District, was a long way from the beautiful Danube landscape of today. The Prater amusement park (today the oldest amusement park in the world) was establishing itself with cafes, swings and carousels and a giant Ferris wheel. Nearby the Barnum and Bailey Circus advertised: 'the greatest aerial feats and shows of strength, sword swallowers, expanding and contracting men, human pin cushions, armless and legless humans, and other things and amazing sights that could be seen nowhere else'. These acrobats and artists, capable of such extraordinary acts, would come to Alder in their sickness and weakness. Alder, grounded in his convictions for the mutual respect of all, was inspired by their strength of mind and stamina. It was in this environment that Alder began, surrounded by human exploitation and suffering, to develop what would later become his theories of overcompensation, the inferiority complex and their roles in human personality development. He published the book *Study of Organ Inferiority and Its Psychological Compensation.* This book was a study of people's self-regarded tendencies to judge themselves as deficient in some way or another, and how those inadequacies would drive their behaviours, in what Alder described as a minus or plus action.

Freud's attention was piqued. Initially viewing Alder as his disciple, Freud invited Alder to come and visit him in Vienna and join his Vienna Wednesday Society (which eventually became the Vienna Psychoanalytic Society). Freud, known for the cultivation of his devotees, until they had ideas of their own, quickly entered into a tormentous relationship with Alder. Alder disagreed with Freud on the importance of sexual development. For Alder, sexual development was only a minor influencing factor in the tapestry of developmental experiences that a child is exposed to. As the second sibling in a family of six, birth order was a major clue to a child's socialisation and goals in life. When Alder was 4 years old, his baby brother Rudolf died in bed beside him of diphtheria. This harrowing experience led to the polarisation between Alder and Freud on the notion of the death wish. For Alder, there was no death wish. The human psyche strove for significance and worth in the eyes of others; for Freud it was a battle to return to an inanimate state.

These were more than differences in scholarly opinion. The two had fundamental differences in politics and temperament. Freud's renowned temperament was to dominate, if not in fact to bully; for his version of the psychoanalytical movement to advance, there had to be complete consensus from his followers. As part of this process, Alder was expected to commit to continual self-examination with his peers. Any deviation from absolute compliance to Freud's theories was heavily criticised and could result in expulsion from the society, but Alder was rebellious and insubordinate. The environment was intolerable and by 1904, Alder had decided to leave the Wednesday Society. Perhaps feeling that it was better to have the rebellious Alder contained within the Wednesday ranks, Freud somehow persuaded Alder to stay but he was now seeing Alder's work as a serious threat to his own dominant theories of psychosocial development and the basis of personality.

The polarisation continued to escalate and fester in other areas. Fritz Wittels, Freud's friend and biographer, gave a presentation to the group on the 'natural' position of women in society. Alder found Wittels' gendered opinions objectionable and in return gave a response through his talk on the psychology of Marxism and the class struggle. Alder was now viewed as a fanatical socialist, and hostilities were barely contained. In 1912, in another attempt to keep Alder within the society, Freud offered to step down, suggesting Alder as his replacement. The group, however, voted Alder.

Alder could not face another argument and left, taking with him a small following of dedicated 'Adlerians', who then started their own society for the study of individual differences 'The Psychology of the Undivided Whole', what would become the Österreichischer Verein für Individualpsychologie. Freud would later write that he had hated Alfred Alder for over 25 years. Alder had let him down and he found people who had let him down to be the most hateful people of all.

Having put the Wednesday Society aside, Alder's fresh approach set him apart from other psychologists and soon he was enjoying success, building a movement that directly argued for holistic psychological treatment, well-being and social equality. At a time when Carl Jung was developing his ideas about psychological types, Alder had a small number of personality types that he felt were heuristic devices, that moulded personality. People who had a tendency towards the domination of others, 'the ruling type', were governed by energy forces that sought to overpower others. When their ungoverned ruling energy was turned inwards, they may be drawn into self-harming behaviours, such as addiction or suicide. When the energy source was directed outwards, they would become oppressors or sadists.

The learning type is more likely to use their energy to protect themselves. They will insulate themselves from threats and challenges. They lack energy and to survive sap the energy of others. This inability to lead a useful life leads to anxieties, obsessions and depression. The avoiding type also has such low energy that they avoid life completely, perhaps even retreating into themselves. They may end up in the most extreme situations developing psychosis.

The most useful is the social type: healthy, energised, outward-looking individuals who show an interest in others. Alder designed treatments that were designed to encourage effective social development. At its core, the Alderain method would seek to create equity between the client and the therapist. Both would work together in a collaboration to gain insight and to encourage a sense of community and responsibility as the mechanism by which to effect change, methods that would be familiar to most modern psychologists today.

The Bohemian Viennese life was interrupted in 1914 with the outbreak of World War I. Alfred was called to work as a doctor with the Austro-Hungarian Army while Raissa unwisely took the children to Russia for a holiday. They had hoped the impending war would be delayed until after their return. Russia invaded Eastern Prussia, and, with two further Russian armies ready to fight against the Austro-Hungarian forces, Raissa and the children were promptly arrested as possible traitors. They were held for 5 months until Raissa somehow managed to convince the Czar that she was a loyal Russian citizen who had been forced to marry Alfred.

On return from military service, Alfred began to apply his individual psychology in the treatment of children with behavioural problems. He established child guidance clinics to support early interventions and school involvement as the mechanisms to manage the sources of 'backwardness, delinquency, criminality and neurosis'. By 1927, 27 clinics were established across Vienna. Staffed by Alder's trainees, the Alderains would work with children, parents, teachers, doctors and social workers, building a support community to help children with emotional problems. Alder then began giving lecture tours across Europe and America with the aim of increasing global awareness of his individual psychology and the role that therapy, encouragement and pedagogy can play in improving outcomes for children.

His work was a tremendous success; he published *Understanding Human Nature*, which rapidly sold over 100,000 copies in America alone and in 1929 Alder was invited to Columbia University as Adjunct Professor. Raissa, however, was not keen to move to America. She was now an influential member of the Communist Party in Russia and a move to America was not, to her mind, a politically neutral act. Raissa's position on the move caused tension in Alder's marriage. Alder viewed her attitude as behavioural as domination, something he did not condone politically or in his personal relationship with his wife. Political changes in Europe, however, would settle the matter for the Alders.

The Jewish-Austrian population had enjoyed a period of prosperity under Franz Joseph I. The Emperor's belief that civil rights were not contingent on a people's religion had created a more equal society, but by the 1930s conservative-fascism was making life increasingly harsh; Jews were being expelled from political, economic and social life. Alder's pioneering child guidance clinics were closed, and individual psychology was at a standstill. As active socialists, Raissa and Alfred feared immanent imprisonment, so the family left Vienna for Rotterdam, where they obtained passage to America.

In America, Alder set about the promotion of his individual psychology. When not working as Professor of Medical Psychology at the Long Island College of Medicine in New York, he was touring internationally, delivering talks to mass audiences. By 1937, Alder had published more than a dozen books. He had, however, only been enjoying life in America for 2 years, when he suddenly died on a European lecturing tour. He was unwell before he left for the trip, potentially from exhaustion from his persistent self-drive, and he died on the streets of Aberdeen from a suspected heart attack. This unfortunate event was further compounded for the family when Alder's remains were lost, and, remained so for over 70 years. Alder's ashes were eventually recovered when the Vienna Individual Psychology movement set about trying to resolve the mystery. They lobbied the Austrian consul to Scotland, who eventually tied Alder's cremation down to one of only two possible sites. They were found at the Warriston Crematorium in Edinburgh, and in 2007 Alder's remains were eventually returned to Vienna for burial.

Alder's principles and values were egalitarian; he favoured equality and the right to well-being and fairness for all. He had a strong commitment to the ideas of socialism and the well-being of others, but he never became a staunch follower of communism. In later life, he was vocal in his disagreement with the oppressive and cruel tactics of Lennon and his one-time friend, Leo Trotsky. His egalitarian viewpoints would not only lead to Alfred's exit from Freud's Wednesday Society but also develop the feminist ideology of their daughter Alexandra, who went on to become an even more committed socialist and the first female neurologist in Vienna and in America. In 1935, Alexandra was appointed to Harvard, but only added to the contract research staff list as no women were given faculty positions.

Influenced by the writings of the South African philosopher and statesman Jan Smuts, Alder believed that people are not a collection of disparate elements. To be understood, people are more effectively treated as unified wholes within the context of their physical, social and economic environments. For Alder, personality is related to the 'style of life', which is our style in handling interpersonal relationships, challenges and ourselves. How you live your life is your personality:

> *The style of life of a tree is the individuality of a tree expressing itself and molding itself in an environment. We recognize a style when we see it against a background of an environment different from what we expect, for then we realize that every tree has a life pattern and is not merely a mechanical reaction to the environment.*
> (Alder, 1929, p. 90)

Alder's holism was not as thrilling or sensational as Freud's work, but Alder's approach was practical and adaptable to the realities and complexities of the human psyche. He succeeded in a world dominated by psychoanalysis to psychologists with an alternative perspective. Work that ultimately went on to influence psychologists such as Karen Horney, George Kelly and Carl Rogers.

Alfred Alder's major writings

Adler, A. (1924). *The practice and theory of individual psychology*. Oxford, UK: Harcourt, Brace.
Adler, A. (1927). *Understanding human nature*. New York: Greenberg.
Alder, A. (1929). *The science of living*. Garden City, NY.
Adler, A. (1931). *What life should mean to you*. Oxford, UK: Little, Brown.

Further reading

Grey, L. (1988). *Alfred Alder, the forgotten prophet: A vision for the 21st century*. London: Praeger.

2 Anne Anastasi (December 19, 1908–May 2, 2001)

Anastasi influenced several generations of psychologists through her immensely popular textbooks on the construction and use of psychological tests.

Anne Anastasi's Sicilian father, Anthony, died when she was 1 year old. Soon afterwards, her maternal relatives became estranged from her father's family, and she never met any of them. She was supported by her mother, Theresa Gaudiosi Anastasi, who was the office manager for the Italian newspaper *Il Progresso* and educated at home by her grandmother. She started attending public school at the age of 9 and graduated at the top of her class. Anastasi was particularly drawn to mathematics even to the point where she taught herself spherical trigonometry (the study of figures on the surface of a sphere) while a teenager. She enrolled at Barnard College (at the age of 15) intending to pursue a degree in mathematics. However, she was attracted to psychology, partly through her reading of Spearman's work on correlation coefficients – a statistical measure of the relationship between two variables. After graduating in 1928 she enrolled for a PhD at Columbia University under the supervision of Henry E. Garrett. Garrett wrote extensively on race differences in intelligence and the need for an educational system that could take those into account and was a staunch opponent of racial integration in the southern states of America. As will shortly become apparent, Anastasi took a rather different view.

While working on her doctorate she met her future husband, John Porter Foley Jr., who was also completing a PhD. Jobs were hard to come by so on completion of her doctorate in 1930 Anastasi took a position at Barnard College, New York, and Foley worked more than 200 miles away in George Washington University, Washington, DC. They were married in 1933, and a year later she was diagnosed with cancer, the treatment for which left her unable to have children. In

DOI: 10.4324/9781003229179-3

1944, Foley secured a position with the Psychological Corporation in New York City. This meant that Foley and Anastasi were able to reside full-time at the home they had purchased shortly after their marriage. It was through her husband that Anastasi became acquainted with the work and ideas of the anthropologist Franz Boas and the psychologist Jacob Kantor. Boas introduced her to his concepts of cultural relativism and historical particularism: the suggestion that differences between groups of people are the product of historical, social and geographic conditions and that each culture has a unique history, and one cannot presume the existence of general laws about how cultures change. Kantor was a behaviourist who coined his approach 'interbehaviourism' because he considered both the organism and stimulus objects surrounding it to be equally important. The significance of interactions between an organism and its environment is a key feature of Anastasi's work. She was particularly interested in process accounts of human abilities: she wanted to understand how genetic and how environmental factors influenced the development of human abilities but argued against attempts to quantify the relative contributions of each.

'Anastasi' came to be synonymous with psychometrics (the design and use of psychological tests and the application of statistical and mathematical techniques to psychological testing) and with differential psychology (the quantitative investigation of individual differences in behaviour) for several generations of students and professional psychologists because of the popularity of the numerous editions of her standard texts on the topics. Some of the earliest insights into the importance of individual differences can be found in Plato's writings. When Plato set out his vision of an ideal state, he considered one of its most important principles to be the correct assignment of individuals to the tasks to which they are best suited. More than two thousand years later, Binet and his student Victor Henri started publishing studies that constitute the first systematic examinations of the aims, scope and methods of differential psychology – the analysis of differences between individuals. Fifty years on, Anastasi published *Psychological Testing* (1954), a carefully crafted encyclopaedic introduction to psychological assessment that brought the reader through the fundamentals of test design, selection and interpretation. She worked on updates of *Psychological Testing* well into her 80s. Anastasi's intellectual influence was also due to the lucidity of her writing on complex topics and to her forthright approach to politically sensitive debates on the role of genetic and environmental influences. Her textbooks grew out of courses; she began to teach early in her career. In those texts, as in her teaching, one of her key objectives was to try to explain difficult statistical and psychological concepts in readily understandable ways. Her books and her research reflect a generalist orientation similar to that of the experimental psychologist Harry Hollingworth, in whose department at Barnard College she worked for 9 years. In *Fields of Applied Psychology* (1964), for example, the reader is introduced to a wide range of applications, from engineering psychology to clinical psychology, and considerable attention is given to interrelationships between disciplines and the importance of corroborating findings. Her interest in integrating research from diverse areas is also illustrated within the treatment of single topics, such as the formation of psychological traits, which draws from such varied data sources as animal experimentation, observations of infant behaviour, educational psychology and personality research.

In an autobiographical piece, she identified 'chance encounters and locus of control' as a theme running through her career. She illustrated these in anecdotes. For instance, her first full-time academic position arose from a chance encounter with Hollingworth – they met crossing 119th Street on Broadway. He asked whether she had plans for the fall of 1930 and on hearing she had none he offered her a position. The appointment was subsequently confirmed in a brief letter from Hollingworth. Another happy accident occurred in 1947 when she was elected President of the Eastern Psychological Association. She described her response as 'astonishment bordering on shock. . . . What caused my surprise was that I was only an assistant professor' (1988, p. 62). This discrepancy between the great esteem in which she was held by peers – she was the third woman President of the American Psychological Association – and her self-assessment of her contributions, she attributed to her single-minded focus on completing the tasks that needed to be done. In 1987, President Reagan conferred on her a National Medal of Science in recognition of her contribution to the development of differential psychology – Skinner was also honoured with a medal in the same year. Notwithstanding this and other laurels of recognition, Anastasi was not driven by a need to attain status and prestige, nor by winning the acceptance, admiration and approval of others. She was primarily motivated by a desire to pursue the tasks she had chosen for herself and to be immersed in that subject matter. Much of her work stemmed from a concern with prevalent misconceptions about psychological tests and common forms of misuse. Such misuse and misinterpretations became a problem in the 1920s and 1930s, following the development of group tests and the popularisation of fast, affordable testing. By the late 1960s, she had come to the view that psychologists

have been devoting more and more of their efforts to refining the techniques of test construction, while losing sight of the behavior they set out to measure . . . the isolation of psychometrics from other relevant areas of psychology is one of the conditions that have lead to the prevalent public hostility towards testing.

(Lindsey, 1980, p. 297)

During the 1970s, the notion that a pure, culture-free measure of intelligence, aptitude or achievement could be devised gained popularity partly because such tests seemed to offer the potential of resolving some of the disputes on racial differences in these areas. However, Anastasi argued that attempts to devise such tests were inherently flawed because they could never avoid measuring some of the effects of gender socialisation, ethnic or racial influences. This was not a particularly popular message because it clearly implied that 'pure' measures of any aspect of human psychology – intelligence, personality, aptitude or whatever – are an impossibility.

In a reflective piece, written at the age of 83, she examined the role of advanced statistical techniques in the rapprochement between mainstream experimental psychology and the psychometric tradition. She concluded that the psychometric approach – the construction and use of psychological tests – had much to offer than the experimental approach, which favoured laboratory-based studies of behaviour. Within the experimental approach, there is a tendency to regard variability in the behaviour of research participants as something of a nuisance. Anastasi took a different view:

> When dealing with human behavior, in any form and from any angle, you will encounter variability – extensive and pervasive variability. If you ignore this variability, it will come back to haunt you in the form of incorrect conclusions in basic research and wrong decisions in applied research and practice.
>
> (1991, p. 71)

Underlying much of Anastasi's writing are questions about the role of genetic and environmental factors on the development of behaviour. She was a forceful exponent of the cognitive differentiation hypothesis – the suggestion that the development of human intelligence involves a process of differentiation and specialisation of abilities as a function of age, education and other, less formal, learning experiences. This is illustrated in her analyses of the relationship between intelligence and family size; her research on creativity in children and adolescents; and a long-term project on drawings by hospitalised psychiatric patients, which suggested that many alleged signs of pathology were more closely related to educational, occupational and other aspects of an individual's experiential history than to specific pathology. She also argued that questions of heredity and environment are involved in the nature and origins of psychological traits and therefore in the interpretation of psychological test scores. Anastasi was concerned with understanding the underlying causes of ability long before models concerned with the processes of trait formation – how psychological characteristics are formed – were popular. Her books tell a convincing story of how properly constructed, well-validated and psychologically well-founded tests can prove valuable in both theoretical and applied fields, provided that the underlying socio-cultural, developmental and cognitive processes are well understood.

Anastasi's major writings

Anastasi, A. (1937). *Differential psychology*. New York and Cambridge: Macmillan.
Anastasi, A. (1954). *Psychological testing*. New York and Cambridge: Macmillan.
Anastasi, A. (1964). *Fields of applied psychology*. New York: McGraw Hill.
Anastasi, A. (1967). Psychology, psychologists, and psychological testing. *American Psychologist, 22*(4), 297–306. https://doi.org/10.1037/h0024521
Anastasi, A. (1991). The gap between experimental and psychometric orientations. *Journal of the Washington Academy of Sciences, 81*(2), 61–73. Retrieved from www.jstor.org/stable/24531448

Further reading

Hogan, J. D. (2003). Anne Anastasi: Master of differential psychology and psychometrics. In G. A. Kimble & M. Wertheimer (Eds.), *Portraits of pioneers in psychology* (Vol. 5, pp. 263–296). American Psychological Association; Lawrence Erlbaum Associates Publishers.

3   John Robert Anderson
(August 27, 1947–)

Anderson developed a computer-based system capable of simulating a wide variety of intelligent behaviour and used that system to build a tutoring system for mathematics and computer programming.

Born in Vancouver, John Robert Anderson grew up in a poor section of the city. During his childhood, he pursued several possible pathways, and his parents were supportive of them all. One of those dreams was to become a writer and that was one of his aspirations when he enrolled at the University of British Columbia. Although his High School performance was good, his progress as an undergraduate student was often characterised by poor preparation coupled with doubts about whether he was really cut out for a career in psychology. Pulling out all the stops in his final year, he graduated in 1968 at the head of his class and was awarded the Governor-General's Gold Medal. For his senior thesis, he worked with Arthur S. Reber on the perception of clicks in linguistic and non-linguistic messages. Undergraduate programmes of the 1960s typically included courses on learning theory, the psychology of language and cognitive psychology (the psychology of thinking and problem-solving), but connections between the three were few and far between. Anderson was particularly interested in the relationships between language and thought and an opportunity to pursue investigations in this area arose when he was offered a doctoral position at Stanford. That opportunity provided working relationships with Gordon Bower, who had published ground-breaking work on mathematical models of human learning; Richard Atkinson, who was working on computer-assisted instruction; Herbert Clark, who was running studies on the comprehension and use of language; and Edward Feigenbaum, who was working on knowledge-based systems. He had intended pursuing a PhD in mathematical psychology but his doctoral work, supervised by Bower, on the structure

DOI: 10.4324/9781003229179-4

of memory recall was the start of another, lifelong dream: to develop a theory of human thought processes sufficiently well specified that it could be implemented in a computer simulation. The case for such a formally specified theory has been stated by Baddeley: 'While simple qualitative conceptual models have proved very useful, one eventually reaches a point at which some form of detailed and preferably quantitative model is necessary if the concepts are to develop' (1994, p. 363). His first attempts were implemented in the FRAN (Free Recall in an Associative Network) computer simulation of memory and later the human associative memory (HAM) theory. HAM was a model of the structures and processes of human memory and dealt in detail with how human memory processes language.

After graduating from Stanford in 1972, Anderson took a position at Yale University as Assistant Professor. He remained there for a year, teaching undergraduate and graduate courses on the psychology of thinking during which time his interest in cognitive psychology broadened to include cognitive processes and structures. He moved to the University of Michigan, where Lynne Reder was a graduate student. They married in 1973 and formed a close intellectual partnership. During his 3-year stint at Michigan, his interests in language and learning developed, and he designed a computer simulation of language acquisition. His association with James G. Greeno, who was working on learning and reasoning, directed his interests to the application of cognitive psychology to education. Both developments were to become significant later in his career. During this period, he developed the HAM theory and conducted experiments that were to lead to ACT (adaptive control of thought) theory. ACT, like HAM, was a computer model of human memory but with an important extension that dealt with the ways cognitive procedures, such as problem-solving, interact with memory. His work with HAM was concentrated on developing a model of factual information or 'declarative knowledge' about the world. ACT built on this by employing an ordered set of rules called a production system. For example, if you were making a cake, the declarative knowledge would consist of the list of ingredients and the production system would be the rules dictating how they should be put together. If you are using an unfamiliar recipe, it is usually impossible to keep all of the ingredients and all of the production rules in memory at one time. ACT attempts to simulate this in a computer model of working memory – a temporary memory store where different pieces of information and rules are brought together.

When Anderson left Michigan, he returned to Yale, where he continued to develop and test the ACT theory, focusing on how past knowledge interacts with and influences the acquisition of new knowledge. John and Lynne moved to Carnegie Mellon University in the fall of 1978 where, in the company of Herb Simon and Alan Newell, the emphasis in his work shifted to computer simulation of problem-solving. Anderson uses the term 'cognitive architecture' to refer to the design and organisation of the mind and in *The Architecture of Cognition* (1983) he gave an account of the fully evolved theory, ACT* (ACT star), which he described as a theory of the basic principles of operation built into cognitive systems. It examined high-level cognition, the elements that give direction to thought such as planning, and how production systems constrain adaptive processing choices in the human cognitive system. Consider the following analogy: the quantity of declarative or factual knowledge about the world stored in a computer might be increased enormously over several years but the usefulness of that information will be limited by the rules determining how it can be combined and applied. In this sense, ACT* is a simulation of the kinds of processing limitations that constrain human problem-solving and learning.

In 1980 and 1985, Reder and Anderson had two sons, Jay and Abe. Anderson's fascination with the development of their cognitive abilities is reflected in a simulation of his eldest son's language acquisition in *The Architecture of Cognition* (1983). His earlier interest in the application of cognitive psychology to education rekindled, and he became involved in their education by tutoring them in mathematics. His attempts to develop a computer that could teach mathematics involved generating a cognitive model of the mathematical skill that was to be learned (e.g. subtraction) and emphasised the use of real-time cognitive modelling in instruction. He did this by trying to develop a set of production rules that solve a class of problems, such as subtraction problems, in the same way and at the same speed that students should solve the problems. In other words, Anderson's computer-based math tutor tried to simulate the world as a learner would understand it. A good computer model of the learner's world should be able to diagnose the sources of any errors made by the learner and then provide appropriate assistance through carefully guided instruction.

ACT* was so titled because Anderson believed that ACT theory had gone just about as far as it could. Since then, he has embarked on two major attempts to 'break' ACT theory. One of those involved the development of an intelligent computer-based tutor based on ACT theory. The basic idea was to build into the computer a model of how ACT would solve a very complex thinking task like generating proofs in geometry. The computer-based tutor used ACT's theory of skill acquisition to get the student to emulate the model stored in the computer. To Anderson's surprise, this approach to the development of computer-based tutors proved remarkably successful, and it is often cited as one of the most fruitful intelligent tutoring initiatives. His second attempt to do away with ACT theory began with a sabbatical, in 1987, to Flinders University, Australia. There he focused on how cognition might be adapted to the uncertainty that is an essential feature of any environment. He developed what he called 'rational analysis' based on the idea that to understand human thinking, it is *not* necessary to develop a theory of its mechanisms. Rather it is only necessary to understand the organisation of uncertainty – the probabilistic structure – of the problems facing the person trying to solve a problem. This led to successes in developing theories of human memory and categorisation and to a computer program capable of accounting for a wide range of data collected in studies on humans solving different kinds of problems. He went on to develop a new theory of procedural learning that incorporates rational analysis. This, the ACT-R theory, was published in *Rules of the Mind* (1993), with an accompanying ACT-R simulation on a PC disc. ACT-R emphasises the importance of practice in learning the components of any skill. Its basic assertion is that in order to learn a complex skill, each component must be mastered individually. This position contrasts with the Gestalt claim (see Wertheimer for a fuller description) that learning includes moments of insight or transformations when whole knowledge structures become reorganised or learned – akin to 'eureka!' insights when, after minutes or hours of problem-solving, a solution suddenly becomes apparent.

In his more recent work, Anderson has addressed the discrepancy between psychologists' preferences for conducting experiments on psychological effects spanning tens of milliseconds and the achievement of significant educational outcomes that may take hundreds of hours that are the concern of educationalists. His analysis recapitulates some of the issues that taxed Wundt and Bartlett, both of whom were concerned about the relationship between minuscule psychological events studied under laboratory conditions and gigantic phenomena such as language and culture. Anderson poses the question: 'Is there any reason to believe that learning can be improved by paying attention to events that are measured in tens of milliseconds?' (2002, p. 86). His answer employs Alan Newell's suggestion that there are 'four bands of cognition': biological, cognitive, rational and social. The millisecond level of analysis is situated within the biological band, whereas significant educational achievements lie within the social. Some have argued that trying to link biological processes to large-scale educational outcomes is a bridge too far, but Anderson argues for the plausibility of three smaller 'bridges' of consecutively longer spans: biological-cognitive, cognitive-rational and rational-social. He contends that learning that takes place over hundreds of hours can be meaningfully decomposed to learning

20   *John Robert Anderson*

events spanning tens of milliseconds while also recognising that further empirical work is required to underpin his arguments concerning the 'bridges' between the cognitive-rational and the rational-social bands. Using this approach, Anderson has shown how his own work on the computer simulation of the minutiae of human thought processes can be linked with much larger phenomena. The power in Anderson's approach lies in his demonstration of how a common architecture or structure might be used to perform a very wide range of cognitive tasks, from the simple to the relatively complex. The common architecture approach used in ACT contrasts with that taken by others who maintain that each mental function (e.g. memory, language, perception) has its own distinctive structure and must be studied on its own merits. Whatever the final outcome of this debate, there is general agreement that there are many other features of human memory, such as retrieval, that remain to be properly simulated. Notwithstanding this limitation, the prognosis for the future of ACT theory is not bad; it is certainly a long way off being broken.

John Robert Anderson's major writings

Anderson, J. R. (1976). *Language, memory, and thought*. New York: Lawrence Erlbaum.
Anderson, J. R. (1982). Acquisition of cognitive skill. *Psychological Review, 89*, 369–403.
Anderson, J. R. (1993). *Rules of the mind*. Lawrence Erlbaum Associates, Inc. Learning and Memory. UK: Wiley.
Anderson, J. R. (2002). Spanning seven orders of magnitude: A challenge for cognitive modeling. *Cognitive Science, 26*(1), 85–112. https://doi.org/10.1016/S0364-0213(01)00062-3
Anderson, J. R. (2007) *How Can the Human Mind Occur in the Physical Universe?* New York: Oxford University Press.
Anderson, J. R., & Bower, G. H. (1972). Recognition and retrieval processes in free recall. *Psychological Review, 79*(2), 97–123. https://doi.org/10.1037/h0033773
Singley, M. K., & Anderson, J. R. (1989). *The transfer of cognitive skill*. Cambridge, MA: Harvard University Press.

Further reading

Fodor, J. (1983). *The modularity of mind*. Cambridge, MA: MIT Press.
Kolodner, J. L. (1983). Reconstructive memory – A computer model. *Cognitive Science, 7*, 281–328.
Laird, J. E., Newell, A., & Rosenboom, P. S. (1987). SOAR: An architecture for general intelligence. *Artificial Intelligence, 33*, 1–64.
Simon, H. A. (1981). Information-processing models of cognition. *Journal of the American Society for Information Science, 32*, 364–377.

4 Alan D. Baddeley (1934–)

Baddeley developed a sophisticated theory of memory that has been fruitfully applied in a wide range of settings.

The second son of Donald and Nellie Baddeley, Alan grew up in the working-class district of Hunslet, Leeds. His father was a compositor, his mother, a homemaker. His academic performance at Cockburn High School was less than mediocre, and it was not until his mid-teens that he acquired a serious interest in academic pursuits and started to think about the possibility of going to university. His ambition to enter either Oxford or Cambridge was largely motivated by a desire to play rugby for one or the other, but this was thwarted by their lack of interest in enrolling him. Thoughts about taking a degree in philosophy were weighed against the poor employment prospects after graduation, but psychology offered an attractive compromise, and he was offered a place at University College London. The American experimental psychobiologist Roger W. Russell had been appointed to the chair in 1950 and provided Baddeley with an introduction to both the North American and British tradition. After graduating, he went on to complete an MA at Princeton, based on work on a cognitive approach to secondary reinforcement in rats – a perspective that favours the idea that animals are capable of creating crude but effective representations, such as memories, of things in their environment. He returned to England only to find jobs as scarce as ever, and he spent some time as a hospital porter and schoolteacher. Talking of an opportunity to study the beneficial effects of alcohol at the Burden Neurological Institute, Bristol – it was to be funded by Guinness the brewers – appeared to offer many attractions but the post never materialised. However, he secured a position at the Medical Research Council's Applied Psychology Unit (APU), financed by the Post Office, which was funding research on the design of postal codes. It was during

DOI: 10.4324/9781003229179-5

this 5-year stint at the APU that he married Hilary Anne White; they had three sons one of whom, Roland, pursued a career in psychology and computational neuroscience. Time at the APU (at that time directed by Broadbent) was followed by a period as Lecturer and Reader at Sussex University. He was joined at Sussex by Graham Hitch, his first post-doctoral fellow, and they commenced a career-long collaboration on memory. A sabbatical at the University of California offered opportunities to collaborate with George Mandler, who was working on structural and organisational factors in memory, and Donald Norman who was working on memory and attention. On returning to the UK, Baddeley took up a Chair at Stirling University. This was a short appointment – just 2 years – because Baddeley took the post at a time when Stirling's plans for expansion were annulled by the Government's policy to curtail public expenditure in universities. When Broadbent retired from the APU, Baddeley returned to Cambridge where he served as Director between 1974 and 1995. He then moved to the position of Professor of Psychology at the University of Bristol. Although Baddeley's name is inexorably linked with the study of memory both within the discipline of psychology and in the public mind (a feat attributable to his capacity to communicate complex ideas in a non-technical style that engages the lay reader), he has also made valuable contributions in the fields of language development and breakdown, developmental disorders and cognitive aspects of rehabilitation. Some of this work (e.g. on Alzheimer's disease) has included research collaborations with his wife Hilary.

Baddeley's first appointment at the APU sparked his interest in human memory and in the application of psychology outside laboratory settings. While a graduate student, he became interested in diving and was intrigued by the problems of measuring diver performance in the open sea and continues to work in this area. An interest in short-term and working memory came from a project where he tried, unsuccessfully, to develop ways of evaluating the quality of telephone lines. In one study, he used immediate memory for similar and dissimilar words, and was struck by the robustness of the phonological similarity effect. He discovered that similarity of meaning had a much less powerful effect than phonological similarity in immediate memory, while for long-term learning exactly the opposite occurred, with phonological similarity being unimportant and semantic similarity dominant. This finding led him to regard memory as having separate long-term memory (LTM) and short-term memory (STM) components. A similar conclusion came from collaborative work with Elizabeth Warrington on amnesic patients who showed normal performance on a STM task but grossly impaired functioning on a task requiring LTM.

Baddeley was publishing his theory of memory at a time when the simple dichotomous view of memory as comprising a system of interlocking but separate storages, short-term and long-term memory, had been superseded by Fergus Craik's levels of processing account. According to Craik, stimulus information is processed at multiple levels simultaneously, depending upon its characteristics. The 'deeper' something is processed, the more it will be remembered. For instance, information that involves strong visual images or many associations with existing experience and knowledge will be processed at a deeper level. While regarding this approach as a useful re-conceptualisation of earlier findings on the role of coding in memory, Baddeley's approach was to accept the limitations of earlier unitary concepts of STM proposed by Broadbent and others, and to elaborate it into a multi-component model of working memory. Baddeley and Hitch (1974) proposed that STM comprised at least three components: a central executive and two subsidiary systems – the articulatory loop (later re-named the phonological loop) and the visuo-spatial scratch-pad. The central executive is responsible for organising and planning cognitive activities and is intimately involved in processes to do with understanding, planning and the control of actions. Brain injury to the frontal lobes is reflected in damage to the central executive, as indicated by evidence showing that people who suffer such injury endure particular difficulties structuring and controlling their actions. The visuo-spatial scratch-pad is that part of the system responsible for visual mental imagery and is so called to accommodate evidence indicating that mental images appear to have both visual and spatial properties. The phonological loop allows speech-based information to be available to the central executive for extended periods of time but, rather like an old-fashioned looped tape recording, the quantity of information it can hold is quite limited. Evidence supporting the existence of neurological processes underpinning the phonological loop can be found in studies of people with brain damage who manifest specific deficits in memory span without total loss of short-term memory.

While the central executive is the most important component of the model, it has proved least tractable. Attempts to fractionate the attentional control mechanism have postulated a hypothetical split between the capacity to focus attention (switch focus) and to divide attention across two concurrent tasks. Studies of patients with Alzheimer's disease suggest that dual-task performance is markedly impaired in a manner consistent with Baddeley's predictions. Other evidence does not fit the model, such as that of a densely amnesic patient who retained a capacity to play bridge, even to the point of remembering the contract and the cards played earlier in the hand. Cases of this type point to the existence of some type of storage involving the temporary activation of long-term representations in order to create and maintain novel cognitive structures – something akin to long-term working memory (Baddeley & Hitch, 2000). In order to accommodate the growing corpus of evidence bearing on the operation of the central executive, Baddeley has postulated a fourth component of working memory – the Episodic Buffer. This is hypothesised to be a limited capacity system that provides temporary storage of information held in a multi-modal code. It is thought to be capable of binding information from the subsidiary systems, and from long-term memory, into a unitary episodic representation. Conscious effort is required to retrieve information from the buffer. This expansion of the model places greater emphasis on understanding processes of information integration rather than on the segregated analysis of the subsystems. In so doing, it provides a more robust theoretical base from which to fractionate the more complex aspects of executive control in working memory.

The Baddeley and Hitch model has proved both robust and fruitful, being applied to a range of situations from the analysis of adult reading to the breakdown of memory in aphasic patients, and from the development of memory in children to the memory deficit of patients suffering from senile dementia. The model works well because it allows continuous theoretical development based on empirical research, as illustrated by the addition of the Episodic Buffer, and offers a robust model that is applicable to a wide range of real-world problems. Ever concerned with the need to refine and elaborate the model, Baddeley concluded thus:

> Postulating a new component after 25 years does not solve the deep and important problems underlying the issues tackled. It does however focus attention on the need for our working memory model to be able to account for the integration of information from multiple sources.
>
> (2000, p. 135)

Alan Baddeley's major writings

Baddeley, A. D. (1976). *The psychology of memory*. New York: Basic Books.
Baddeley, A. D. (1978). The trouble with levels: A re-examination of Craik and Lockhart's framework for memory research. *Psychological Review, 85*(3), 139–152.
Baddeley, A. D. (1982). *Your memory: A user's guide*. London: Penguin.
Baddeley, A. D. (1986). *Working memory*. Oxford: Clarendon Press.
Baddeley, A. D. (1996). Exploring the central executive. *Quarterly Journal of Experimental Psychology, 49*, 5–28.

Baddeley, A. D. (2000). The episodic buffer: A new component of working memory? *Trends in Cognitive Sciences, 4*, 417–423.

Baddeley, A. D., & Hitch, G. J. (1974). Working memory. In G. A. Bower (Ed.), *Recent advances in learning and motivation* (Vol. 8, pp. 47–89). New York: Academic Press.

Baddeley, A. D., & Hitch, G. J. (2000). Development of working memory: Should the Pascual-Leone and the Baddeley and Hitch models be merged? *Journal of Experimental Child Psychology, 77*, 128–137.

Further reading

Collins, A. F., Gathercole, S. E., Conway, M. A., & Morris, P. E. (Eds.). (1995). *Theories of memory I*. Psychology Press.

Conway, M. A., Gathercole, S. E., & Cornoldi, C. (Eds.). (1998). *Theories of memory II*. Psychology Press.

Tulving, E., & Craik, F. M. (Eds.). (2000). *The Oxford handbook of memory*. Oxford: Oxford University Press.

5 Mamie Phipps Clark (1917–1983) and Kenneth Bancroft Clark (1914–2005)

The Clark's worked to correct the impact that attitudes and behaviours towards race had on children. They were advocates for integration and a whole child approach to addressing the compounded impact of poor housing, education, social and economic segregation, and family breakdown.

1920s Harlem was a progressive world of publishing houses, visual arts, scholars, blues music, gay culture and feminism. Artists, writers and intellectuals created a community still described today as the place that shifted the image of African Americans from uneducated peasants to cosmopolitan sophistication. Growing confidence, self-determination and even militancy shaped racial consciousness and progressiveness that was both symbolic and real. However, by the time the stock market crashed in 1929, the black population has swollen to a point that 215,00 humans were crammed into each square mile. Buildings were barely habitable, unemployment rates doubled, and life expectancy fell. Harlem was an unhealthy place to live. Racism was as pervasive as tuberculosis, cancer and accidents, with devastating consequences for Harlem's 'near delinquent' children.

Hundreds of children who should have been given institutional care were incarcerated in prisons or left neglected because of the refusal of agencies to accept children of colour. There was an epidemic of child poverty, delinquency, maladjustment, trauma and discrimination, and where help was available the methods were often punitive. Little improved until the end of World War II, when finally, philanthropists and professionals in psychiatry and social welfare began lobbying hard for an end to the inhumanity. Clinics that specialised in child guidance were needed for the diagnosis and treatment of children who were becoming permanently lost to their community.

In 1945, two young psychologists from Columbia Kenneth Bancroft Clark and Mamie Phipps Clark approached almost every social service

DOI: 10.4324/9781003229179-6

agency in New York City with a modest proposal – that the limited mental health programmes in Harlem be expanded to provide social work, psychological evaluation and remediation for the children of Harlem. Through their applied psychological approach, the Clarks aimed to build children's self-esteem so that they could better cope with life in the slums and issues such as lack of privacy and discrimination. Objections to the Clarks plans were, however, ample. It was considered both that there was adequate provision to meet the needs of the Harlem community and that as 'mere' psychologists, the Clarks were ill qualified to run an institution. Rapidly realising their approach was not going to work, the Clarks concluded that they may as well open the clinic themselves. As such, on March 1, 1946, the Northside Centre for Child Development was born along with a lifelong battle between the psychologists and the psychiatrists who believed they should be running the show.

Kenneth Bancroft Clark was born in the Canal Zone of Panama in 1914. His mother Miriam and father Arthur were both Jamaicans. Arthur was chief timekeeper for the Panama Agencies Company and the Grace Steamship Company, and Miriam would later become one of the first black women to become a shop steward for the International Ladies Garment Workers Union. Arthur and his wife Miriam separated when the children were very young, and to secure the best possible education for the children, Miriam moved Kenneth, aged 4 and his 2-year-old sister Beulah to New York. The family lived in a predominantly white area in the west side of Harlem. His schooling was strict, with teachers expecting the same level of performance from all children regardless of their skin colour. Kenneth recalled never having any memorable issue with race until, in fifth grade, a black teacher joined the school. He was so proud and joyful at seeing this black teacher that he went home and told his mother. However, the pattern of integration in Harlem was starting to change. Slowly, fewer and fewer white children attended school, the area was increasingly becoming a black neighbourhood and Kenneth was becoming increasingly aware of a segregated way of life. By the time he graduated Junior High School, there was only one white child in his class.

Resisting the strong steer given to him by his guidance counsellor to pursue a vocation, Kenneth entered George Washington High School, eventually graduating in the top of his class. Opportunities were, however, limited for black high-school graduates in the early 1930s. Most colleges practised open discrimination admitting few, if at all any, black students. Kenneth eventually chose Howard University, an elite African American university which became central to the early civil rights movement. Kenneth was taught by an array of eminent black scholars, who were focused not only on their subject matter but also on the teaching of values and the perspective of life and race through activism for racial justice, social and economic reform. In particular, the eminent leader in educational reform Francis Cecil Sumner had a substantive influence on Kenneth's thinking. Sumner was the first African American to receive a PhD and the first African American President of the American Psychological Society. Sumner's work focused on refuting racist and biased theories that were commonly used to conclude that African Americans were inferior, work that he found throughout his career was impossible to fund. Kenneth referred to Sumner as being his intellectual father (Clark, 1938):

> *he didn't just teach psychology. He taught integrity. And, although he led the way for other Blacks in psychology, Sumner would permit no nonsense about there being anything like 'Black Psychology' -any more than he would have allowed any nonsense about 'Black astronomy.' In this and many other ways, Sumner was a model for me. In fact, he has always been my standard when I evaluate myself.*
> (Clark quoted in Hentoff, 1982, p. 45)

After a rejection from Cornell University, citing that Kenneth would be 'uncomfortable or unhappy' with the close and intimate work of psychology with faculty and students', Kenneth eventually became the first African American to study for a PhD in psychology at Columbia University. Following graduation, however, Kenneth found it impossible to secure a position at Columbia or any other elite university. There seemed to be an assumption that as a black man, Kenneth would automatically seek a post that would support the education and development of 'his' people at a black college. Both out of guilt and the challenges of securing a position elsewhere, Kenneth accepted a position at Hampton Institute.

Mamie Phipps (Clark) grew up in the spa town of Hot Springs, Arkansas, where her West Indian father managed a hotel and spa and practised medicine for the town's black citizens. Mamie had a middle-class lifestyle in a largely liberal town, which helped to insulate her from the worst of racial segregation. While her family's position helped her cross more lines than the average African American, she still had to learn how to navigate the 'dos' and the 'do nots' of a segregated society, which bathroom to use, where she could travel to and where she ought to avoid.

Mamie was just 16 years of age when she enrolled at Howard in 1934. Her plan was to study mathematics and eventually become a teacher, but with the help of a young teaching assistant called Kenneth Clark, Mamie soon realised that her true passion was for the social sciences. Psychology would satisfy not only her intellectual curiosity but also her ambition to work with children. Kenneth and Mamie became engaged in 1937, and following sustained protests from Mamie's parents, they eloped to be married the following year. Married students were not permitted at Howard University and so the marriage was kept a secret until Mamie's graduation. After her graduation, Mamie took up a position at the Washington law offices of the pioneering civil rights attorney Charles Huston and began plans with Kenneth Clark for her master's degree at Columbia.

Research

Inspired by Ruth and Gene Horowitz's work with preschool children on self-identification, Mamie focused her thesis on issues of race and identity in children. Securing access to 300 African American children, Mamie went on to make some important observations about the development of racial consciousness. Nursery school children were shown line drawings of coloured and white children, along with images of different animals; very young children would often choose animals as their personal depiction. With age, children would increasingly choose images that were more like them and by the age of 4, they were able to accurately identify themselves as black or white.

Impressed by the magnitude of the findings, Max Meenes offered to have Mamie's thesis presented at the meeting of the American Psychological Society. Realising that this presentation while prestigious, would in all likelihood be given by Meenes at the expense of credit to the Clarks, Kenneth and Mamie rapidly turned their work into a series of academic papers that became instrumental in securing funding from the Rosenwald Foundation to explore racial identity through what would later become known as the coloured dolls test.

By asking a series of questions,

- *show me the doll that you like the best or that you'd like to play with.*
- *show me the doll that is the 'nice' doll.*
- *Show me the doll that looks 'bad.*
- *give me the doll that looks like a white child.*
- *give me the doll that looks like a coloured child.*
- *give me the doll that looks like a Negro child.*
- *give me the doll that looks like you.*

the Clarks determined that most black preschool children preferred to play with white dolls. Children would describe white dolls in positive terms, but black dolls would be ascribed negative characteristics. Black children would also become emotional when asked to describe the doll which represented them, often describing their skin colour not as black, but rather yellow or white. The conclusions from these studies played a pivotal role in the Supreme Court's 1954 ruling that segregation was causing psychological harm to children and that racial segregation in public schools was unconstitutional – specifically that prejudice, discrimination and segregation were developing negative self-perceptions and even self-hatred in black children.

The Northside Centre for child development

By 1945, Mamie had decided that she needed to strike out on her own with the singular purpose of helping Harlem's children. There were virtually no mental health services in Harlem and those that did exist were inadequate in their capacity to address the needs of the black community.

> *One thing leads to another, and you begin to think about the security in children, and you being to wonder, how can you give these children security?*
>
> (*Mamie Clark cited in Markowitz & Rosner,*
> *2000, p. 35*)

A racially and socioeconomically integrated child guidance clinic providing help, security, diagnostic and treatment services to Harlem's children would be a model for mental and social health in Harlem. However, following repeated rejections from the more established social services agencies, Mamie and Kenneth rapidly realised that the only way to work around resistance was to open a clinic themselves. Securing a small loan from Mamie's father, they began to renovate some small rooms called Dunbar Apartments; a garden apartment complex named after the eminent African American poet and novelist Paul Lawrence Dunbar, financed by John D. Rockefeller to be the first cooperative building to home African Americans affordably. They then set about persuading psychiatrists, psychologists, paediatricians and psychiatric social workers to provide professional support to the clinic for free. For the first 12 months, only the secretary and a remedial teacher were paid. The lack of funds, however, did little to dampen the attraction to Northside. The Clarks were becoming quickly recognised as significant professionals in the city. Their objectives to distance the clinic from ideas of a charity service for poor African Americans, to provide an integrated service for people from all localities, and to surpass the quality and levels of historical provisions resonated with New York families and mental health professionals.

In 1947, with a budget of only 34, 932 dollars, Northside treated 156 children. By 1974, with a budget of over 900 thousand, Northside was supporting nearly 1,300 children. With this increase in budget and scope, however, came new challenges.

Northside was developed to respond agilely to the needs and problems of an impoverished community. The 'whole child' treatment approach required attention to emotional, behavioural, educational, familial and socio-economic factors. Breaking down barriers between the mental health professions, social workers, educators, researchers and clerical workers was essential to its effectiveness. However, not all staff responded well to such professional integration. Psychiatrists felt that they should be the core professional base at Northside, but the Clarks believed that a successful whole child approach requires the merging of professional identities and therapeutic approaches, with a blurring of lines between the child, its family and staff. Staff began aggressively lobbying for unionisation. Demands for salary increases that could not be met and the threat of the union shop (a form of clause that requires all employees to be union members) was undermining the sense of a warm family atmosphere that the Clarks had tried to instil at Northside. Unionisation threatened to remove freedom of choice and re-establish boundaries between professional and non-professional staff.

An even more serious issue was that the racial integration of the Northside teams was now under threat. When the first vote to unionise was triggered, the board was split down the middle on racial lines. A move to unionise would now result in the loss of Kenneth and Meme Clark; however, failure to unionise would almost certainly result in strike action and the possible closure of Northside. In the end, the board voted 3 to 1 to reject unionisation and the Clarks set about preparing the children and families of Northside for possible strike action. The year 1970 was the worst for casework development at Northside. A lost year where staff morale, the spirit of cooperation and common community evaporated. However, the Clarks continued to work closely with staff, ensuring their clients were adequately served. With patience, wisdom and humour, they made it possible to reach a compromise agreement that stabilised Northside.

Legacy

Mamie Clark was Director of Northside until her retirement in 1979. Mamie inspired and shaped the support services of the Northside Centre for Child Development in a very real way. From a centre that had begun as a consultation and guidance centre, Northside expanded and adapted to address issues of education, poverty and the social policies of race. By the 1980s, Northside was managing a double tragedy which threatened to eradicate an entire generation of Harlem's children: the spread of the HIV/AIDS virus and the crack cocaine, which brought with it an epidemic of neglect, physical and sexual abuse, homicide and incarceration. Their goals, however, remained steadfast: '*to improve children's self-esteem in order to minimise the pernicious impact of racism and discrimination*' (p. 247, Harris, 1989 cited in Markowitz & Rosner, 2000). In 1973, Mamie was awarded the American Association of University Women achievement award and in 1983 the National Coalition of 100 black Women awarded her the Candace Award for humanitarianism. She died from lung cancer the same year.

Kenneth Clark was Co-Founder and Research Director of the advanced Northsides boarder social agenda. In addition to his involvement in the 1954 *Brown v. Board of Education*, US Supreme Courts desegregation decision, Clark founded Harlem Youth Opportunities Unlimited (HARYOU). HARYOU was dedicated towards developing education and job opportunities, and also provided him with the opportunity to carry out extensive sociological research in Harlem. Work which helped him reorganise Harlem's schools to help improve the performance of black children. Kenneth was awarded the Presidential Medal of Liberty by President Ronald Regan in 1986 and the outstanding achievement award by the American Psychological Society in 1994.

Columbia University Department of Psychology established the Mamie Phipps Clark and Kenneth B. Clark Distinguished Lecture Award to recognise extraordinary contributions of a senior scholar in the area of race and justice.

Kate Harris, Kenneth and Mamie's daughter and Northside's executive director, argued that despite the war on poverty, and the black power movements of the 1950s, 1960s, and 1970s, and her parents' famous social-science brief to the US Supreme Court, white racism towards black children never ceased. Forty years later, African American children were still rejecting the black doll.

Mamie Phipps Clark's and Kenneth Bancroft Clark's major writings

Clark, K. B. (1938). *Indices of a racial inferiority feeling among American Negroes.* Unpublished Manuscript, 10 January 1938, p. 2, box 168, folder 5, Kenneth Bancroft Clark Papers, Manuscript Division, Library of Congress, Washington, DC.

Clark, K. B. (1940). *Some factors influencing the remembering of prose material.* Unpublished doctoral dissertation, Columbia University, New York.

Clark, K. B. (1944). Group violence: A preliminary study of the attitudinal pattern of its acceptance and rejection: A study of the 1943 Harlem Riot. *Journal of Social Psychology, 19*(2), 319–337.

Clark, K. B. (1945). A brown girl in a speckled world. *Journal of Social Issues, 1*(2), 10–15.

Clark, K. B. (1948, January). Social science and social tensions. *Mental Hygiene, 32*, 15–26.

Clark, K. B. (1950). Racial prejudice among American minorities. *International Social Science Bulletin, 2*(4), 506–513.

Clark, K. B. (1952). The effects of prejudice and discrimination. In H. L. Witmar & R. Kosinsky (Eds.), *Personality in the making, the fact-finding report of the midcentury white house conference on children and youth* (pp. 135–158). New York: Harper and Brothers.

Clark, K. B. (1955). *Prejudice and your child.* Boston: Beacon Press.

Clark, K. B. (1965). *Dark ghetto: Dilemmas of social power.* New York: Harper and Row.

Clark, K. B., & Phipps Clark, M. (1939). The development of consciousness of self and the emergence of racial identification in Negro preschool children. *Journal of Social Psychology, 10*(4), 591–599.

Clark, K. B., & Phipps Clark, M. (1940). Skin color as a factor in racial identification of Negro preschool children. *Journal of Social Psychology, 10*, 159–169.

References

Brown v. Board of Education. (1954). 347 U.S. 483.

Clark, K. B. (1938). KBC interview, 25th January.

Hentoff, N. (1982). The integrationist. *The New Yorker, 58*, 37–73.

Markowitz, G., & Rosner, D. (2000). *Children, race and power, Kenneth and Mamie Clark's Northside Centre.* New York: Routledge.

6 Albert Bandura (December 4, 1925–July 26, 2021)

Bandura pioneered the development of a theory of social learning that has been particularly influential understanding aggression and how a wide range of human behaviour is motivated and regulated by self-evaluations.

Albert Bandura, the only son in a family of five older sisters, grew up in Mundare, northern Alberta, Canada. He spent his elementary and high school years in the village's one and only school. His career in psychology came about by chance. He commuted to the University of Iowa in a carpool of engineering and pre-med students whose day started early. A psychology course with an early morning start was available, so he took it and was soon hooked. At Iowa, he studied with the learning theorist Kenneth Spence, an associate of Hull, and in 1952 earned a doctorate in clinical psychology under the supervision of the clinical neuropsychologist Arthur L. Benton. While working on his doctorate, he met Virginia Varns, an instructor in the nursing school. They married and later had two daughters. In 1952, he moved to Wichita, Kansas, to a 1-year internship at the Wichita Guidance Center. He then moved to Stanford University.

At the start of his career, Bandura focused on learning. Most of the research at that time was concerned with learning from direct experience. At that time, it was widely assumed that learning could only occur by responding to stimuli and experiencing their effects. Bandura felt that this line of theorising was at odds with informal evidence that virtually all learning resulting from direct experience occurs on a vicarious basis – by observing other people's behaviour and its consequences for them. Whereas behaviourism tended to emphasise the influence of the environment on behaviour, Bandura was interested in the influence of behaviour on the environment. In this respect, his position is closer to that of Jacob Kantor, whose 'interbehaviourism' argues that

DOI: 10.4324/9781003229179-7

the organism and stimulus objects surrounding it should be treated as equally important, a position that presaged the emergence of ecological psychology. Bandura referred to his concept of environment-behaviour interaction as 'reciprocal determinism' – the notion that the environment and a person's behaviour cause each other. He developed this idea to a point where he began to consider the interaction between the environment, behaviour, and the person's psychological processes. When he started to consider a role for mental imagery, he ceased to be a strict behaviourist and became a cognitive psychologist. Indeed, he is often regarded as a 'founding father' of cognitive behaviourism. His theoretically ambitious *Social Learning Theory* (1977) set out to 'provide a unified theoretical framework for analyzing human thought and behaviour' (p. vi). While his introduction of cognitive concepts into behaviourism marked a clear departure from traditional behaviourism, it also marked a point where Bandura began to consider observational learning (modelling) and self-regulation. This interest led to a program of research on the determinants and mechanisms of observational learning and modelling of rule-governed behaviour. He distinguished between three kinds of models: live (e.g. the behaviour of a friend), symbolic (e.g. the behaviour of an actor on TV) and verbal (e.g. the behaviour of someone described in a short story or novel). The enormous advances in communication technology through the last century (from radio to television and the internet) mean that the symbolic environment plays an increasingly powerful role in shaping values, ideas, attitudes and lifestyles so Bandura's work is particularly relevant to contemporary developments in the growth of information and communication technology.

Bandura paid special attention to the role of symbolic modelling in the social diffusion of new ways of behaving and is most closely associated with a classic investigation called the 'bobo' doll study, in which he examined whether young children could learn aggressive behaviours by watching adult models perform aggressive acts. Children between 3 and 6 years watched either an aggressive model (an adult who hit a bobo doll with a mallet), a non-aggressive model (an adult who played quietly with toys and ignored the doll), or no model (a control group who did not see any model). Children who had seen the aggressive models tended to imitate the violent behaviours they observed more often than children in the other two groups. Bandura's social cognitive theory has offered one of the most influential psychological explanations of how people may come to regard their injurious actions against others as trivial and even acceptable. Bandura and his colleagues identified several cognitive mechanisms that offenders may use to minimise their perceptions of the impact of their actions on others. These include moral justification (e.g. 'I lied to protect my family'), euphemistic labelling of severe assaults (e.g. 'I messed him up a bit') and denial of consequences (e.g. 'I only steal from big chain-stores').

Another major line of interest for Bandura aims to clarify the different mechanisms of personal agency. This work is concerned with how people exercise control over their own motivation and behaviour and over their environment. One focus of this research is on how human behaviour is motivated and regulated by internal standards and anticipatory self-evaluative reactions – how I will feel if I do such and such. Bandura argues that among the mechanisms of personal agency, none is more central or pervasive than people's perceived efficacy to exert control over different aspects of their lives. His studies of familial causes of aggression, with his first graduate student Richard Walters (who died at a young age in a motorcycle accident), promoted an increasing emphasis on the role of modelling in personality development. Like the personality theorist Walter Mischel, he developed a social cognitive theory that considers the person as an active agent using cognitive processes such as memory, problem-solving to reflect on experiences of the world and to make decisions and plan behaviour. This contrasts with views in which the person is regarded as a more or less passive respondent to environmental circumstances or a victim of unconscious drives. In fact, Bandura, like Eysenck, is highly critical of psychoanalysis for its reliance on concepts that cannot be clearly defined and for promoting the use of therapeutic methods that he contends have failed to demonstrate their effectiveness in achieving sustained changes in psychological functioning. He is also critical of its emphasis on the seemingly unavoidable consequences of early childhood experiences. In this regard, he can be considered closer to the more optimistic and humanistic psychology of Rogers. Unlike Rogers, his approach reflects a significantly stronger commitment to empirically guided theory development and to the therapeutic importance of actual experiences rather than to the creation of a therapeutic climate conducive to change.

Bandura's emphasis on the study of processes that account for the acquisition, maintenance and change of behaviour contrasts with that of trait theorists who place greater value on the import of innate dispositions. Social cognitive theory sees the adaptively functioning person as a well-tuned organism capable of adapting to the environment and of changing parts of the environment to suit themselves. The self is considered not as a fixed structure but as a set of cognitive processes: the person does not have a psychological structure called the 'self' but self-processes that are part of the person. Bandura regards the self-efficacy belief system as the foundation of human motivation, well-being and personal accomplishments.

In other words, unless people believe that they can bring about desired outcomes by their actions, they have little incentive to act or to persevere in the face of difficulties. There is a good deal of empirical evidence to support his argument that personal-efficacy beliefs shape just about every aspect of people's lives – whether they think pessimistically or optimistically, their vulnerability to stress and depression, and the life choices they make. However, critics contend that self-efficacy theory misses the point that it is outcome expectancies that actually guide behaviour: if people believe they can perform the tasks presented in a particular situation, then it is the expectation of receiving a positive outcome that motivates their actions. Bandura has replied that well-designed empirical studies should resolve this type of dispute, and he points to the corpus of evidence showing that empirical self-efficacy beliefs can predict behaviour more accurately than measures of outcome expectancy.

Self-efficacy theory has proved particularly effective in clinical interventions. For instance, self-efficacy analysis suggests that phobias, such as snake phobia, result from people losing their sense of self-efficacy – their sense of being able to effectively respond to the situation presented to them. Because people are most convinced that they can manage a situation by actually managing it, therapeutic interventions emphasise ability to overtly perform specific behaviours, such as handling snakes. While Bandura concurs with Eysenck's position that therapies are effective because they reduce anxiety reactions, he does not agree that therapeutic interventions should focus on attenuating levels of emotional distress. Instead, the focus should be on developing a person's sense of belief that they can cope effectively. The therapist's role is to promote successful outcomes by bringing to bear various techniques that will engage the client with frightening tasks and help them perform those tasks proficiently. For example, people who develop anxieties and fears may do so because their planning abilities either switch off or diminish in effectiveness, and the person focuses on planning to cope with their emotional distress rather than planning to address the reality of the situation as it is presented to them. Bandura suggests that a therapist's role may initially involve vicarious mastery: a client with a snake phobia would observe others handling snakes. As therapy progresses, the client and therapist work in closer collaboration in order to sustain a reciprocal interaction between increases in self-efficacy and greater performance successes. Although this type of protocol has enjoyed considerable success, critics point out that it does not address the source of a person's phobia, underplays the role of unconscious processes that may be implicated in the phobia and often requires a fairly sophisticated, adult-like, development for the client to benefit from a therapeutic intervention.

Bandura's social learning theory has influenced a diverse range of applied work as illustrated in John Farquhar's classic 'Three-Community Study', in which matched farming communities received one of three interventions. One community received messages about the prevention of heart disease by mass media and direct mail; another received additional instruction for those considered at high risk and a third acted as a control. The mass media were found to be as effective as direct instruction in reducing heart disease risk. More generally, Bandura's ideas have enjoyed considerable influence and respect across five decades. Their impact is due in no small part to his readiness to embrace empirically founded ideas from a range of sub-disciplines within psychology. This willingness is indicated by the changes to the name given to his theoretical position from observational learning, which reflected a more traditional behavioural position, to social learning theory, which reflects a stronger emphasis on the ways in which social behaviours are learned by watching other people, to social cognitive theory which emphasises the greater role given to cognitive processes in mediating social learning.

Albert Bandura's major writings

Bandura, A. (1969). *Principles of behavior modification*. New York: Holt, Rinehart, & Winston.

Bandura, A. (1977a). Self-efficacy: Toward a unifying theory of behavioral change. *Psychological Review, 84*(2), 191–215.

Bandura, A. (1977b). *Social learning theory*. NJ: Prentice-Hall.

Bandura, A. (Ed.). (1995). *Self-efficacy in changing societies*. Cambridge: Cambridge University Press.

Bandura, A. (2000). Exercise of human agency through collective efficacy. *Current Directions in Psychological Science, 9*(3), 75–78. https://doi.org/10.1111/1467-8721.00064

Bandura, A., & National Inst of Mental Health. (1986). *Social foundations of thought and action: A social cognitive theory*. NJ: Prentice-Hall, Inc.

Bandura, A., & Walters, R. H. (1959). *Adolescent aggression*. New York: Ronald Press.

Bandura, A., & Walters, R. H. (1963). *Social learning and personality development*. New York: Holt Rinehart and Winston.

Further reading

Evans, R. I. (1989). *Albert Bandura, the man and his ideas: A dialogue*. Greenwood.

Hall, C. S., & Lindzey, C. (1957). *Theories of personality*. Wiley.

Mowrer, R. R., & Klein, S. B. (2000). *Handbook of contemporary learning theories*. Erlbaum.

7 Frederick Charles Bartlett (October 20, 1886–September 30, 1969)

A theorist of human cognition, Bartlett popularised the concept of schema as a basic unit of thought.

Bartlett's childhood was spent in Stow-on-the-Wold, situated about 30 miles from Oxford and 85 from London, where his father ran a successful footwear outlet. The local grammar school being defunct, it was his parents' intention that he and his older brother should go to boarding school. However, a near-fatal attack of pleurisy at the age of 14 put an end to those plans, and Bartlett was left to educate himself, supported by his father's encouragement and the library of a local minister. He enrolled as an external student at London, taking courses in philosophy and logic offered by the University Correspondence College, based at Cambridge. His first-class degree prompted the Correspondence College to offer him a position as tutor. While filling that role, he read for a University of London MA and gained distinctions in sociology and ethics. This was followed by a decision to make a fresh start as an undergraduate at Cambridge. He achieved a first-class degree, and while it was his intention to continue with a career in anthropology his tutor, the physiologist and psychologist William Rivers, encouraged him to take charge of the course in experimental psychology because it would broaden his career opportunities. World War I shaped his career through the departure of several psychologists, Charles Myers, William McDougall and William Brown, to military service. A combination of poor health and lack of medical training meant that Bartlett could not enlist. It fell to him to fill Myers' role, and he was appointed Assistant Director of the Psychology Laboratory. In 1924, he became Reader in Experimental Psychology and Director in the same year when Myers left to found the National Institute of Industrial Psychology, London.

DOI: 10.4324/9781003229179-8

It was during the war years that he met his wife to be, Mary Smith. They collaborated on the perception of weak intensity sound, the work being of importance to the operation of hydrophone anti-submarine detection equipment. During this period, he completed a thesis based on the studies. Several years later, these studies formed the core of his classic text *Remembering* (1932). Notwithstanding the demands imposed by his new responsibilities, Bartlett found time to spend on his love for social anthropology. Travel to undertake fieldwork was out of the question, but he was able to apply his psychological expertise in a novel analysis of the social and cultural transmission of memory through devices such as myth and folklore, reported in *Psychology and Primitive Culture* (1923). This aspect of his work is reminiscent of Wundt's Völkerpsychologie (social psychology).

Bartlett is best known for his investigations into memory and in particular for his book *Remembering*, which examined the influences of social factors on memory. His first account of the effects of those social influences was a product of his knowledge of anthropological accounts of the outcomes of cross-cultural contacts on conventions. He defined the process of 'conventionalisation' as one in which 'cultural materials coming into a group from outside are gradually worked into a pattern of a relatively stable kind distinctive of that group. The new material is assimilated to the persistent past of the group to which it comes' (1958, p. 280). He drew a connection between these ideas and his experimental data on memory that implied that, after repetitive recall, the participants protocols reached a fairly stable form and that any changes in recall usually demonstrated the impact of old information on new. However, although he originally regarded his research to be 'an all-out experimental attack upon conventionalizing' (1958, p. 143), he became disillusioned with this approach because conventionalisation seemed less like an explanatory concept and more like a tag for a similarity between phenomena in different disciplinary domains.

Bartlett's strongest influence is in his theory of schemata: a schema (singular for schemata) is constantly changing in the light of new experiences, but it provides a dynamic framework or model into which new experiences are interpreted and structured. Bartlett was not the first to use the term – Piaget also made considerable use of the concept in his theory of cognitive development. Bartlett's concept of schema was developed in part through discussion with the physiologist Sir Henry Head, who used 'postural schema' to explain how past information about the position of one's body informs current actions and to account for disorders of body orientation. Bartlett's observations on making tennis strokes capture the core elements of his idea of movement schemata: 'When I make the stroke I do not, as a matter of fact, produce something absolutely new, and I never merely repeat something old. The stroke is literally manufactured out of the living visual and postural "schemata" of the movement and their interrelations' (1932, p. 202).

The concept of schema posed a fundamental challenge to the prevailing views on memory that were exemplified in the classic work of Hermann von Ebbinghaus. Ebbinghaus had argued that in order to study memory in its purest form, it was necessary to establish experimental conditions that would remove potentially confounding variables. His experiments were designed to uncover rudimentary laws of memory by using nonsense syllables to create situations where the memory content was meaningless and therefore isolated from other memories and prior experience. He contended that more complex forms of memory could be explored once the simpler laws describing its structure and operation had been uncovered. However, Bartlett argued that if a psychologist is concerned with understanding relatively high-level processes like recall and proceeds to try and isolate the response – the memory to be recalled – by making the stimulus extremely simple, she has performed a very different kind of procedure. This kind of experimental procedure does not lead to the identification of simpler laws because when people learn nonsense syllables, they typically use a variety of strategies to *impose* meaning on the task, such as contriving associations between the meaningless stimulus and meaningful memories. In other words, human memory has emergent properties that are not captured in highly simplified memory tasks, and even the very simplest tasks can never fully exclude those properties because people invariably attempt to impose meanings on the material they are learning. Not only were Bartlett's ideas counter to those of Ebbinghaus, but they were also hostile to the behaviourist school which, at the time Bartlett was publishing, was eschewing the study of any kind of covert mental entity. Thus, his concept of schema was relatively neglected until the emergence of cognitivism, an approach that focuses on the analysis of higher mental processes such as problem-solving, and artificial intelligence. For example, Broadbent (1970) concluded that

> the term 'schema' appears to have become completely disused . . . the schema itself had no list of defining properties, but was simply a label for something whose operation was illustrated by experimental results. . . . Theoretical concepts of this kind, without public definitions, are almost bound to be self-defeating.
>
> (p. 4)

Moreover, there is a good deal of argument and evidence that Bartlett presented two versions of schema theory, an official version in which he contends that memory is a constructive process and an unofficial or private version (Ost and Costall, 2002). The latter has a place for the concept of the memory trace and acknowledges that if memory is a process of construction and reconstruction, there must be some entity on which to base the construction. Notwithstanding these ambiguities, for a period of time the vagueness of the notion of schema provided a useful theoretical anchor for the nascent cognitive sciences, an interdisciplinary approach to the way the brain processes information.

With the outbreak of World War II, Bartlett, a member of the Air Ministry's Flying Personnel Research Committee, was drawn into the analysis of psychological problems revealed by the expansion of the RAF. His close association with Kenneth Craik, who joined the Cambridge laboratory in 1936, was indispensable. Craik had the ingenuity and engineering talent required to fabricate the experimental simulations that were needed to study pilot behaviour and fatigue. Their work was supported with the establishment of the Medical Research Council's Applied Psychology Unit in 1944. Craik was its head, but he died in a road traffic accident just before the end of the war. This was a profound personal loss to Bartlett. Later, Bartlett adapted Craik's methods in his investigations of remembering and thinking. As a practical activity, he considered thinking to involve the completion (by interpolation or extrapolation) of some previously incomplete state of affairs and he devised experimental procedures to explore this idea systematically. His book *Thinking* (1958) is less remarkable than the earlier *Remembering*, although in many ways it reveals more of his personal attitudes and thinking (e.g. his involvement with anthropology, sociology, and philosophy) than any of his earlier published work.

Bartlett twice switched his interests from lively academic fields to ones where there were practical problems to be solved. The first was a switch from sociology and anthropology to the experimental psychology of perception and remembering. The second was from a purely academic psychology to the application of psychology in occupational settings. He occupies a pre-eminent position in the development of psychology in Britain. Starting with just one laboratory assistant in 1922, he was guiding the efforts of more than 70 staff and researchers some 30 years later, and most of the important psychological appointments in Britain during the middle of the 20th century were made from among those who had been trained under him.

Frederick Bartlett's major writings

Bartlett, F. C. (1916). An experimental study of some problems of perceiving and imaging. *British Journal of Psychology*, *8*, 222–266.

Bartlett, F. C. (1923). *Psychology and primitive culture.* Cambridge, UK: Cambridge University Press.

Bartlett, F. C. (1932). *Remembering: A study in experimental and social psychology.* Cambridge, UK: Cambridge University Press.

Bartlett, F. C. (1934). *The problem of noise.* Cambridge, UK: Cambridge University Press.

Bartlett, F. C. (1937). Psychological methods and anthropological problems. *Africa, 10,* 401–420.

Bartlett, F. C. (1958). *Thinking: An experimental and social study.* London: Allen and Unwin.

Bartlett, F. C. (1929). Experimental method in psychology. *Nature, 124,* 341–345.

Further reading

Brewer, W. F., & Nakamura, G. V. (1984). The nature and functions of schemas. In R. S. Wyer, Jr., & T. K. Srull (Eds.), *Handbook of social cognition* (Vol. 1, pp. 118–160). NJ: Erlbaum.

Broadbent, D. E. (1970). Frederick Charles Bartlett 1886–1969. *Biographical Memoirs of Fellows of the Royal Society, 16,* 1–11.

Ost, J., & Costall, A. (2002). Misremembering Bartlett: A study in serial reproduction. *British Journal of Psychology, 93,* 243–255.

8   Daniel Ellis Berlyne (April 25, 1924–November 2, 1976)

Daniel Berlyne was a complex and fascinating psychologist who made experimental and theoretical contributes to areas such as curiosity, aesthetics, physiology, arousal, attention, play, humour and thinking.

Born in a working-class area of Salford, Manchester, in 1924, Daniel Berlyne (Dan) was aware that his family was different. Daniel's family was of Russian-Jewish descent; his paternal grandparents were refugees from White Russia (paternal). His maternal grandparents were from Latvia. His parents were moderately observant Jews, keeping dietary laws, but not necessarily activities forbidden on a Saturday. Daniel describes a 'feeling of isolation', 'being peculiar' and being viewed with 'blatant hostility'.

Daniels's father built up a glass business specialising in stained glass windows and mirrors, and this wealth in an impoverished area of Manchester further created a sense of difference; the Berlyne family comprised the only people in the street with a car and electric lights. Daniel had two siblings, both younger. A brother, 10 years younger who was taken out of school early by his father. A sister, 5 years younger, who after a period at Cambridge enjoying the social life more than academic pursuits also trained as a psychologist.

Daniel described himself as a thin, pale, faddy child who refused to eat meat. His home as 'unintellectual' and his parents 'low brow'. While his mother had been an elementary-school teacher, neither parent had strong academic leanings. They were interested in education as a means to rise in the social scale but were indifferent to intellectual pursuits and would in fact disapprove of 'highbrow' pursuits such as classical music. His parents did however provide Daniel with piano lessons – because that was the 'thing to do'. Daniels's father expected him to go into the family profession, and there was never any idea that Daniel would move into any profession or intellectual activity.

DOI: 10.4324/9781003229179-9

Miss Williams, his primary-school teacher, was a major formative influence on the young Berlyne. Knick nicknamed her the 'Mighty Atom'. Miss Williams selected Daniel for coaching for entrance to the scholarship examination to the Manchester Grammar School. He attributes his first memory of psychology to Miss Williams as she described psychologists as the kind of people who examine the behaviour of boys who do not come to school because of tummy aches. This special attention, however, further added to a sense of difference and isolation. Miss Williams expected great things from scholarship students; they were held up as an ideal. This however was not something that most of the class were destined towards, and Daniel became isolated from the remainder of his class.

At the Manchester Grammar School, Daniel found his forte in modern languages and struggled at mathematics. This weakness Daniel attributes to a dislike of productive thinking. It did not fit with his investigative tendencies and impatience. Art was also something that Daniel struggled with. He felt this reflected awkwardness in his motor co-ordination, and he found himself to be careless. This carelessness and untidiness spilled over into other areas of his academic performance, and because at the time this carelessness was considered a moral deficit, he found his teachers demonstrated considerable impatience with him. Aptitude must however have shone through because Daniel was encouraged to apply for a scholarship to Cambridge.

Daniels family was less than enamoured with this news, considering Cambridge to be something for the knobs. It was rather like being presented at the Royal court. However, his family were starting to realise that Daniel joining the family business was perhaps not such a good idea, and his father agreed that Daniel could go to university, but not to Cambridge. He should attend Manchester University and study for a Bachelor of Commerce degree. Daniel struggled with this idea and began to try to persuade his father that he might want to work in some other business. His father found this difficult, that Daniel's career path seemed unclear and precarious. Daniel never entertained the idea of being a university teacher, too lofty a pursuit, a remote possibility. He was, however, certain that whatever came out of going to university would be better than going into the family business. Mr Hislop (his teacher) was quite persuasive that Danielss's skills in modern languages would do well in the civil service. Although Daniel was very unclear about what 'one does all day in the civil service', he was strongly attracted by the £1000 per year described by Mr Hislop.

While at the Grammar School war broke out, and Daniel was evacuated to Blackpool at the beginning of the war. During this time Sigmund

Freud died. A friend had obtained a copy of Freud's introductory lectures from the school library. Daniel found this rather interesting, possibly initially for its salacious appeal but the works did however leave a lasting impression on Daniel. The evacuation to Blackpool was timed badly, and it lasted only 5 weeks at a time when there was no bombing. When the blitz started, Daniel was actually back in Manchester again.

At the age of 16, Daniel won four scholarships to Cambridge: a modern languages scholarship, a state scholarship, a Manchester scholarship and a Salford scholarship. He started University at 17. Berlyne describes this period as some of the most satisfying years. Perhaps this was his first sense of belonging. The environment was intense and while there was something of a shortage of food, there was an intense social life, plenty to do, drinking tea and crumpets and talking late at night. He describes a sense of belonging to an elite but with very little snobbery.

Berlyne was attracted to the philosophical teachings of Russell and Wittgenstein, although this romance did not last long. He reports finding Wittgenstein's style unusual and rambling and rude. Wittgenstein would 'hold' people in his rooms, but only those he found interesting. This was not quite legal; anyone could listen to a public lecture so to get around this problem Wittgenstein would gate-keep by being rude to people he did not want there and by prohibiting 'lecture tourists'; you either came to all the lectures or you did not come back.

Daniel reports a similar lack of enthusiasm about his language lecturers. He was not taken with any of their teaching styles, but this may be in part because he knew that they could be called up at any time into the army. This insecurity created a sense of disengagement. Initially, government policy was that graduates would have one uninterrupted year, but as his studies progressed it became clear that this protection would be rescinded. The war also meant that learning German was difficult. Many of the German lectures had left the university and only a few refugees remained. He was learning a language from a culture from which he was cut off. At this time, Daniel read *General Psychology* (Sprott). Up until this point, Daniel had focused on Freud and hypnosis and this book opened Daniels's mind to other areas of psychology.

Berlyne in his first set of examinations (part one of the tri-pass) in modern languages got a first in French but was very disappointed with his 2.1 in German. The subject matter in modern languages began to change 'insidiously' from learning the language to understanding the literature. Berlyne enjoyed the language but not the literary criticism. 'Woke up' to this and although he enjoyed the criticism, he realised he did not want to make a career out of this. Recognising that he did not want to study languages and elected to change degree course and study psychology.

Despite his early negative experiences of the Wittgenstein group, Berlyne decided he wanted to study philosophy. There was small group/tutorial teaching, which he enjoyed but it was a risky degree course because really the only thing you could do was become a University Lecturer and his father would not understand. Psychology seemed like a less risky option. On visiting the psychology department, Berlyne met his first psychology 'subject' (participant) and assumed that this poor person was a neurotic arriving for psychotherapy.

Berlyne changed degree track and commenced studying psychology at a time when psychology was a wing of the physiology lab and only 10 or 15 people were taking the topic. Again, Berlyne was less than enamoured with the lecturer's style, and he found the content uninteresting and out of date. He read Bartlett's *Remembering*, several times and fell asleep on each occasion. Again, Berlyne talks about isolation from other parts of the departments, knowing that interesting work was taking place but not being exposed to it.

In 1943, Berlyne was called up into the army. Based on his modern language skills, Berlyne was sent to the intelligence corps as a private. This experience of a drop in social status was not something that Daniel liked; he was used to porters at Cambridge calling him Sir and reinforcing his feelings of belonging to an elite. His knowledge of German was also not a particular advantage because most of the interceptions were in cipher. Daniel ended up mostly doing dull clerical work, travelling to Tunisia, Italy, Corsica and Malta. Unappreciative of the protection and safety provided to Daniel by this role, he felt strongly that his skills and abilities could have been used in a better way. He was frustrated that there was a war going on and he was assigned to such dull work, yet perhaps the early signs of development in aesthetics were emerging as he spent time in Italy getting to know the citizens, visiting art galleries and gaining an appreciation of art. At 22, Daniel returned to Cambridge. Life was satisfying but much more serious. There was no sense of affectation and an increased sense of lost time. His self-confidence was low; he was unsure about what he would study, and he started self-medicating with Aspirin, which seemed to have a tranquilising effect. Daniel went back to see Bartlett for careers advice and enrolled on the Cambridge psychology program and graduated in 1 year, obtaining his first class in BA in 1947 and later in 1949 his MA.

After a series of unsuccessful academic interviews, he obtained his first academic post at St Andrews University, Scotland. He describes St Andrews as 'a nice place to visit, but you would not want to live there'. So before accepting the post at St Andrews, he wrote to the University and asked how much notice he would have to give when he wanted to resign. He found St Andrews an odd place, where psychology was not allowed to flourish. The University was very small about 1,200 students; there were about 30 psychology students in total and there was much competition between academics about how the subject should be taught. Here, however, Berlyne saw his first experimental maze, with a rat. Taken with this, he began to consult with others doing rat work with the aim of examining curiosity. He published his first paper in 1949, 'Interest as a psychological concept', in *British Journal of Psychology*, beginning an academic publishing profile career in interest and curiosity. After a 'decent' period (2 years), Berlyne decided it was time to leave St Andrews and travel to the United States, learn what was taking place and bring back the knowledge to the UK.

In 1951, he went to Yale University. At Yale he didn't feel he learned a lot about learning theory but learned much more about other areas such as statistics and research design, compensating for what he felt was defective training in these areas at Cambridge. More generally he learned more broadly about psychology in the USA. At the end of the first year, the subject of taking a PhD came up. Daniel had explored this possibility while at St Andrews, but since no one had taken a PhD at St Andrews since 1928 it was deemed unnecessary. An agreement was reached that if he would stay on for an additional year, he could teach at Brooklyn College and take a PhD. Aspirations were higher at Yale. Students had a higher level of insecurity and fear of failure. He describes again the teaching as uninspiring, the experience as distressful and he was not always sure that he was coping. Again, a drop in social status bothered him. As a graduate student, his status as a lecturer at St Andrews was no longer acknowledged.

In 1953, Berlyne married Hilde Strauss in Bridgeport, Connecticut (with whom he had three daughters). The same year he obtained his PhD from Yale (Some aspects of human curiosity); however, because of visa problems he was unable to obtain a permanent post. He was also starting to accept that his ambition to work in Cambridge or Oxford was becoming less likely.

As such the couple travelled back to the University of Aberdeen, where Daniel would take up a teaching post 'fresh and full of ideas.

Daniel remained at Aberdeen until 1956 when he took a sabbatical from Aberdeen and travelled to California, where he became a Fellow at the Centre for Advanced Study in the Behavioural Sciences at Palo Alto, California. Berlyne found the environment unusual because he found it difficult to meet with faculty members and collaborate on projects. Initially, he used this as a period to write, and began writing *Conflict, Arousal and Curiosity*. This work integrated Berlyne's work with developments in the areas of exploratory behaviour, arousal and curiosity. Laying the framework for a theory of collative motivation, the book had application in the areas of art, thinking and humour, as well as neurophysiological and information theory. The book was ahead of its time and not widely cited at the time. However, its popularity has continued to grow. The following year, he began working with Jean Piaget as Membre-resident at the Centre International D'Epistemologie Genetique in Geneva, Switzerland, and from there he returned to North America in 1959–1960 at the National Institute of Mental Health in Maryland. In 1960, he took up an Associate Professorship at Boston University, then because of resourcing issues, the lack of academic community and the expectation that he would teach child psychology (something he felt was outside of his specialism), he resigned to join what he felt to be a more ambitious department at the University of Toronto. He joined in 1962 as Associate Professor, becoming Full Professor the following year where he remained for the rest of his life.

Theory of aesthetics

Berlyne's interviews with the Canadian Psychological Association reveal himself an erudite theoretician and integrator. A continuing source of inspiration in experimental aesthetics, his work is often described as the study of collective motivation (Konečni, 1978). The crux of Berlyne's theory was the effects of and reactions to curiosity and arousal and how those effects impact organisms on a psychophysical, environmental and collective level. The latter is related to the hedonistic qualities of arousal through aspects such as novelty, complexity, surprisingness, and incongruity. Berlyne argued that there was a curvilinear relationship with complexity and preference. Specifically, that complexity increases linearly with preference until an optimum level of visual arousal is reached. At this point, further increases in complexity would elicit a downturn in arousal and preference would decrease. People will seek to maintain a level of arousal that supports their preferred level of stimulation. Individuals who are highly aroused will seek out certainty, whereas those low on arousal will seek more stimulating environments. He co-authored some 7 books and 150 scientific papers, Berlyne received accolades, including Fellow of the Royal Society of Canada and the British Psychological Society, and the Fellows of several divisions of the American and Canadian Psychological Society.

Daniel Ellis Berlyne's major writings

Berlyne, D. E. (1949). 'Interest' as a psychological concept. *British Journal of Psychology*, *39*, 184–195.

Berlyne, D. E. (1960). *Conflict, arousal, and curiosity*. New York: McGraw-Hill Book Company. https://doi.org/10.1037/11164-000

Berlyne, D. E. (1970). Novelty, complexity and hedonic value. *Perception and Psychophysics*, *8*, 279–286.

Berlyne, D. E. (1971). *Aesthetics and psychobiology*. New York: Appleton.

Berlyne, D. E. (1971). *Studies in the new experimental aesthetics*. Washington, DC: Hemisphere.

Berlyne, D. E. (1975). Behaviourism? Cognitive theory? Humanistic psychology? To hull with them all!, *Canadian Psychological Review*, *16*, 69–80.

Berlyne, D. E., & Piaget, J. (1960). *Théorie du comportement et opérations*. Paris: Presses Universitaires de France.

Further reading/listening

Cupchik, G. C. (1988). The legacy of Daniel E. Berlyne. *Empirical Studies of the Arts*, *6*(2), 171–186. https://doi.org/10.2190/FLM8-6NQ7-N5WM-WLLT

For a full list of publications see the University of California (1986). Daniel E. Berlyne 1924–1976 Notes and comments. *Music Perception*, *4*(2), 227–234. Retrieved from http://konecni.ucsd.edu/pdf/1986%20Ten%20Years%20D.%20E.%20Berlyne%20MP.pdf

Interview with Daniel Berlyne, International Association of Empirical Aesthetics with the Canadian Psychological Association, Boston & Toronto.

Konečni, V. J. (1978). Daniel E. Berlyne: 1924–1976. *The American Journal of Psychology*, *91*(1), 133–137. Retrieved from www.jstor.org/stable/1421829.

9 Alfred Binet (July 8, 1857– October 18, 1911)

Binet invented the intelligence test and used it to quantify children's intelligence.

Alfred Binet was born *Alfredo Binetti* in Nice on July 8, 1867. His parents were wealthy, his father was a physician and his mother an artist, but the marriage was not a happy one and they divorced when Alfred was quite young. Alfred lived with his mother in Paris after the divorce. His father was a harsh man who viewed his son as weak and cowardly. To toughen him up, he used to make Alfred view and touch corpses, which only made matters worse. Albert developed a lifelong fear of his father.

Binet attended the Lycée Louis-le-Grand, Paris, which was named after King Louis XIV of France in 1682 and to this day plays an important role in the education of elite French society. Alfred was a competent student, receiving several awards during his time at Louis-le-Grand in areas such as literary composition and translation. He obtained a degree in law in 1878, obtaining his practising licence at the age of 21. He began studying for a doctorate but found he detested the discipline, describing law as '*the career for men who have not yet chosen a vacation*' (Binet, 1904, cited by Wolf, 1973, p. 3).

Like his father and grandfather before him, he turned to medical studies at the Sorbonne. Studying in the embryological laboratory of Edouard-Gérard Balbiani, he studied botany and zoology, developing skills in systematic observation and experimental methods. His doctorate was awarded in natural science in 1894, and he married Laure, the daughter of Edouard-Gérard. Laure and Alfred went on to have two children: Madeleine and Alice. Binet described Madeleine as a 'reflective' child, whereas Alice was more impulsive. He continued to observe differences in their developmental style throughout their lives, as he studied their development and individual mental processes at his laboratory.

DOI: 10.4324/9781003229179-10

Binet's career however remained fraught with difficulties and conflicts, which predictably circled around cadavers and his estranged father. His pursuit of psychology was not through formal education but self-directed through the study of articles and books by the British Philosopher John Stuart Mill and the philosopher, biologist and sociologist Herbert Spencer.

In 1892, after several years of self-study, Binet was introduced to the neurologist Jean-Martin Charcot. Charcot soon became his mentor, and the two began working together at the Salpêtrière Hospital in Paris. This was an unpaid position, but Binet had independent means and this supported him to study and give over his time as he pleased. Under Charcot's guidance and inspiration, Binet commenced on one of the most productive periods of his career. Charcot's work on hypnosis, however, caused Binet considerable embarrassment. Charcot had claimed to present evidence that hypnotic states could be influenced using magnets, and Binet was a forceful supporter of Charcot's position. The work did not however stand up to scrutiny and was discredited. Binet had to retract his position and ultimately severed his connections with Charot over the fiasco.

Binet's work explored several areas: fetishism, hallucinations, perception and suggestion, visual imagery, memory, chess performance, music, fear and religion, depression, deaf mutes and mental fatigue. He was establishing himself as a prolific writer when he began working, as Associate Director at the first French psychological laboratory, the L'École Pratique des Hautes Études at the Sorbonne in 1889. This was again an unpaid position. At that time, Henri-Étienne Beaunis was Director. His philosophy was in the introspective model of Wilhelm Wundt, but he gave Binet license to study as he wished. Binet became Director in 1894. This was a prodigiously productive year for him. He produced a book on experimental methods and a book on expert calculators, four papers that studied childhood abilities, two papers on dramatists and one on spatial orientation, and a methodological piece on recording piano-playing techniques, and he founded the first French journal dedicated to the study of psychology; *L'Année Psychologique*.

The following year, Binet began collaborating with Victor Henri on a series of studies investigating the abilities of Parisian school children with the intention of developing a battery of tests that would permit a more systematic examination of ability. Binet and Henri were convinced that a fuller understanding could be arrived at by studying the abilities of children outside of the normal range of abilities, particularly those who were below average.

Termed 'Psychologie Individuelle', Binet became the most power-ful promoter and advocate of the study of individual differences. By 1899, Binet was collaborating with the physician Théodore Simon and both became committed members of the Société Libre pour l'Etude psychologique de l'enfant (The Free Society for the Psychological Study of the Child). Profoundly sceptical regarding the utility of the so-called objective assessments by parents, teachers and doctors. Binet set about trying to convince its members that systematic observation and the experimental method were the way forward for the study of child development and steered the organisation towards the psychological training of teachers and research into educational psychology.

By 1901, Binet was heading the French Ministerial Commission in Paris, which aimed to track underperforming or 'abnormal' children with the aim of identifying those who would not benefit from formal State education. In May 1905, Binet and Simon had established the first Laboratory of Experimental Psychology in a Parisian school. Here they could refine their work into a test battery which would evaluate all levels of abilities testing digit span retention, vocabulary, paper folding, comprehension, block design reproduction, similarities and differences. The sample sizes, however, remained small and unrepresentative, which is surprising, given Binet's standpoint for the importance of sound experimental methods and robust research design. What made the test unique, however, was its capacity to increase in difficulty. It ranged from using simple tracking tests, to the more advanced analysis of older or gifted children through testing with complex sentence completion. The test would, in theory, enable assessments of children which would determine what mental age that child was performing at, permitting comparisons between a child's mental age and the average performance of children in a chronological age group.

The first Binet-Simon test was published in 1908 and the later 1911 revision helped answer some of the issues around representation. The groups tested were more diverse in age, intellect and socio-economic status. Binet's intention was that it could help him advocate for the education of all children and to better help teachers understand their individual needs, and he spent much of his professional time and research efforts on educational reform. The test, however, remained largely ignored in France. It was Henry Goddard, the prominent American psychologist and eugenicist, who discovered Binet's work and translated it into English. Lewis M. Terman administered the test to North American children with the intention of understanding the genetic basis of intelligence. The test then went through further revisions at Stanford University, where Terman was working as Assistant Professor in the School of Education; resulting in the Stanford-Binet intelligence test.

Binet died unexpectedly in 1912. He was only 54 years of age and his wife was also in poor health. We know very little about the personality or personal life of Binet, few records exist. His daughter Madeleine described him as a

> *lively man, smiling, often very ironical, gentle in manner, wise in his judgments, a little sceptical of course.* . . . *Without affectation, straightforward, very good-natured, he was scornful of mediocrity in all its forms. Amiable and cordial to people of science, pitiless toward bothersome people who wasted his time and interrupted his work.* . . . *He always seemed to be deep in thought*
>
> (cited in Wolf, 1973, p. 36)

Binet is described as happiest when he had a blank sheet of paper to fill, and outside of the psychology laboratory, he had a passion for the theatre, attending plays and sharing his home with playwrights, actors and directors. He wrote, co-authored and produced dramas, four of which were performed in Paris at the Grand-Guignol and Sarah-Bernhardt theatres. These plays typically had a dark, morose, psychological side, examining the grave consequences of greed, pompousness and stupidity.

Binet mostly resisted theoretical speculations about the inherited or theoretical nature of intelligence. From 1908, he was advocating a constructionist perspective but was hampered by a lack of understanding about the structure of complex intelligence. The closest Binet came to a theory of intelligence was a manifestation of comprehension, memory and good judgement, and that a complex number of specific processes combined into a whole.

In his study of judgement, Binet distinguished between direction, adaption and criticism. Direction was the strength of task focus and problem-solving strategy. These operated to support idea generation in the face of distractions and failure. Adaptation was the extent to which an individual could make appropriate choices from alternative options and their capacity to refine their solutions to fit any task constraints. Criticism was the internal monologue which provided feedback to help evaluate potential solutions to a problem. Binet's work on this area relates closely to modern-day ideas about the role of metacognition in intelligence, particularly current thinking on learning to learn as a predictor for academic performance. Binet's study of his own children and their differences in temperament also laid out the blueprint for future work on cognitive styles and the work of psychologists such as Howard Gardner who argued for different patterns of strengths and weaknesses in ability.

Binet's legacy is in his contribution to psychometric testing through the development of an easy-to-use test that examined mental functioning. The nature of intelligence, for Binet, was what his test could measure and the scale embodied ideas that are still relevant today. The best way to understand performance is to reference it against what is normal or typical, and, rather than observing simple processes, understand that the largest differences between individuals will reside in complex mental functions. It would follow that those functions should be assessed in a variety of ways and that what is considered intellect would be the sum of those measures.

Binet did not, however, consider the impact such labels would have on children who performed poorly on the test. He believed that intellectual potential was malleable. While inheritance might place a ceiling on potential, special education, simulation and support would compensate for any deficits. For Binet, the value of his test was in the opportunities it provided to children because they could be reliability measured and reliability supported. The test was, however, heavily weighted towards scholastic experience, particularly verbal ability. The sampling of children included in the study remained to narrow usefully record performance at higher levels; it was too easy at lower levels and too difficult at the upper end. There were a number of technical problems with the test, including misplacements of test items relative to mental age, the same number of psychological functions were not always assessed at each age level and because mental age could be arrived at differently from person to person. In particular, when a child was expected to be verbally developed, the test began to disproportionately favourable performance on verbal test items, to the point at which at the top end of the scale the test could be said to capture only verbal ability. Test takers with poor verbal ability, or for whom French or English was not their first language, were automatically penalised.

The test, which was doubtless a major improvement on previous processes, was still inadequate. Binet was aware of at least some of these problems and did make attempts at improvements. It would be Lewis M. Terman who would ultimately go on to make the most substantial improvements, revising the test into a more comprehensive and easier-to-use tool.

Alfred Binet's major writings

Binet, A. (1890). *La Suggestibilité*. Paris: Schleicher Frères.
Binet, A. (1890). Perceptions d'Enfants. Revue Philosophique de la France Et de l'Etranger, *30*, 582–611.

Binet, A. (1891). *Études de psychologie expérimentale*. France: O Doin.

Binet, A. (1892). *Les Altérations de la Personnalité*. Paris: Alcan.

Binet, A. (1893). *L'Etude Expérimentale de l'Intelligence*. Paris: Schleicher Frères.

Binet, A. (1898). *La Fatigue Intellectuelle*. Paris: Schleicher Frères (with V. Henri).

Binet, A. (1898). La Mesure en Psychologie Individuelle. *Revue Philosophique, 46*, 113–123.

Binet, A. (1908). Le développement de l'intelligence chez les enfants. *L'Année Psychologique, 14*, 1–94.

Sur la nécessité d'établir un diagnostic scientifique des états inférieurs de l'intelligence. Binet, A., & Simon, T. (1905). *L'Année Psychologique, 11*, 163–190 (with Th. Simon).

Further reading

Fancher, R. E. (1985). *The intelligence men*. New York: W.W. Norton.

Wolf, T. (1973). *Alfred Binet*. University of Chicago Press.

10 Donald Eric Broadbent (1926–1993)

Broadbent used experimental methods to understand and enhance human behaviour in a wide range of settings particularly through his work on selective attention.

Donald Eric Broadbent was born in Birmingham, the son of an executive in a British-based multinational company who left both the company and his family at the start of World War II. For the early part of the war, he lived with his mother in the small Welsh village of Llandyman and later they moved to Mould. His mother supported them with income as a clerical assistant in local business offices. He was educated at Winchester College, the fees being paid from his father's pension fund, an 'exhibition' and a school bursary. He enlisted for military service in 1944, and his RAF training was undertaken in North America, where he first encountered the subject of psychology – then largely unheard of by most young people in England. He was drawn to considering the problems that can arise when people are required to work with complex technologies, and this motivated a switch from engineering to psychology. Thus, he was originally attracted to psychology by the need to design technological environments suitable for human use. Throughout his career, he remained committed to the idea that psychologists should develop sound theories capable of delivering applications that could be used in the public interest, and he provided numerous powerful demonstrations of how attempts to solve practical problems can motivate and inform theoretical innovation. The Cambridge Department of Psychology, headed by Bartlett, was a particularly appropriate place for someone with such interests. The admissions committee at Pembroke College were sure that he should study for a degree in chemistry but, after much persuasion, relented.

Wartime work on developing applications of cognitive psychology for resolving user-technology problems had led in 1944 to the foundation

DOI: 10.4324/9781003229179-11

of the Medical Research Council's Applied Psychology Unit at Cambridge. On graduation, Broadbent joined the unit and commenced work on topics relating to the influence of environmental stressors on human cognitive performance, a theme throughout his career. In 1958, he became Director and over the next 16 years he shaped the Unit, creating an enduring blend of pure and applied research.

Donald married Margaret E. Wright in 1949, and they had two daughters before the marriage was dissolved in 1972. He married Margaret Gregory (who had been married to Richard Gregory) in the same year. A couple of years later, Broadbent moved to Oxford to pursue his own work without the administrative responsibilities of the Unit. Much of this work was conducted in collaboration with his second wife. The death of his daughter Liz, following a road accident in 1979, had an enduring impact on his life and almost certainly contributed in part to his renunciation of his previously strong Christian faith (Weiskrantz, 1994).

Broadbent was trained in Cambridge at a time when the influences of Alan Turing, an intellectual pioneer of artificial intelligence, and the gifted experimentalist Kenneth Craik created an atmosphere sympathetic to his interests in designing technological environments suitable for human use and to the idea of explaining human behaviour in terms of the computational processes that must be undertaken by any system that behaves as people do. Although Craik had died in a road accident just before Broadbent arrived, the influence of his thinking on cybernetic and hierarchical control systems was well established. During the 1950s, he worked on a variety of applied problems, first on the effects of noise on cognitive performance and then on the difficulties of handling a large number of speech messages simultaneously. These problems were readily handled in terms of the conceptual frameworks due to Craik, Turing, Bartlett and other influences on the Cambridge group; but problematic to handle in the terminology current in psychology laboratories at that time. Consequently, he encountered some difficulty in publishing early work in the mainstream academic journals. His work on auditory selective attention (the perception of some stimuli in the environment relative to other stimuli of lesser immediate priority) was seminal for two reasons. First, it provided a methodology for investigating the psychology of attention at a time when behaviourism had rejected attempts to investigate such phenomena. Second, it exploited new information processing concepts being developed in mathematics and engineering to develop a model of human cognition that proved both theoretically sound and useful in practical matters.

Perception and Communication (1958) summarised many of the results obtained in his own laboratory and in a variety of others. In it, Broadbent adopted an information processing framework and argued for its advantages over statements about the connections between stimuli and responses. The publication of the book proved timely and became widely quoted by psychologists turning to a cybernetic, information processing, or cognitive approach to explaining human behaviour. The book set the agenda for what subsequently became known as cognitive psychology, and it is probably the contribution for which he is best known. It is often not fully recognised that the perspective proposed in the book was a by-product of research undertaken for applied reasons. This reflects an important feature of the individuality of his contribution: he demonstrated that psychological theory is best when grounded in the empirical analysis of practical problems.

A central theme of *Perception and Communication* is that a person undertaking several tasks might experience interference between the central processes involved in each of them, that it could be reduced by practice, and that in some cases certain tasks are selected rather than others by a 'filtering' mechanism. The conception was however determinate and, like many psychologists at that time, Broadbent thought of one internal event as succeeding another in a straightforward causal fashion. During the 1960s, he and others produced a great deal of evidence to indicate that the central processes are not like that; on the contrary, each momentary event 'inside' a person is only statistically related to the things that have happened before, so that stable and efficient behaviour depends on the averaging of many separate processes. From this perspective, errors become very important as a way of sorting out the details of the process; it is also in principle impossible ever to eliminate human error totally. These arguments altered quite considerably conceptualisations of attention and workload, and they raised a number of questions about the role of probability and motivation in perception. The revised views were presented in *Decision and Stress* (1973), but this had less impact than *Perception and Communication*. Broadbent attributed this to a failure of presentation and communication on his part and not to problems with the underlying arguments and evidence. In subsequent work, he continued to be concerned to argue against psychological theories that assume determinate and separate mechanisms of cognition. He argued that it was hopeless to attempt to find 'the' mechanism by which any particular psychological task is performed. Different people perform the same task differently, and the same person may perform it differently on different occasions. This led to his arguing for two lines of attack in psychology: first, the need to study the implications of one strategy of cognition rather than another – which ways of thinking show which kinds of advantages and disadvantages? Second, one should look at the external circumstances that cause one strategy to be adopted rather than another.

This change of emphasis coincided with a change in the practical needs of society; away from quick-fix cures for problems created by particular technological devices that have been badly made, to a demand for a more planned approach to the design of devices that might not be constructed for a long time ahead. Thus, his move from the Applied Psychology Unit to Oxford afforded opportunities to demonstrate that the gradual accumulation of evidence from laboratory experiments on different styles of attention and memory could be linked to lengthy life experiences of the individual in the world outside. These efforts took him through the 1970s and into the 1980s and produced a number of important detailed findings, including evidence that people in certain kinds of jobs develop certain psychiatric symptoms. The kinds of symptoms that develop depend on the particular characteristics of the job, and the process is linked to particular individual patterns of selective attention that the person can be shown to display in the laboratory. Thus, in later years he addressed the effects of powerful, pervasive social stressors in the working environment. As part of this work, he developed the Cognitive Failures Questionnaire, a widely-used measure of absent-mindedness. His breadth of research interests – attention and memory, perception, stress, individual differences in temperament, occupational health, and copying styles – address problems and applications which are related through an underlying theoretical fabric. In lighter moments, he would suggest that he was trying to contribute to establishing a new topic called 'Dyccop': Dynamic Cognitive Clinical Occupational Psychology.

Broadbent was firmly convinced that the test of the intellectual excellence of a psychological theory, as well as its moral justification, lies in its application to practical considerations. Moreover, psychology could clarify many of its major questions by considering the resemblances between all adaptive systems – whether mechanical, electronic or social. He applied this view in his assessment of his own contribution to psychology:

> at the end of a career, it is worth realising that the advance of knowledge is actually a network, not a single module, the interaction between individuals reduces the damage done by the errors of any one and the continual review of past outputs makes the final symbolic formulation increasingly accurate.
>
> (1973, pp. 59–60)

Donald Broadbent's major writings

Broadbent, D. E. (1957). A mechanical model for human attention and immediate memory. *Psychological Review*, *64*(3), 205–215.

Broadbent, D. E. (1958). *Perception and communication.* London: Pergamon Press.
Broadbent, D. E. (1961). *Behaviour.* London: Eyre & Spottiswood.
Broadbent, D. E. (1971). *Decision and stress.* London: Academic Press.
Broadbent, D. E. (1973). *In defence of empirical psychology.* London: Methuen.
Broadbent, D. E. (1984). The Maltese cross: A new simplistic model for memory. *Behavioral and Brain Sciences, 7*(1), 55–94.
Broadbent, D. E., Fitzgerald, P., & Broadbent, M. H. (1986). Implicit and explicit knowledge in the control of complex systems. *British Journal of Psychology, 77*(1), 33–50.

Further reading

Baddeley, A., & Weiskrantz, L. (Eds.). (1993). *Attention: Selection, awareness, and control: A tribute to Donald Broadbent.* Clarendon Press/Oxford University Press.
Weiskrantz, L. (1994). Donald Eric Broadbent. *Biographical Memoirs of Fellows of the Royal Society, 40,* 33–42.

11 George Herman Canady (1901–1970)

Herman George Canady was the first African American social psychologist to study the influence and role of race as a bias factor in IQ testing.

George Herman Canady, the son of the Reverent Howard T and Anna Canady was born in the railway town of Okmulgee, Oklahoma, in 1901. The arrival of the railways triggered much prosperity in Okmulgee. A building boom was followed by an expansion of agriculture, coal mining and several new industries such as glass and bottle factories, foundry, and machine shops. By the 1920s, Okmulgee had more millionaires per capita than any other place in the country.[1]

Canady attended Douglass Elementary School, Favour High School, and eventually graduated from George R. Smith College in Sedalia Missouri in 1922. Initially, Canady had ambitions of following his father's calling to the ministry. Having secured the Charles F. Grey scholarship, George began studying Theology at Northwestern University Theological School. However, he quickly realised that his passions lay more towards the behavioural sciences. Canady switched subjects, graduating in 1927 with a major in sociology and a minor in psychology, followed by an MA in clinical psychology in 1928,[2] a Chair of the Psychology Department at West Virginia State University, and his PhD from Northwestern in 1941.

Contribution to the black psychology movement

With interests in clinical problems, intelligence, race and bias, Canady's major contribution to psychology, explored the role that the dynamic between the test administrator (examiner) and test taker played in the measurement of IQ; the suggestion being that black children may not be able to connect with a white examiner and that this dynamic may

DOI: 10.4324/9781003229179-12

impact on the accuracy of measured IQ. Additionally, since white examiners rarely encounter black children, those examiners may carry preconceived and biased notions about the mental attributes of black children. Attitudes could impact on the objectiveness of the data collection and analysis. Additionally, distrust was so ingrained in the black communities that the test takers themselves placed barriers to the process by deliberately providing inaccurate data in an attempt to hinder personal disclosure. Black children had also learned to placate and to please those they viewed as being in more powerful positions. They were more likely to be paying attention to pleasing the examiner than completing the test to the best of their abilities, rendering the value of the results to nothing more than a test of 'good-will'.[3]

Results from Canady's research suggested that there was a tendency for black children to perform systemically worse if test administration was performed by a white examiner and that this pattern was presented also in white children. They would perform worse if tested by a black test administrator. The average IQ gain that black students experienced when tested by a black examiner was the same as the average drop of white students tested in the same way. Canady reported a respective gain and loss of 6 points which, for some students, increased/decreased to over 10 points. Canady's results were not found to be statistically significant spawning future studies and controversy over the capacity of other researchers to systematically replicate his findings.[4,5,6,7,8] Nonetheless, Canady's work has been significant in contemporary psychological theory, for example, where perceived negative stereotypes play a role in triggering ingroup anxiety when those group members interact with outgroup members. For example, children who are then wary or mistrustful of white authority figures will experience anxiety which impacts on their performance. Additionally, theories such as stereotype threat have been able to demonstrate that where there is an expectation of discrimination, performance will diminish.[9] Taken together, stereotype threat and ingroup anxiety can lead to poor performance, loss of interest in subject matter and diminished confidence and self-esteem.[10]

Canady was not just interested in the study of race in individual differences, he was also one of the first people to challenge the idea that there were demonstrable gender differences in intelligence. His 1943 paper 'A Study of Sex Differences in Intelligence-Test Scores Among 1,306 Negro College Freshmen'[11] demonstrated no gender differences in general intelligence, but perhaps some differences in favour of women on subtests on verbal subtests, and in favour of men in subtests addressing numerical aspects of performance.

He lobbied to bring psychology to black institutions to provide more psychology programmes and to provide a better standard of research methods training. Canady surveyed the range of psychological education available, the types of programmes, resources, and faculty support. Only 30% of the 47 institutions provided some degree of psychology training, with only 4 providing comprehensive psychology programmes where students could major in the discipline. Research methods were particularly poorly addressed, with only one institution making laboratory work a requirement,[12] and only 8 of the 88 psychology lecturers across all institutions had published research within 5 years of the survey. This publication was possibly the only scholarly work at that time examining the training and research of psychologist in black universities and colleges and was fundamental in changing the perceptions, development and employment of black scholars to the field.

Canady continued to make significant efforts to raise the profile of psychology to black students and institutions, and his organising efforts led in 1938 to the formation of Division 6, a Department of Psychology within the American Teachers Association. This was one of the very first professional organisations for psychologist of colour, and through Canady's efforts the Division 6 team were not only able to directly address issues related to African American education, issues which had previously been examined through a largely white-centric psychological lens, but also contribute to the restructuring of the American Psychological Association during World War II. Ethnic minority psychologists were still in small numbers, but their voice was growing.

George Herman Canady married Julia Witten in 1934, and together they had two children, Joyce and Herman George Jr. Herman was one of the first African Americans to attend law school, and later became a circuit court judge and activist against segregated public spaces.

For his contributions to science and psychology, George Herman Canady was honoured as Fellow by the American Association for the Advancement of Science and the American Psychological Association. After 40 years as Chair of the Psychology Department at West Virginia State University, he retired in 1968 and died 2 years later, on January 1, 1970.

Notes

1 Schultz, J. (2005). Most millionaires/capita to own and out: Can they come back? *Boomtown USA*. Retrieved from http://webcache.googleusercontent.com/search?q=cache:y5sOXQc9dYMJ:boomtownusa.blogspot.com/2005/05/most-millionairescapita-to-down-outcan.html+&cd=2&hl=en&ct=clnk&gl=us

2 Guthrie, R. (1998). *Even the rat was white: A historical view of psychology* (2nd ed.). Boston: Allyn and Bacon.
3 Canady, H. G. (1936). The effect of "rapport" on the IQ: A new approach to the problem of racial psychology. *Journal of Negro Education, 5*, 209–219. https://doi.org/10.2307/2292157
4 Moore, C., & Retish, P. (1974). Effect of the examiner's race on black children's Wechsler preschool and primary scale of intelligence IQ. *Developmental Psychology, 10*(5), 672–676.
5 Thames, A., Hinkin, C., Byrd, D., Bilder, R., Duff, K., Mindt, M., Arentoft, A., & Streiff, V. (2013). Effects of stereotype threat, perceived discrimination, and examiner race on neuropsychological performance: Simple as Black and White? *Journal of the International Neuropsychological Society, 19*, 583–593.
6 Thames, A., Hinkin, C., Byrd, D., Bilder, R., Duff, K., Mindt, M., Arentoft, A., & Streiff, V. (2013). Effects of stereotype threat, perceived discrimination, and examiner race on neuropsychological performance: Simple as Black and White? *Journal of the International Neuropsychological Society, 19*, 583–593.
7 Graziano, W., Varca, P., & Levy, J. (1982). Race of examiner effects and the validity of intelligence tests. *Review of Educational Research, 52*(4), 469–497.
8 Terrell, F., & Terrell, S. (1983). The relationship between race of examiner, cultural mistrust, and the intelligence test performance of black children. *Psychology in the Schools, 20*(3), 367–369.
9 Gilovich, T., Keltner, D., & Nisbett, R. E. (2006). Being a member of a stigmatized group: stereotype threat. In T. Gilovich, D. Keltner, & R. E. Nisbett (Eds.), *Social psychology* (pp. 467–468). New York: W.W. Norton.
10 Gilovich, T., Keltner, D., & Nisbett, R. E. (2006). Being a member of a stigmatized group: Stereotype threat. In T. Gilovich, D. Keltner, & R. E. Nisbett (Eds.), *Social psychology* (pp. 467–468). New York: W.W. Norton.
11 Canady, H. G. (1943). A study of sex differences in intelligence test scores among 1306 Negro college freshmen. *The Journal of Negro Education, 12*, 167–172.
12 Canady, H. (1938). Psychology in Negro institutions. *The Journal of Negro Education, 7*(2), 165–171.

George Herman Canady's major writings

Canady, H. G. (1936). The effect of "rapport" on the IQ: A new approach to the problem of racial psychology. *Journal of Negro Education, 5*, 209–219. https://doi.org/10.2307/2292157
Canady, H. G. (1942). The American caste system and the question of negro intelligence. *Journal of Educational Psychology, 33*(3), 161–172. https://doi.org/10.1037/h0062680
Canady, H. G. (1943). A study of sex differences in intelligence-test scores among 1,306 Negro college freshmen. *The Journal of Negro Education, 12*(2), 167–172.

12 Raymond Bernard Cattell (March 20, 1905–February 2, 1998)

Applied advanced statistical techniques to make fundamental contributions to the measurement and understanding of the structure of personality and ability.

Raymond Bernard Cattell was born in Hill Top, Staffordshire, England, on March 20, 1905, to Alfred Earnest Cattell and Mary Field. His family were second-generation owners of several manufacturing plants in the United Kingdom. They were mechanical engineers and the inventors of engines and automobiles, World War II military equipment and the new internal combustion engine. Cattell was the second of three sons, and the family moved to the seaside town of Torquay in Devonshire when he was 6 years old, triggering a love of the sea that would last a lifetime. Later in his life, Cattell would publish a personal account of his sailing experiences around the coastline and estuaries of Devon.

Cattell quickly demonstrated an aptitude for literature and science. By the age of 10, he was reading H.G. Wells and Arthur Conan Doyle. His academic competence put him in conflict with his less able brother, but the problem was soon resolved when Cattell won a scholarship to attend Torquay Boys' Grammar School and his brother was moved to a school which could more address his education outside of forthright academic study. Cattell's talent developed quickly in this new environment, and he eventually became the first in his family to pass the university entrance examination to study Chemistry at Kings College London. Cattell graduated in 1924 at the age of 19 with a first-class degree in physics and chemistry. Always open to the works and ideas of others, Cattell browsed far outside of his science, attending the lectures of Bertrand Russell, H.G. Wells and Aldous Huxley, who Cattell said, converted him to vegetarianism for almost 2 years.

The works of Sir Cyril Burt and of Francis Galton and their arguments to secure a better future for mankind, merged with the destructive

DOI: 10.4324/9781003229179-13

aftermath of World War I, influenced Cattell's decision to use the new science of psychology to solve human problems, and he began studying for a doctorate in psychology with the psychologist and priest Francis Aveling. His PhD was undertaken to resolve problems raised by Spearman's Principles of Cognition and the nature of mental energy. Cattell was closely involved in developing a new factor method to further study Spearman's theory of general intelligence, work which would eventually lead to an invitation to work at Thorndike's lab at Columbia University.

Following the successful completion of his PhD in 1929, Cattell secured a post at Exeter University and his first son Herry was born to his childhood sweetheart Monica Rogers. Cattell was studying for an MA in education at the time and soon moved to Leicester to organise the development of one of England's first child guidance clinics. He was awarded a Darwin Fellowship from the Eugenics Society, which enabled him to conduct research into declining population intelligence. During these productive year's, Cattell finally published his book *Under Sail Through Red Devon*, however, unable to tolerate his consistent neglect, his wife left him after only 4 years.

Cattell's MA work was his first systematic attempt to articulate what would become the lynch-pin of his career, his ideas on the structure and function of personality, but it was his work on intelligence which captured the notice of Edward Thorndike and in 1937 Thorndike offered him a research position at Columbia University. The following year, 1938, he became the G. Stanley Hall Professor at Clark University, Massachusetts, which was a role primarily aimed at the study of developmental psychology.

Clark was another disappointment for Cattell. Depression ensued, largely because he felt there were limited opportunities to research. In 1941, Cattell moved to Harvard to work with Gordon Allport and Henry Murray on more serious personality research but was again disappointed. He and Allport spoke a different personality language, which was near impossible to reconcile. World War II finally settled Cattell's career path, he was invited to work on psychological measurement issues for selection purposes, he caught the attention of the APA President Herbert Woodrow and he was invited to occupy a new professorship at the University of Illinois, which had the first electronic computer owned by an educational institution.

Soon after joining the faculty at Illinois, Cattell met and married the mathematician Karen Schuettler, who would become instrumental in supporting him with the statistical aspects of his work. Karen and Cattell went on to have three daughters (Mary, Heather and Elaine-Devon) and a son (Roderic). The marriage ended in 1980.

At Illinois, Cattel could complete the most advanced large-scale factor analyses of his career. With his wife, he founded the Laboratory of Personality Assessment and group behaviour and the commercially successful Institute for Personality and Ability Testing. Cattell remained in Illinois until 1973, only leaving at the mandatory retirement age. He continued to write up results from research projects after retirement, eventually moving to Hawaii, which enabled him to pursue his love of sailing while working part-time advising at the University of Hawaii. The Hawaiian low-altitude environment also enabled Cattell to better manage his worsening heart condition.

The researcher and clinical psychologist, Heather Birkett, became Cattell's third wife. They moved to a lagoon near Oahu (called the gathering place), where Cattell continued to publish and sail until old age made navigation hazardous. Heather would become fundamental to the development and publication of the most robust of Cattell's tests; the 16PF became the one of the most well-known personality tests in research, occupational selection and clinical practice for decades.

Throughout the course of Cattell's career, he authored 56 books, 500 journal articles and book chapters, and 30 standardised testing manuals. He was doubtlessly one of the most significant psychologists of his time. Awards included the Educational Testing Service Award for distinguished service, the Behaviour Genetics Association Memorial Award for eminent research and the Distinguished Lifetime Contribution to Evaluation, Measurement and Statistics from the American Psychological Association. In 1997, the American Psychological Society named Cattel as their Gold Medal Award for a Life Time of Achievement in Psychological Science; an award which risked the destruction of his legacy. Cattell, now aged 92, was accused of supporting white supremacism and segregation.

Although an eminent and prolific psychologist, Cattell's style throughout his career was divisive and grandiose. He was so contentious that a common belief was that the award was delayed until he was 92 years old because, by then, almost everyone he had ever offended would have died. Psychology is too difficult for psychologists, he would argue, and that teachers and researchers in psychology were mediocre. Cattell was also reluctant to discuss or acknowledge the works of others in his field, something noted by Arthur Jensen in his review of *Intelligence* (1987). Cattell's book did not contain a single reference to developments reported in leading journals. His writing was also neologic and lacking in clarity. He also shared an attitude with Hans Eysenck that re-writing was an encumbrance that distracted him from the next scientific endeavour. Cattell wrote faster than most people could read, but it did not always follow that this writing was good, '*an assault on the English language*', '*an alphabet soup so thick a parenthesis drowns*'. Perhaps seeing the irony in his own works, Cattell described psychology as '*describing things which everyone knows in language which no one understands*' (1965, p. 18).

Cattell's study of intelligence had always been a branch from his study of personality. His interest largely focused on the idea that personality factors could explain why some individuals of similar intelligence were unequal in achievement. The trait of perseverance offered fertile ground, and he characterised individuals into racial categories, using hair and eye colour, stature and cephalic index, to analyse if there was a possible hereditary factor to perseverance. This work, much to his frustration, was largely ignored and he discontinued this line of investigation in favour of more empirically grounded research into personality.

He did, however, remain interested in defending the study of racial difference and saw nothing instrumentally wrong with segregation. Cattell went as far as attacking the integrity of those who were interested in the scientific study prejudice for attempting to introduce false values into science. Cattell published *Beyondism; Religion from Science* in 1972. The book described his socio-moral beliefs and his arguments against human rights, humanism and social justice because, he argued, they interfered with genetic progress. Group competition increased positive evolutionary progress. Those who were reluctant to investigate racial differences were 'ignoracists' and more dangerous than racists.

For Cattell, interrace relationships were not the issue, rather what he called for was genetic management, where the genetically unproductive would not be permitted to have children. While not overtly racist in its central thesis, the book championed intellectual elitism even though his research into the decline of intelligence had been defunct by James R. Flynn.

This was at a time when America was becoming a more culturally diverse and integrated nation. Unsurprisingly, there was a limited inclination towards the kind of values, scientific and religious, that Cattell was advocating. Ignored by mainstream science, he began an association with *Mankind Quarterly*, a marginal anthropological journal which had been started in part as a response to UNESCO's declaration that race was not a biological construct. The journal's editorial team included a leading Nazi anthropologist and a British anthropologist who had contributed to the Nazi literature on racial hygiene. The outputs from the journal could be reasonably described as racist. Whether Cattell and the editorial team were completely ideologically compatible, remains to be seen. However, *Mankind Quarterly* gave Cattell an outlet for *Beyondism* and he joined the editorial team, but he was now firmly tied to extremist arguments that attempted to apply scientific justification for racial policies.

Two weeks before the award ceremony, Barry A. Mehler, who was Director of the Institute for the Study of Academic Racism issued a press release about Cattell's lifetime commitment to eugenics, and Cattell, who was largely unknown to the public, became the surprise target of mainstream news. The Foundation delayed the award and began investigating the allegations.

Cattell attempted to address the misconceptions of his work in an open letter published in the *New York Times*. He attempted to clarify that his ideas had developed over the years and now only believed in voluntary eugenics and that there was no valid evidence to support the argument that there were racial differences in intelligence. He attempted to correct the misconceptions and attacks against him. '*I believe in equal opportunity for all individuals, and I abhor racism and discrimination based on race. Any other belief would be antithetical to my life's work*'. Cattell was now in poor health; he withdrew his name from the nomination and died a few months later, on February 2, 1998, surrounded by his family and his two dogs.

Cattell was one of the first psychologists to use this 'mental model' framework to make some categorisations about the traits that make up personality. He defined personality as that which may predict what a person will do in each situation and if we can better understand personality, we can then use it to investigate human behaviour.

Initially, Cattell started with thousands of traits, about 18,000 different trait terms in the English lexicon. This technique is known as the 'inductive-hypothetico-deductive spiral' approach (Cattell, 1978), eventually condensing those vast numbers down into 16 primary traits using the statistical method of factor analysis. The inductive approach is a cyclic process whereby theories that emerge from the data are used to generate testable hypotheses and then fed back into the cycle. At that time, it was possibly one of the first truly objective approaches to the measurement of personality because it broke away from what is sometimes referred to as the Barnum effect – the tendency for people to latch onto general descriptors about personality – towards the breaking of personality into useable workable constructs which were grounded in a theory of personality that could be used to interpret behaviour. This shifted thinking in the field away from 'grand theories' of personality as a state, changing over time, towards a nomothetic trait definition of personality as a constant characteristic that remains stable, more or less, over time.

In part to answer Gordon Allport's criticisms that Cattell was relying on statistical analysis over individual observations, he developed four key research methodologies. A method whereby a person's scores on several measures are compared across different situations and over time (the P-technique). Correlations of large numbers of different measures (the Q-technique), the R-technique, whereby individuals are compared in terms of their scores or performance on many specific measures, and Differential-R, which measures individuals on different occasions and examines changes and similarities.

Using his methodology, he could present evidence for ability, temperament and dynamic traits, and, surface and source traits. Ability relates to skills and intelligence, temperament to the emotional life and dynamic to the motivational life. Surface traits are the behaviours and attitudes that manifest from the source traits from which they are formed.

Despite Cattell's exhaustive efforts to map out an analytically derived model of personality, his refusal to acknowledge that personality could be represented in a smaller number of dimensions (despite identifying a three-factor model), combined with difficulties in replicating the 16-factor model, resulted in psychologists falling out of favour with the Cattellian personality measures towards a 'global' five-factor model.

Cattell's extensive and pioneering work played an important role in what is often remembered as the 'Big 5 (Goldberg, 1981)' or the OCEAN (McCrae & Costa, 1985) five-factor model of personality (openness, conscientiousness, extraversion, agreeableness and neuroticism).

Raymond Cattell's major writings

Cattell, R. B. (1950). The main personality factors in questionnaire material. *Journal of Social Psychology, 31*, 3–38.
Cattell, R. B. (1951). P-technique: A new method for analysing personal motivation. *Transactions of the New York Academy of Sciences, 14*, 29–34.
Cattell, R. B. (1965). *The scientific analysis of personality*. Harmondsworth: Pelican.
Cattell, R. B. (1970). *Personality and learning theory*. London: Springer.
Cattell, R. B. (1971). *Abilities: Their structure, growth and action*. Boston: Houghton Mifflin.
Cattell, R. B. (1973). *Personality and mood by questionnaire*. Oxford, UK: Jossey-Bass.
Cattell, R. B. (1978). The position of factor analysis in psychological research. In *The scientific use of factor analysis in behavioral and life sciences*. Boston, MA: Springer. https://doi.org/10.1007/978-1-4684-2262-7_1
Cattell, R. B. (1982). *The inheritance of personality and ability*. New York: Academic Press.
Cattell, R. B. (1987). *Beyondism: Religion from science*. New York: Praeger.
Cattell, R. B. (1987). *Intelligence: Its structure, growth and action*. Amsterdam: North-Holland.
Horn, J. L., & Cattell, R. B. (1966). Refinement and test of the theory of fluid and crystallized intelligence. *Journal of Educational Psychology, 57*, 253–270.

Further reading

Goldberg, L. (1981). Language and individual differences: The search for universals in personality lexicons. In L. Wheeler (Ed.), *Review of personality and social psychology* (pp. 141–165). Beverly Hills, CA: Sage Publication.

McCrae, R. R., & Costa, P. T. (1985). Updating Norman's "adequacy taxonomy": Intelligence and personality dimensions in natural language and in question-naires. *Journal of Personality and Social Psychology*, *49*(3), 710–721. https://doi.org/10.1037/0022-3514.49.3.710

Tucker, W. (2009). *The Cattell controversy: Race, science, and ideology.* Chicago: University of Illinois Press.

13 Katherine Cook Briggs (1875–1968) and Isabel Briggs Myers (1897–1980)

Founders of a psychological instrument grounded in the appreciation of human differences.

Isabel Briggs was born on October 18, 1897, to Lyman J. Briggs and Katherine Briggs. She was born in Columbia, South Carolina. She grew up in Washington, where she was homeschooled by her mother while her father worked as a doctor. She was, throughout her early life, her mother's project. Isabel's nurse was promptly dispatched after advising Katherine that the child's feet were ill matched and that they should never feed her hog meat at it would make the child coarse. These attitudes were incompatible with Katherine's permissive child-rearing beliefs, attitudes which quickly changed when she discovered her infant child waving a carving knife around the kitchen and lessons in obedience commenced.

In her heart, Katherine was an author. She had driving ambition, but her schooling had equipped her inadequately. She is quoted as saying that whoever had taught her to read and write had done so badly. At a time in history when it was still believed that excessive education would diminish a women's fertility, Katherine managed to secure a college degree, studying geology with the emerging field of psychology. She developed an academic career but sacrificed it to support her husband's medical career, but she remained an avid reader and writer throughout her life. This career path was unorthodox for a woman of that time, but it was a grounding that enabled Katherine and her husband to evolve a new educational system for their children Isabel and Albert.

Katherine's bond with Isabel was intense. She began to keep a detailed diary so that in the future they would, together, explore the ideas and ideals, the influences and the methods of their lives which would inevitably shape little Isabel's character. When baby Albert died

DOI: 10.4324/9781003229179-14

at 18 months, Katherine's grief was recorded in this leather-bound book, which she later attempted to publish as a novel called *The Life of Suzanne*. After failing to publish as a novel, her writings were printed in a series of 300-word editorials in the *Ladies Home Journal* and some feature articles under the pseudonym, Elizabeth Childe.

Katherine's exhaustive efforts meant that by the time Isabel was entering kindergarten she could read. Following a bout of measles, however, Isabel was not returned to school and remained at home.

Public school education was to Katherine, plagued by rules, definitions, drill, confusion and haste. She had a very modern philosophy that the knowledge that a child has does not make them clever. Rather, it is their attitude to what they do not know that does. Katherine wanted to encourage curiosity in Isabela so that she would try out her own ideas about her education without interference. Nobody was needed to intercede between the knowledge seeker and where the knowledge existed. Isabel's school days were not fixed or planned; there was a great deal of independent reading, arithmetic and writing. By the age of 7, Isabel had kept a sophisticated log of a month-long journey to Costa Rica, by the age of 8 she was learning German, Latin, French and classics such as Cicero and Vergil.

Katherine's writing success was soon followed by Isabel who, from the age of 14, began submitting editorials and letters. Mostly muses on the irritations of school life, poems and short stories. The only subject Isabel did not seem to thrive at was music, but she was partial to some dancing, particularly throughout her college years. Despite her mother's close supervision, Isabel was turning into a well socialised young woman with an array of hobbies and interests. By her pre-college years, she was managing the attentions of five men before deciding that she wanted to attend the co-educational institution Swarthmore College, where she met Clarence Gates Myers. Known to his friends as the 'Chief', Isabel summed him up to her mother as qualifying 'splendidly on strength and control and the moral code' (letters Dec 16th, 1915). The couple soon became 'secretly engaged', but the imminent threat of conscription to join the fighting in Europe triggered Chief into making an application to the army aviation service. Draft would give no such choice. The couple publicly announced their engagement, and, while they awaited Chief's orders, they returned to study. Isabel remained in Swarthmore. Chief went to Princeton, which had placed its resources at the disposal of the government to support the war effort, and then he went on to train as a bomber pilot. Eventually, the couple secured a brief window of time in which to marry and Isabel was a war bride on June 17, 1918.

Katherine began to struggle in 'letting go' of Isabel. She had been a formidable influence in her life, but her affections were now usurped by Chief. To continue to exert influence, Katherine began to court the involvement of Chief. She would encourage him to write to her and then supply her daily letters of advice to Isabel. This constant stream of advice was causing strain on the relationships between Chief, Isabel and Katherine, and the young couple soon started to put distance in place. That did not prevent detailed lifestyle comments arriving from mother. Regardless of her mother's continued intrusion, Isabel returned home to her mother's care for the birth of her first child. It was a safe, generous and loving space, when her baby boy was delivered stillborn and the following year, the premature birth and death of her second child, a little girl. The Chief, clumsily, wired her a message: 'third time is a charm'.

The couple finally returned home to their now-new Swarthmore home, where Isabel eventually gave birth to a healthy boy in April 1926. 'Peter-baby' was joined the following year by baby Isabel-Ann.

While Isabel was growing her family, the avid reader Katherine had begun directing her attention back to her own education. She started by trying to analyse and understand the basic components of human behaviour by keeping notes on the characters she had read about, such as Benjamin Franklin, General William T. Sherman, Henry Adams (autobiographical accounts of women were a rarity). Then in 1923, she came across Carol Gustav Jung's Psychological Type and is alleged to have said 'this is it'.

Katherine's attempts at turning her ideas into fiction were however failing. She could find no publisher prepared to take on her works, which were stories untangling the secrets of psyche but relied so heavily on the work of Jung and Freud that they were simply over the heads of the average reader. It was Isabel who was to rise to acclaim as an author. In 1928, in response to a newspaper advertisement, Isabel wrote in the space of 5 months, her first manuscript. This book won several literacy prizes, eventually leading to further books and work as a playwright. Katherine never wrote fiction again but something else had piqued her interest.

The *New Republic* (1926) had run an article which suggested how personality type could be used both for profit and for pleasure. This was just before the great stock market crash of 1929 and by 1931 America was amid the Great Depression. Katherine's husband Lyman was unexpectedly promoted, his director died of a stroke at his desk and Lyman inherited a workforce that was inflicted with cutbacks and wage cuts. The difficulties of his position were further compounded by Isabel's belief that they could make money on the wayward stock market. They all lost heavily. Katherine had begun corresponding with Carl Jung, following his publication of psychological types in 1937. She finally met Jung at the Terry Lectures at Yale University and explained how she had, on reading his work, burned her own notes about the human psyche. Jug must have taken her reasonably seriously because he expressed disappointment that she had done this and proceeded to send her his seminar notes. Katherine continued to pursue her interest, gathering momentum in 1942 writing a Reader's Digest article entitled '*Fitting the Worker to the Job*'.

Such measures had been in circulation since the early 1900s. Popularised by the Taylorism search for efficiency and a tidy solution for people sorting, but quality in industry was widely variable, if not completely fraudulent and prejudiced. As the world prepared for World War II, developing a code that could identify the human psyche and facets of resilience that contribute to society and make the world a safer place was becoming a national infatuation. Isabel discovered the Humm-Wadsworth Temperament Scale and hoped that the test would prove efficacious in helping match people to the right positions; the tool was a failure. Katherine's response to her daughter was that she should develop her own tool.

The 'indicator' was born from Katherine and Isabel's ideas about Jung's personality types, funded by their family and driven by Isabel's passion. Never deterred by lack of knowledge on a subject, Isabel studied everything she could about statistics and psychology; she then drew up some preliminary questions in a forced-choice format and began testing increasingly larger samples of people. The basic premise was that 'the indicator' would identify the personality profile of its takers, profiles which would be differentiated on the dimensions of sensing versus intuition, thinking versus feeling, judging versus perceiving and introversion versus extraversion. These dimensions assigned 16 personality types, and those types would further diverge from one another by the extent to which they were dominant or auxiliary drivers, one is the driver and one is the helper.

Jung was still in sporadic correspondence with Katherine and had historically expressed dislike of the theory and rationale behind the measurement device that the device was in no way aligned with his work. A letter does exist, signed by Jung, which seems to contradict his usual position. The letter states, '*The Type-Indicator will prove to be of great help*' (Jung letters to Myers Briggs, 1950), which would seem to completely contradict that this type of measurement was to Jung a parlour game. There is however strong evidence that the then 75-year-old Jung was not in effect signing his own letters and that the content represents little more than the platitudes of his secretary Marie-Jeanne Schmid. It is not difficult to imagine, however, that this was the encouragement that Isabel needed to persist.

In 1956, the Educational Testing Service's (EAS) interest was piqued. They were already the publisher of the Standardised Assessment Test (SATs) that were being implemented for college admission. The test was highly profitable and the indicator offered an opportunity for expansion into personality and, by 1962, the newly titled 'Myers-Briggs Indicator' was being printed for research purposes. The publishing staff were, however, less enthusiastic. Deriding it as unscientific rubbish. The supporting manual was produced by a young test developer, Larry Stricker, and contained a harsh critique of the test. This was not something that Isabel was going to passively accept. Isabel penned the *trademark* of the academic feud; a 24-page missive to the publishing house and filed the manual in a folder labelled '*Larry Stricker, Dam him*'.

Then, much the way as her mother had helpfully supplied a constant stream of advice, Isabel began to make daily (and nightly) visits to the publishing offices in a bid to gather evidence and re-write the manual. Fuelled by what she described as the perfect energy drink (milk, yeast and heresy bar), victory was assured. Stricker was replaced and a new version of the manual was finally published in 1962. This achievement is even more remarkable when we consider that from 1956 Isabel was fighting a malignant tumour in her lymph glands, even delaying surgery so that she could give a symposium.

Isabel had turned into a formidable character. EAS was, however, losing money on the project and staff, who did not ask for the day off or hide when Isabel was in the office and were voicing discord with her nocturnal reconnaissance missions. At the end of 1965, EAS terminated any consulting arrangements with Isabel and, after 10 years of losses, they ceased publication in 1975.

Isabel's test was in danger, but there were greater threats. In 1963, Isabel's father Lyman died and Katherine died 2 years later. Isabel's cancer returned in 1972. Peter and his wife Betty were divorcing, and her daughter Ann was embroiled in an affair with a college professor. Isabel and the Chief were working hard to support Ann and her children, when Ann suddenly died from a pulmonary embolism. The death of a child is a grief like no other. Seventy years earlier, in her leather-bound book, Katherine Brigg's had written of Albert to Isabel, 'If sorrow comes to you, my little girl, and I should not be there to help you bear it, remember this, the message from my grief to yours'. Bereavement and sorrow are as much a part of life as birth and joy. Isabel would later respond to her mother, as she wrote 'a Credo for Living' and her search for meaning and comfort in God. In 1975, at the age of 78, Isabel's clashes with EAS were at an end. The Myers-Briggs Type Indicator, which had started as a family affair, became the venture of Consulting Psychologists Press, who would turn it into one of the most well-known personality measures in the world. Isabel spent the final years of her life continuing to support and promote her work and she died from cancer on May 5, 1980.

Legacy

Based on Jungian theory, the Myers-Briggs Type Indicator [MBTI] the term 'test' is frequently associated with this measure, but the MBTI is an indicator of personality and not a test per se. The confusion about what the MBTI does and does not do has often led to allegations of poor psychometric validity, misuse, misunderstanding and the scientific and academic community being reluctant to adopt the test in mainstream research. For example, publications citing the MBTI have progressively fallen since 2017, while trait measures such as Costa and McCrea's the 'Big 5' continue to rise. The disparity in application is puzzling, given that it has been known for some time that there is significant overlap between the two measures (Furnham, 1996). The British Psychological Society Testing Centre, who offer independent reviews of psychometric tests, also provides a favourable account of the measures.

Katherine Cook Briggs' and Isabel Briggs Myers' major writings

1962. Inferences as to the dichotomous nature of Jungs types, from the shape of regressions of dependent-variables upon Myers-Briggs Type Indicator Scores. *American Psychologist, 17*(6), 364–364.
1962. *The Myers-Briggs type indicators.* Princeton, NJ: Educational Testing Service.
1964. *Relation of medical students' psychological type to their specialties twelve years later.* Center for Applications of Psychological Type.
1967. *Relation of psychological type to dropout in nursing.* Gainesville, FL: Center for the Applications of Psychological Type.
1974. *Relevance of type to medical education.* Paper to be included in The Myers-Briggs Type Indicator in Medical Education.
1974. *Type and teamwork.* Gainesville, FL: Center for Applications of Psychological Type.
1976. *Introduction IO type.* Gainesville, FL: Center for Applications of Psychological Type.
1976. *Introduction to type*.* CPP.

1977. *The Myers-Briggs type indicator: Supplementary manual.* Consulting Psychologists Press.

1979. *Type and teamwork.* Center for Applications of Psychological Type.

1980. *Gifts differing* (with Paul Myers-Briggs).

Further reading

Furnham, A. (1996). The big five versus the big four: The relationship between the Myers-Briggs Type Indicator (MBTI) and NEO-PI five factor model of personality. *Personality and Individual Differences, 21*(2), 303–307.

Saunders, F. W. (1991). *Katherine and Isabel; Mother's light, daughters journey.* CA: Consulting Psychologists Press Inc.

14 Sir Cary Cooper (April 28, 1940–)

Cary Cooper was born in Los Angeles, California, on April 28, 1940, to Harry Cooper and Lillian Greenberg. His parents were of Eastern European Jewish background. His Russian father was born in Buky, a small Jewish shtetl, in what would later become Ukraine (following the emergence of the Soviet Union). Harry, his younger brother, and his mother Ida (Kuperman) were forced to flee Ukraine around 1920 in response to the waves of anti-Jewish pogroms (state-sanctioned purgative attacks aimed at ethnic cleansing) that were wrought upon the Jewish population by the White Volunteer Army and the Cossacks. Tens of thousands of Jews were subjected to persecution and antisemitic discrimination. They were terrorised, raped, had their property stolen and in the end, many Jews, particularly the younger ones, chose to abandon Buky in the hope of finding safer locations, education and better work opportunities. Harry's father had already managed to make it to Canada. He sent the family money to make the journey and, at the age of 10, Harry and his family walked over 1,600 miles from Buky to Murmansk in northwest Russia, where they were able to find a ship willing to take them to Canada.

Harry was a bright child and could already speak Russian, Yiddish and German. Onboard the ship, he began to quickly develop his English skills, adding again to his language repertoire. When the family arrived in Canada, Harry began to work, supporting his family by cutting hair. Eventually, Harry emigrated to America to open a barber's shop in Los Angeles.

Lillian's family had emigrated from Romania to America to escape the increasingly harsh policies of discrimination and anti-Semitism which, even before Romania joined the Axis alliance of 1940, were already commonplace in Romania. The family settled in mid-west Nebraska, where they lived a comfortable middle-class lifestyle. Lillian's father worked as a porter for the Nebraska State government, which

DOI: 10.4324/9781003229179-15

meant that the family was sufficiently secure financially to send Lillian to university, something largely unheard of in the 1920s. However, ineffectual land management policies triggered the Dust Bowl drought and failed crops, and the stock market crash of 1929 devastated the region. Like millions of American families, their financial stability and security became perilous. The family lost all their money. Lillian was forced to leave University, and she travelled to Los Angeles with ambitions of becoming an actress.

Lillian was only 21 when she met Harry. Harry was 9 years her senior and had already been married twice and had four children. His first marriage was 'shot gun' and after the baby was born, the relationship only lasted about another 12 months, and the family no longer kept in touch. His second wife died of a blood disease shortly after giving birth to her third child. They settled in a poor part of East LA, but an area with a strong Jewish community. Harry ran a barbers shop, which became a focal point for the community. It was a buzzing environment with people always coming in and out of the shop, and perhaps attracted by Harry's illegal side hustle, an off-course, bookmakers running out of the back of the shop. Cary recalls often having as a child to pick up the phone and note down some betting fundamentals and agreed-upon odds.

These activities were often a source of discomfort if in fact shame but that was perhaps nothing in comparison to trying to process the treatment of his half-siblings (Murray, Beverly and Sally). Lillian had not felt able to cope with Harry's children from his previous relationships, and they were placed in a Jewish Orphanage. Cary's lasting memories were that he would go at the weekends to see his brothers and sisters and play with them while his father would cut their hair. Cary could never understand how his siblings had ended up in an orphanage and that by some misfortune not of his own making, his birth had caused his siblings to end up in care. These experiences had a profound and lasting impact on Cary. A complex range of emotions whereby Cary could see his mother as both loving and caring, but conversely someone who had placed his father's children into care. In his opinion, she should never have taken on his father if she was not also prepared to take on his children. Eventually, Cary's grandmother stepped in and brought Harry's children to live with her, and Cary spent the rest of his life working to stay close and meaningfully involved with his siblings and their children.

Cary's father was not particularly educationally ambitious for his children, but Lillian was determined that her two children (Cary and Tabi) would attend university. Harry was cautiously supportive but made it clear if that was what the kids wanted to do, they had to pay for it themselves. Cary managed to secure a place at the highly competitive UCLA, studying business management and economics during the day and working every night and at weekends. He held jobs serving legal subpoenas and sold dishes and magazine subscriptions door to door in order to support himself through his studies, flipping between living at home when money was tight, and with friends when times were better. Like many students, Cary's early studies suffered. Not just because of juggling work and study commitments but also because of associated socialisation that comes with freshman years and fraternity membership. He did manage, however, to pull things around and by the final year of his study, his was talent was spotted and given the opportunity to work on a special assignment for a top UCLA professor in the aerospace industry in California. This was the first time he began to think of himself as possibly being academically talented. As the first in his family to go to university, it had taken some time to develop a sense of belonging. University was an intimidating place, and it took him a while to learn to study effectively. The perceptions of others that Cary was somehow very smart became a reoccurring motivation in Cary's life. With a deep-seated lack of belief in his own intelligence, he had a passion to prove that he was actually as smart as people thought he was.

His learning was interrupted by military service. He joined the Navy Air Force Reserve eventually specialising in naval photographic intelligence and was trained in Memphis, Tennessee, and latterly in San Francisco. These were formative and wonderful experiences that enabled Carry to work and socialise with a diversity of individuals from different cultural and religious backgrounds, but it was in Memphis where he first substantively experienced racist incidents, discrimination, harassment and violence – experiences which resulted in him joining the civil rights movement.

After military service, Cary returned to California. He planned to start studying his MBA in the fall and in the interim, he took up a position as a social worker with the Bureau of Public Assistance for the city of Los Angeles, in one of the most deprived areas of Los Angeles, Watts! The white flight to suburbia had effectively created a black indigent area in South-Central LA, which was starved for investment and government services. Seeing the extent of the deprivation and its' consequences on the mental health and well-being of the families he was dealing with, and of the widespread deprivation of the black community, had a powerful impact on Cary.

Cary was serving Watts, a neighbourhood in Southern LA, described by Martin Luther King as having been bypassed by the progress of a decade. Cary was the only white social worker in the office, but he felt a strong sense of community and as a Jew who had experienced anti-semitism he could relate to his clients. He had always been involved in the civil rights movement in some form because he had seen so much hostile behaviour, prejudice and discrimination. He could identify with what the blacks were experiencing and wanted to make a difference, but the job was harrowing particularly when the focus of his role shifted towards supporting those with the most insurmountable problems: the most impoverished, homeless and drug addicts in the city centre of LA. The value of his work in Watts and with the homeless led to an offer that he might continue in his role while studying for his MBA. An agreement was reached that he could study during the day and visit his clients in the afternoon and at night.

Cary had always believed that he was intent on a position as a corporate lawyer, and his decision to build upon his undergraduate business and economic training, with an MBA, was solidifying that pathway. But then three things came together to tip the balance into psychology. His profound experiences working with the most vulnerable, his ability to study psychology with his MBA (something almost unheard of today) and working with Professor Fred Massarik, one of the top organisational psychologists in California. Massarik applied his understanding of psychology to all of organisational behaviour from sociology, phenomenology and social anthropology, conducting research in areas of human experience such as financial institutions, organisational development and small group training environments. Inspired by Cary's talents and capabilities, he persuaded Cary to travel to England to study his PhD at Leeds University, who was in partnership with UCLA analysing the impact of 'T-Groups', a form of sensitivity training often used in human relations or counselling work whereby participants learn about themselves, their interactions with others and more generally how group processes shape behaviour.

Cary brought his unique set of skills in management, economics, finance, psychology and social processes (a combination he describes as making him an outlier) to the Department of Management Studies at the University of Leeds and began working with Professor Peter Smith to evaluate the impact of T-Groups and their impact on people who had to deal with other people. From teachers, to businessmen, to clergymen Cary explored the negative and positive aspects of T-Group engagement and trainees self-actualisation concluding that the T-Group processes were significant in supporting independence, spontaneity, flexible and sensitive attitudes towards their own needs and the needs of others.

Cary secured his first academic position at the University of Southampton and began working prolifically with the educational and social psychologist Professor Peter Robinson. Peter and Cary were the only applied psychologist in the department with a single-minded experimental focus, and the two soon became firm allies and friends. Research was fruitful and impactful, but at the same time the culture of the organisation was career limiting, and Peter soon began nudging Cary to commit now fully to the study of occupational psychology and workplace well-being.

The time came for transition in the form of a golden opportunity to prove his expertise when Sir Roland Smith, Captain of Industry, Chairman of Manchester United Football Club and Head of the UMIST's Manchester School of Management spotted his talent. Roland had been told about Cary from colleagues in Manchester and called him up saying, '[Y]ou need to leave Southampton and come to work up north, where there are opportunities working with big businesses and industry'. Lacking in self-confidence and needing people to see something in him, Cary reluctantly boarded a train for Manchester, where he was met by Roland Smith, a Rolls Royce and a suite at the Midland Hotel (where it is thought that Rolls met Royce). After a tour of Manchester, Roland takes Cary to the offices at the UMIST, where an interview with Lord Boden is sprung upon him and he is offered a job. If you take this job, in 1 year you will be Professor, argued Roland. He was right, at 33 Cary secured his Professorship, and Sir Roland Smith became his confidante, peer-father figure and lifelong friend.

Professor Sir Cary Cooper, CBE, has worked for over 50 years, influencing senior executives to create a mentally healthy workplace in their organisations. Mental health and well-being are at the heart of what he believes make UK companies and public sectors more productive. Value and trusting your employees enhance their self-esteem, which translates back into their home life, creating a virtuous circle that enhances home, work and society.

He is the 50th Anniversary Professor of Organizational Psychology and Health at the ALLIANCE Manchester Business School, University of Manchester, UK (2015–today). He has been Pro Vice Chancellor and Distinguished Professor of Organizational Psychology and Health at Lancaster University (2003–2015), President of the Chartered Institute of Personnel and Development, President of Institute of Welfare and past Chair of the Academy of Social Sciences, past President of the British Association of Counselling and Psychotherapy and the British Academy of Management. He is the author/editor of over 250 books, over 450 scholarly articles and a regular contributor to radio and TV.

He was knighted by the Queen in 2014 for his contribution to the social sciences.

He is the Editor-in-Chief of the Wiley-Blackwell Encyclopedia of Management (14 volumes), Editor of Who's Who in Management, Editor of the Wiley-Blackwell WELLBEING volumes (six), Founding Editor of the *Journal of Organizational Behavior*, Founding and Former Chair of the UK government think tank The Sunningdale Institute and lead scientist on the UK Government Office for Science Foresight project on Mental Capital and Wellbeing, and was Chair of the Global Agenda Council on Chronic Diseases and Mental Health of the World Economic Forum. He has also worked closely with the European Commission, the European Council, the European Central Bank and the UN's World Health Organisation and ILO in the health and well-being arena. Over several years, he was voted by *HR Magazine* as the Most Influential HR Thinker and was elected to the HR Hall of Fame. He is an Honorary Fellow of the British Psychological Society, Royal College of Physicians, The Royal College of Physicians of Ireland (Occupational Medicine) and many more; and has Honorary Doctorates from a number of universities (e.g. Sheffield, Bath, Aston, Heriot-Watt, Middlesex, Wolverhampton, Chester and Bolton). Professor Cooper created, and is Chair, of the National Forum for Health and Wellbeing at Work, an employer's organisation of over 40 global employers (e.g. BP, Microsoft, BT, Shell, Rolls Royce, GSK, NHS Employers, UK Government (Wellbeing Lead), John Lewis Partnership, Fujitsu, Aon, etc.), and represented by HR Directors, Chief Medical Officers and Directors of Health & Wellbeing of these organisations.

Cary has been married twice, to June Cooper (Scott and Beth) with whom he had two children, and to Rachel where he had two additional children (Laura and Sarah). He has seven grandchildren ranging from 6 months to 11 years old and retains strong personal ties with the children and grandchildren of his half-siblings from his father's marriages.

Sir Cary Cooper's major writings

Cooper, C. (2014). *Wellbeing: A complete reference guide* (Vol. 1–VI). London, UK: Wiley Blackwell.

Cooper, C. L., & Davidson, M. J. (1982). *High Pressure: Working lives of women managers*. Oxford: Fontana Press.

Cooper, C. L., Field, J., Goswami, U., Jenkins, R., & Sahakian, B. J. (Eds.). (2009). *Mental capital and wellbeing*. London: Wiley-Blackwell.

Cooper, C., & O'Mera, S. (2019). *The apology impulse*. New York: Kogan Page.

Robertson, I., & Cooper, C. (2011). *Wellbeing: Productivity and happiness at work*. London: Palgrave Macmillan.

15 Erik Homburger Erikson (June 15, 1902–May 12, 1994)

Erikson extended and modified Freud's ideas regarding the structure of human development across the lifespan and laid particular emphasis on the importance of inter-personal relationships and the creative qualities of the person.

Erikson's Danish parents separated before his birth, and he was brought up in Karlsruhe in Baden, Germany, by his mother and his German paediatrician whom she married when Erik was a few years old. He kept his stepfather's name as his middle name. As a schoolboy, his interests lay in art, language and history. As a teenager, he considered himself to be morbidly sensitive. After leaving school, he hitchhiked across Europe, studied art in Munich and settled for a time in Florence before moving on to Vienna, where a friend had invited him to help run a small school developing and applying innovative teaching methods. Anna Freud had her professional practice there, and several of the children in analysis with her were attending the school in which Erikson was teaching. Erikson underwent training analysis with Anna Freud and routinely participated in the intensive seminars held by the Viennese Psychoanalytic Society. He was in close contact with the group around Freud and occasionally met with him, usually at Freud's house where Erikson went for his analytic sessions and occasionally at social events. Erikson remained in Vienna for 6 years, studying Maria Montessori's methods of education, as well as teaching at the school and continuing to paint. In 1929, he married a Canadian (Joan Serson), whom he had met some years earlier while she was studying at The European Schools of Dance. The early 1930s were a disturbing time – the Nazis had begun to burn Freud's books in Berlin and were threatening Austria. With their two young sons Kai and Jon (Susan, their third child, was born in America), the Eriksons joined the exodus of professional people, including many of their analyst friends. In

DOI: 10.4324/9781003229179-16

1933, they moved to Copenhagen where he tried, without success, to revert to his Danish nationality. Later, in autobiographical writing, he recalled that much of his theoretical work was influenced by early feelings of confusion and alienation, a theme that emerges in his work on identity crisis. After a short stay in Copenhagen, the Eriksons moved to Boston where he set up practice as one of the first child analysts. Three years later, he took up a full-time academic appointment at Yale University Institute of Human Relations.

In 1939, the Eriksons moved to the University of California at Berkeley, where he was engaged in a longitudinal study of child development. They remained on the West Coast for 10 years, during which time he took up a permanent teaching post at the University of California. That was to prove a brief appointment. He felt forced to resign this position when, with several other staff at the University, he refused to sign a mandatory oath of loyalty dissociating himself from groups and individuals associated with the Communist Party. This was a point of principle for Erikson; he had no links with, nor allegiance to, communist politics. His first book, *Childhood and Society* (1950), was published towards the end of his period on the West Coast. He returned to Massachusetts to take up an appointment at the Austen Riggs Center, a clinic specialising in psychoanalytic training and research. Although he did not have a primary degree, he was appointed Professor of Human Development and Lecturer in Psychiatry at Harvard. There he came in contact with numerous academics, including Gregory Bateson, who worked on the science of communication and control in animals and machines (cybernetics) of social life, the personality theorist Henry Murray and the Gestalt social psychologist Kurt Lewin, who shaped his attempts to integrate psychoanalysis with psychology and anthropology with particular reference to lifespan development. He focused much of his teaching and research on his notions of the cycle of psychological development across the lifespan.

Erikson is associated with the psychoanalytic tradition of ego psychology. One of the major innovations of ego psychology was the inclusion within psychoanalytic theory of the influences of the external environment. The ego is considered to develop and function through a combination of internal processes and external events. Thus, Erikson built on the work of Sigmund and Anna Freud, and much of his work is a direct descendent of Freudian theory. He did not attempt a fundamental re-statement of psychoanalytic propositions but rather sought to elaborate, clarify and extend some of them by introducing new considerations concerning the creative qualities of the ego and placing greater emphasis on interpersonal influences rather than intrapersonal or intrapsychic forces.

Erikson developed a theory of ego development using concepts from embryology, especially the principle of epigenesis. The principle states that a new living organism develops from an undifferentiated entity that is programmed to develop all of the organism's parts in sequence. The ego is thought to develop in a planned sequence of stages. Each stage consists of a unique developmental task that confronts individuals in the form of a crisis or challenge that must be faced. For Erikson, this crisis is not a catastrophe but a turning point of increased vulnerability and enhanced potential. The more an individual resolves the crises successfully, the healthier their development will be.

Erikson defines eight developmental stages. Trust-mistrust is Erikson's first psychosocial stage. It is experienced in the first year of life. A sense of trust requires a feeling of physical comfort and a minimal amount of fear and apprehension about the future. Trust in infancy sets the stage for a lifelong expectation that the world will be a good and pleasant place to live. Autonomy versus shame and doubt is the second stage of development. It occurs in late infancy (1–3 years). After developing a sense of trust in their caregivers, infants begin to discover the impact of their behaviour on others. They start to assert their sense of independence and autonomy. Erikson's theory suggests that if infants are restrained too much or punished too harshly for expressing this sense of freedom, they are likely to develop a sense of shame and doubt.

Initiative versus guilt is the third stage of development, and it occurs during the preschool years. As preschool children encounter a widening social world, they are challenged more than when they were infants. Active, purposeful behaviour is needed to cope with the challenges. As they mature, children are encouraged to assume responsibility for their bodies, their behaviour, their toys and their pets. Developing a sense of responsibility increases initiative. Uncomfortable guilt feelings may arise though, if the child is irresponsible and is made to feel too anxious. Erikson suggests that most guilt is quickly compensated for by a sense of accomplishment. Industry versus inferiority is the fourth developmental stage, occurring approximately in the early primary school years. Children's initiative brings them in contact with a wealth of new experiences. As they move into middle and late childhood, they direct their energy towards mastering cognitive skills. Thus, at no other time is the child more enthusiastic about learning than at this stage. One danger in the primary school years resides in the potential for developing a sense of inferiority – of feeling relatively incompetent.

Identity versus identity confusion is the fifth developmental stage, encountered during the adolescence. At this time, individuals are faced with finding out who they are and where they are going in life.

Adolescents are confronted with many new adult roles. If these are explored in a healthy manner, the adolescent arrives at a positive path to follow in life and a positive identity will be achieved. If an identity is forced on the adolescent by parents or peers, if the adolescent does not adequately explore many roles and if a positive future path is not defined, then identity confusion is likely to result. Intimacy versus isolation is the sixth development stage. It characterises development during the early adulthood years. At this time, individuals face the developmental task of forming intimate relationships with others. If the young adults form healthy friendships and an intimate close relationship with another individual, intimacy will be achieved, if not, isolation will result.

Generativity versus stagnation is the seventh developmental stage, which individuals experience during middle adulthood. A chief concern for this stage of development is to assist the younger generation in developing and leading useful lives – this is what Erikson means by 'generativity'. The feeling of having done nothing to help the next generation is referred to as stagnation. Integrity versus despair is the final developmental stage, which individuals experience during late adulthood. In the later years of life, we look back and evaluate what we have done with our lives. Through many different routes, the older person may have developed a positive outlook in most or all of the previous stages of development. If so, the retrospective glances will reveal a picture of a life well spent, and the person will feel a sense of satisfaction. A sense of completeness may be achieved. If the older adult resolved many of the earlier stages negatively, the retrospective glances will likely yield doubt or gloom and may be experienced as a sense of incompleteness and despair. It is important to bear in mind that while Erikson's stages are presented chronologically, he never suggested that, once a stage has been completed, it is forever in the past. Rather, the developmental challenges associated with each stage are always present in all of our lives; it's just that the relative emphasis tends to vary across the lifespan.

Four criticisms have been directed against Erikson's theory. First, whereas Freud could be considered to be overly pessimistic of the human condition, Erikson is often considered to be overly optimistic. Erikson has countered that this is not true and that for each psychosocial stage, there is a crisis and a specific negative ego quality (e.g. shame, mistrust) that may be a lifelong source of potential anxiety. Second, it has been argued that Erikson has exaggerated the role of the ego at the expense of the id and the unconscious. This is probably true, but it does not seriously impact on the integrity of his position. Third, it is sometimes argued that Erikson's theory places too great an emphasis on the need for the individual to adjust to the norms and expectations of society. However, Erikson's argument is that our sense of identity develops within the possibilities offered by society and these may include stability or change. For example, in *Gandhi's Truth* (1969), he demonstrates a profound interest in people who create and sustain a healthy sense of identity through radical social upheaval. Finally, Erikson has been criticised for the nature of his research designs, which (except for some studies of children's play) are primarily based on personal observation rather than controlled experimentation. Thus, while Erikson offers a considerable corpus of empirical evidence in support of his theory, much of the evidence has been collected in ways that favour support for his position. Despite these criticisms, Erikson's contributions are significant: He emphasised the psychosocial as well as the instinctual basis for behaviour and development; his account of development embraces the whole life cycle and his theoretical position explicitly acknowledges that the individuals often look as much to their future as they do to their past.

Erik Erikson's major writings

Erikson, E. H. (1950). *Childhood and society.* New York: Norton.
Erikson, E. H. (1954). *Insight and responsibility.* New York: Norton.
Erikson, E. H. (1968). *Identity youth and crisis.* New York: Norton.
Erikson, E. H. (1969). *Gandhi's truth.* New York: Norton.
Erikson, E. H. (1974). *Dimensions of a new identity.* New York: Norton.
Erikson, E. H. (1975). *Life history and the historical moment.* New York: Norton.
Erikson, E. H. (1982). *The life cycle completed: A review.* New York: Norton.

Further reading

Coles, R. (1970). *Erik H. Erikson: The growth of his work.* Little, Brown.
Erikson, K. T. (1975). *In search of common ground: Conversations with Erik H. Erikson and Huey P. Newton.* Norton.
Stevens, R. (1983). *Erik Erikson.* Open University Press.

16 Hans Jurgen Eysenck (March 4, 1916–September 4, 1997)

Hans Eysenck was a prolific writer, a researcher with a prominent public profile and one of the most prominent figures in the field of individual differences, 80 books or so, hundreds of papers, test manuals, even an interview with the men's magazine *Penthouse*. He is possibly the best known and most divisive of psychologists; his lasting message was that psychology should trust numbers rather than people, facts over ideology and that psychologists had a duty to speak out regardless of the social taboo: '*a scientist owes the world only one thing, the truth as he sees it*'.

Eysenck's blistering attack on the propaganda of psychoanalysis and the efficacy of a 'talking cure' raised ethical issues around the application of the technique, ultimately leading to its marginalisation in favour of behavioural based therapies. Eysenck's words were clear, direct, fundamental and fierce. The psychoanalysts fought back arguing that Eysenck was simply trying to usurp Freud as the figurehead of psychology.

There is very little known about the early part of Han Eysenck's life. He has written a biography, but the content is written in a style of self-preservation. Eysenck's parents, Eduard and Ruth, were actors who divorced when he was 2 years old. His mother had a moderately successful career on the German silent screen. While she pursued her career, Hans was raised by his grandmother Antonia Werner, whom he described as loving and lenient. Han's mother remarried the producer Max Glass. However, his production companies were shut down by the Nazi/National Socialist government and the family had little option but to go into exile in France. This move was not, however, far enough away from the Nazis. When Paris was overrun, Ruth found herself in an internment camp. Glass spent a king's ransom on bribes to secure her release and then the couple fled to South America.

Eduard Eysenck fared much better. He could trace his German Aryan lineage back through centuries. With the Jewish acting competition in exile, or worse, Eduard enjoyed considerable professional success. He

DOI: 10.4324/9781003229179-17

remained, however, a reluctant Nazi, only joining the party when it became compulsory in 1937.

Hans entered the Bismarck Gymnasium in 1925 and then Prinz-Heinrichs-Gymnasium for the next stage of his adolescent education. The school is described by some of Hans peers as an inclusive conservative school with military connections, but Hans describes it as being run by right-wing nationalists. His physical size, sporting prowess and combative style meant that he was mostly able to avoid being beaten up for his left-wing political views. School failed to inspire Hans; he was bored. He describes his teachers as disengaging and his peers stupidly pedantic. Matters were somewhat improved by his mother who would intersperse his German education with periods of study at public school on the Isle of White and Exeter College.

Hans left Germany, via France, for England in 1934 to pursue a degree in physics at University College London. His lack of Nazi party membership had barred his entry to theoretical physics in Berlin. The worrying ideologies and political behaviours made the decision easy. He had left Germany as a principled protest at fascism, although one could argue that taking a political stance on Nazism was a luxury he was not afforded. If he had stayed, he would have, likely, joined his much-loved grandmother. Despite having few ties with the Jewish community and having converted to Catholicism, his grandmother was identified as Jewish and died in a Nazi concentration camp midway through World War II.

Things were far from straightforward in London. In Germany, students could study most topics of their choosing before commencing their physics degree. This was not the case in England and without realising this; Hans ended up barred from the Physics programme. His only option was to enter psychology, a discipline he openly regarded as unimpressive, unscientific and its members as rather dull-witted. So for him it was easy to gain traction in the field, and he harnessed his 'physics envy' towards this non-robust science.

Hans eventually undertook a PhD in experimental aesthetics under the supervision of Sir Cyril Burt, and his studies were a much-needed distraction from the treatment he was receiving as a German living in England. His German nationality resulted in a rejection from active duty. He was excluded from service and treated with suspicion. Eysenck had little choice but to continue feverishly with his PhD studies which were now being supervised, at a distance, by Burt who had been evacuated to Aberystwyth, Wales. Eysenck could not follow Burt, because his wife was struggling with naturalisation issues. Her residence was confirmed in 1939 and then removed again once war broke out. She was facing the possibility of internment and the couple had to stay in London.

Burt's original plan for Eysenck's PhD was the re-standardisation of the Binet intelligence scale. Working now at a distance from Burt and feeling singularly uninspired, Eysenck soon pivoted towards aesthetic preferences. The idea was that theoretical laws could be applied to aesthetic composition and analysed through the factor analytical method. His work provided some support that facets of personality, attitude and age play a role in aesthetic experience, but to Eysenck's disappointment, not with general intelligence. Despite the lack of evidence to support the role of intelligence in aesthetic experience, Eysenck's work using the Birkhoff formula was formative. He demonstrated that pleasure was a product of order and complexity, triggering new research and insights in the field of psychoaesthetics.

One of Eysenck's early impactful publications came from a development of this work. Historically psychologists had been focused on the number of questions, or test items, as the route to measuring a construct or phenomena. Eysenck was able to demonstrate that fidelity within a population was as much related to the number of persons required for an experimental study. This finding triggered Eysenck's first public spat with Bernard Babington Smith (St Andrews and Oxford Universities), who contended that Eysenck has overreached himself. Eysenck's initial response was typically adversarial, if not in fact outright insulting. Before Eysenck could deliver his offensive, Cyril Burt reigned him in and a more moderate, evidence-based response was delivered. That was the last time that Burt was able to do much to prevent Eysenck, from being 'Eysenck', and as he struck out on his own intellectual path his signature was to deliver criticisms in the most heavy-handed style.

By the close of 1941, Eysenck had published some 11 prestigious articles, including the journal *Nature*. Empirical aesthetics was fruitful, but Eysenck moved on to more contentious subjects and his relationship with his mentor Burt began to decline. Eysenck describes Burt as the only psychologist he ever feared. There would seem to have been some cause. Eysenck became suspicious that Burt was attempting to sabotage his career. Burt would stifle pathways that Eysenck wished to explore, advise him not to publish on certain topics, and there were veiled and not-so-veiled criticisms of his work (a highly critical review of his work on factor analysis had significant input from Burt). Imagined or real, when the scandals around the fabrication of data by Burt emerged, Eysenck briefly jumped to his mentor's defence, only to quickly distance himself when his guilt seemed assured. Burt, in turn, went on to describe Eysenck as a 'boastful Jew' and would not support his continuation as Head of Department at the Institute of Psychiatry. Eysenck was hired to the Maudsley Hospital in 1942. This environment favoured the employment of Jewish-Germans who had suffered professionally during the war. Many of the psychiatrists who worked in the Maudsley had come in direct contact with the worst of the Nazi eugenics practices and had deep sympathy for its victims. It was hoped that Eysenck's work would establish a role for psychology as one of the basic sciences to support psychiatry.

Eysenck's appraisal of the psychiatric literature, particularly psychoanalysis, was typically critical; he began to make many enemies in the psychiatric community. For Eysenck, the works of John Bowlby, Gordon Allport and J.P. Guildford, as well as Ivan Pavlov and Carl Jung ought to be where the focus should fall. Arguably it was Donald W. MacKinnon, the Berkeley Professor and Director of the saboteur and spy processing 'Station S' during World War II, who was Eysenck's greatest influence. His book *The Structure of Personality* became the blueprint for Eysenck's most important works, the study of personality and the beginnings of a strident UK personality movement in a field that was largely dominated by America and Germany.

Eysenck continued to make extensive use of factor analysis; it became the principle of his career, particularly in its application into the empirical pursuit of personality measurement to Jung's typology. Eysenck would explore what was commonly accepted, and test those ideas with rigour, objectivity and reliability. His first study demonstrated that there was no statistical evidence to support the idea that neurotics (particularly female neurotics) were highly suggestable; furthermore, neuroticism had very little to do with introversion. His second study, a landmark in personality, capitalised on the punch-card data management system. Eysenck could factor use the system to systematically analyse data from 700 soldiers diagnosed with neurosis. This work eventually leads to the identification of bipolar personality factors.

The objective of Eysenck's work was to differentiate between what was normal and abnormal personality and to move psychiatrists away from using subjectivity in their decision-making. He wanted to improve diagnostic outcomes for patients and to establish factor analysis as a key instrument for study. Using MacKinnon's work as an archetype, Eysenck eventually identified the two principal factors of personality; extraversion-introversion which is thought to tap into an individual's tendencies towards sociability/assertiveness or aloofness/passivity, and neuroticism-stability, which is related to moodiness/insecurity and emotional stability. Psychoticism which indicates aggressive, cold, antisocial behaviour failed to attract widespread acceptance.

In 1947, he published *Dimensions of Personality*, and this was quickly followed up by several papers which moved the largely historical and philosophical notions behind 'Dimensions' towards a more robust scientific model. This was followed up in 1952 by *The Scientific Study of Personality*, a book which presented more clarity on these arguments for a continuous dimension framework for personality. This book was explicitly critical of psychiatry and drew much more on criterion analysis. Psychologists were bewildered by his unusual approach, and psychiatrists were affronted at his quantitative approach to their work; statisticians just hated it. Yet the core of Eysenck's work was soon replicated through the Cattell 16PF and the five-factor models of personality.

Eysenck, as always, was drawing controversial attention which served mainly to spur him forward. In the search for a biological explanation for extraversion and neuroticism, he drew on the work of Ivan Pavlov, associating personality to the brain's executive structures; the cerebrum, the cerebellum and the brainstem. He had much work to convince himself and his discipline that this work was valuable, but his capacity to bridge personality, genetics and biology was monumental and would ultimately pave the way for the neurophysiological research of the future.

His scientific enquiries between 1953 and 1957 into the relationship between excitation and inhibition empowered Eysenck to move from what had been descriptive accounts of the theories of others towards causal evidence. Introverts were found to be responsive to lower levels of a stimulus than extroverts. Conditioned responses in extroverts were formed more slowly and preserved for much shorter periods of time, and these insights would be the key to understanding neurotic disorders.

His work, however, was attracting increasing criticism. Eysenck was a prolific writer, but this was often at the expense of accuracy. His style was to write and publish quickly, a style which would often lead to vague methodologies that were difficult to replicate, and mistakes. Eysenck was well-aware of these problems, but rather than view them as shortcomings, he simply viewed refinement as getting in the way of the next publication. The double-standard being that Eysenck was openly critical of Cyril Burt for being more concerned about the statistics than the way the data was collected and presented. There were, however, louder voices emerging from colleagues who argued that Eysenck had an established policy for being very selective about what he published. He would omit results that did not support his hypotheses and use diagrammatic illustrations which mislead. His data was also unusually tidy, suggesting that it was not an accurate reflection of the realities of human experimental testing.

His first personality model was not a resounding success, and few were able to replicate his findings and he began to overhaul the theoretical basis for the model and revise the testing techniques. A simpler but more explicit application of the Pavlovian model provided the answer and his revised theory argued that the introverted brain was operating at much higher levels of excitation than the extrovert. Humans sought optimum levels of arousal, and their personalities were manifestations of their usual activation levels. Extraverts needed more stimulation and would seek out experiences that could provide excitation gains. This was not a substantial overhaul, but it was easier to test and reach a consensus.

The problem was that the more Eysenck rose in his field, the more he was on the receiving end of intensive critical scrutiny, and this environment was choking his research and damaging his personal credibility.

Eysenck had become entangled with Sybil Rostal, a research assistant at the Maudsley hospitals. By the 1950s, their affair was quite public, which was scandalising his more conservative colleagues. Loyalties were divided because many of Hans peers were also good friends with his wife. Margaret did not want a divorce, and many saw her as a victim. However, the marriage could not be saved, and Hans married Sybil.

He was also initiating an all-out anti-Freudian offensive, directly attacking the creditability of psychoanalysis and all who sailed in her. His role at the Maudsley meant that their clinical programme 'brand' became increasingly synonymous with science and evidence-based practice, whereas the more interdisciplinary, psychoanalytical department at Tavistock had a much narrow intellectual agenda. When key psychologists at the Maudsley and Tavistock took their feud to the British Psychological Society, Eysenck was ever confident. He had the support of most BPS psychologists, but the BPS medical section, fearing a leadership take-over, offered the Maudsley group their own separate section within the BPS. This tokenism was summarily rejected and in a cunning tactical manoeuvre, supporters of Eysenck who were not BPS members began flooding the organisation with applications for membership.

In what was potentially a bid to stop the 'Maudsley coup', many of the applications were voted down by the panel. There was an almighty argument. Accusations of vote rigging meant that the BPS had to move to suspend further membership applications until November 1956. Eysenck's scorched-earth approach did not win him this battle because the clinicians still blocked the proposed changes, holding onto their psychoanalytical power basis until the mid-1960s.

As criticism increased, Eysenck began to insulate himself within his research group and distance himself from his critics and peers. He became increasingly supercilious, only addressing his critics through his books and papers. Rather than bringing his peers closer, he was creating an impenetrable wall, which only served to increase, what would seem at times as dehumanising back-stabbing from his peers. By 1972, he was not only being denounced, but the public had also taken to punching and kicking him.

Eysenck had long been a member of the British Eugenics Society, and during his early years as a scientist, Eysenck had indeed suggested that in the UK the average IQ was decreasing. He argued that more children were being born to less intelligent, poorer members of the populace. He stopped short at advising on solutions to this problem. The Holocaust was a cautionary note about the role of state-approved ideologies on pro-creation, but Eysenck could transcend this horror story by drawing on his own personal experience as a German of Jewish descent. He made powerful arguments that politics and science are and should remain separate entities.

Then he began to weigh in on the intelligence debate. Eysenck had largely stayed clear of studying intelligence, but in 1967 he launched 'a manifesto on intelligence'. The work was designed to bring the study of intelligence closer to theory by applying the idea that speed of processing offered much promise as a proxy for intelligence measurement and 'g' but the reverse happened. In 1969, Arthur Jensen published his work on racial differences in IQ and social problems. Eysenck backed him, arguing that he had reached similar conclusions to Jensen through his own work. However, Eysenck had not raised the issue because he felt that 'the Negro's . . . were having enough problems' and it was not necessary for him to add another one. Now that Jensen had raised the issue, science had a duty to investigate the problem and the media foray began.

Eysenck asked Jensen if he was prepared to write up his findings as a book; he was not and Eysenck's *Race, Intelligence and Education* appeared 6 months later. This was not a well-conceived publication. It contained no new data and omitted key information on the segregation of children in schooling (which Eysenck was opposed to), and while there was little evidence to support genetic differences in IQ, the book tended to suggest otherwise.

The book was intended to persuade the layperson that the study of biological and racial differences in IQ was worthy of scientific study. To reach the target audience, however, the book was low-brow' and weighted more towards 'Eysenckian' opinion than complex scientific evidence.

The book was largely ignored in a race-wary America. At home, the story was quite different. Eysenck had firmly established himself in opposition to the 'environmentalists', at a time in Britain when Race relations were at their worst. Far-right groups such as the National Front were on the rise. The British MP Enoch Powell gave his infamous 'Rivers of Blood' speech, where he presented a vision of a dystopian Britain that was overrun with a society of dominant, aggressive immigrants. Eysenck was vilified by journalists, academics and students, to the point that his children had temporary name changes to distance themselves from their father's work. To please the public, Hans Eysenck seemed to have lost it all.

There was growing interest from the press not only in Eysenck's work but also about what was happening on campus. His lecturers were becoming disruptive events. Students would try to break up discussion, throwing ink-bombs and being generally unruly. Matters came to a head at the London School of Economics during May 1973. A protest by the Communist Party of England went awry when the protestors invaded the lecture theatre and mounted the stage. Eysenck was physically assaulted.

Ironically, this event helped Eysenck. His refusal to press charges and his immediate return to work gave him martyr status. Eysenck's detractors deplored what had happened, not only physically to Eysenck but also what the invasion and assault stood for more broadly. This was an attack on academic freedom of speech.

Of course, Eysenck never baulked at the opportunity for controversy and he harnessed the media cycle that followed. He would make multiple media appearances discussing his theory of inheritability for traits such as personality and intelligence. When challenged on the social and ethical implications of his work, he would gently allude to his German-Jewish heritage. He stated that he himself had watched his family suffer but that such emotions and concerns had no place in a scientific argument. Thus, the audience had received this powerful personal information and were subtly challenged not to conclude that he was a defacto racist or a Nazi sympathiser.

Eysenck's ideas have had a profound influence on psychology and the volume of his work continues to extend its impact. However, Eysenck's tendency for vague reporting, inaccuracy and overstatement is an undisputable weakness. His dogged persistence for the premier place of science and reasoning is also tested towards the end of his career in his work with the tobacco industry. In the face of developing evidence that demonstrated the link between cancer and tobacco, Eysenck persistently argued that tobacco was a very minor risk factor for disease. Personality, he argued, determined longevity, not tobacco.

The biochemical mechanisms linking smoking and cancer were still poorly understood during the 1980s, but Eysenck (whose work was financed by the tobacco industry to the tune of £800,000) persistently downplayed epidemiological and animal study evidence, arguing the nicotine was not addictive nor carcinogenic. There is no evidence that the tobacco industry tried or could even have actually influenced Eysenck's opinion. He was very much his 'own man'. We might, however, conclude that Big Tobacco was savvy in engaging him. They knew his personal style before engaging him. Once decided on something, Eysenck could be intractable and this personality trait made him a mighty scientific advocate for Big Tobacco.

Hans was the ultimate participant in his own personality-stress experiment. The years before his death were extremely difficult, and he was known to be suffering from stress from ongoing quarrels that were often of his own making. Hans Eysenck died of a brain tumour in 1997. He was survived by his second wife Sybil and his children Connie, Gary, Kevin, Darrin and Michael.

Perhaps still haunted by what had happened to Sir Cyril Burt, Hans followed George Kelly and ordered that all his personal papers be destroyed on his death.

When Eysenck died in 1997, he was the third most cited psychologist in the world (behind only Freud and Piaget). However, in 2020 *The International Journal of Social Psychiatry* and the *Journal of the Royal Society of Medicine* issued expressions of concern relating to seven of Eysenck's papers focusing on the relationship between cancer and personality. Following an investigation by King's College London, 26 papers focusing on personality and cancer were ruled unsafe.

Hans Eysenck's major writings

Eysenck, H. J. (1947). *Dimensions of personality*. London: Routledge and Kegan Paul.

Eysenck, H. J. (1952). The effects of psychotherapy: an evaluation. *Journal of Consulting Psychology, 16,* 319–324.

Eysenck, H. J. (1964). *Crime and personality*. London: Routledge and Kegan Paul.

Eysenck, H. J. (1967). *The biological basis of personality*. Springfield, IL: Thomas.

Eysenck, H. J. (1979). The conditioning model of neurosis. *Brain and Behavioral Sciences, 2,* 155–199.

Eysenck, H. J. (1979). *The structure and measurement of intelligence*. New York: Springer-Verlag.

Eysenck, H. J. (1980). *The causes and effects of smoking*. Minnesota: Sage (with contributions from L. J. Eaves).

Eysenck, H. J. (1980). *The great intelligence debate*. London: Lifecycle Publications (with L. J. Kamin).

Eysenck, H. J. (1989). *Genes, culture, and personality: An empirical approach.* New York: Academic Press (with L. J. Eaves & N. G. Martin).

Further reading

Buchanan, R. D. (2010). *Playing with fire, The controversial career of Hans J. Eysenck.* Oxford: Oxford University Press.

Gibson, H. B. (1981). *Hans Eysenck: The man and his work.* Peter Owen.

Gray, J. A. (1981). A critique of Eysenck's theory of personality. In H. J. Eysenck (Ed.), *A model for personality* (pp. 246–277). Springer.

Kings College London. (2019). *King's College London enquiry into publications authored by Professor Hans Eysenck with Professor Ronald Grossarth Maticek.* Retrieved from www.kcl.ac.uk/news/statements/docs/hans-eysenck-enquiry-final-may-2019.pdf

Modgil, S., & Modgil, C. (Eds.). (1986). *Hans Eysenck: Consensus and controversy.* Taylor & Francis.

O'Grady, C. (2020). Misconduct allegations push psychology hero off his pedestal. *Science*, 15th July. Retrieved from www.science.org/news/2020/07/misconduct-allegations-push-psychology-hero-his-pedestal

Storms, L. H., & Sigal, J. J. (1958). Eysenck's personality theory with special reference to the dynamics of anxiety and hysteria. *British Journal of Medical Psychology*, *31*, 228–246.

17 Sigmund Freud (May 6, 1856–September 23, 1939)

The founder of psychoanalysis, Freud's approach emphasised the importance of unconscious factors in guiding human behaviour and of the value of interpreting dreams as an indirect route to the unconscious.

Sigmund Freud was born in Pribor (Freiberg), Czechoslovakia, on May 6, 1856. His 37-year-old father Jakob had taken his third wife, the 17-year-old Amalie Nathansohn, 12 months before Freud's birth. Sigmund was now the eldest of eight. His father Jacob had two adult sons, Emanuel and Philipp, from his previous marriage to Sally Kanner (who died prematurely in 1852). There is some suggestion of a third wife between Kanner and Nathansohn called Rebecca, however, little is known about her. There are reports that Freud's birth date was recorded as March 6 on official documents but that the family reported the May date to conceal the fact that Amalie was pregnant. Sigmund was largely homeschooled by his mother until he entered formal education at the Leopoldstaedter Realgymnasium in 1865 and the children of his step-brother Emanuel, Jon and Pauline, became Freud's playmates and confidants.

Freud's mother was widely considered to be both beautiful and austere. The family was traditional, patriarchal and authoritative, Freud's sister had to give up her piano lessons because they were disturbing Sigmund's concentration, but it was also united with strong bonds of affection and the light-heartedness of their father. The family was financially stable; there was always enough money for books, music lessons and theatre tickets, and the family would summer at Moravian resorts.

Freud was a bright student; by the age of 20, he had an aptitude for ancient history and the classics. He spoke fluent French, German, English and Spanish. Inspired by a lecture by the physician and anatomist Carl Brühl of Goethe's 'Aphorisms on Nature'. Freud entered Vienna

DOI: 10.4324/9781003229179-18

University in 1873 to study medicine and physiology under the German physician and physiologist Ernst von Brücke. Brücke's influence in what was known as dynamic physiology, an approach in which organisms are treated as part of a system of forces that keep it alive but ultimately led to its demise, was possibly one of the most formative in Freud's career. Freud spent several years in Brücke's lab in comparative study (1877), carrying out brilliant, scientifically precise research, comparing the brains of vertebrates, invertebrates and humans. This was a brief but fruitful period of research. Freud's work on the nervous tissue was the first to help establish the evolutionary continuity between all organisms as well as being the first to describe the structure and function of the medulla oblongata, which is the portion of the hindbrain that controls autonomic functions such as breathing, swallowing, heart and blood vessel function. Work which proved seminal for the discovery of the neuron during the 1890s.

During this period, Freud also studied philosophy under Franz Brentano. Brentano reintroduced the concept of intentionality from scholastic philosophy as well, being one of the first to differentiate between genetic and descriptive psychology. Parts of his work are directly observable in the development of psychodynamics, which emphasises the forces that underlie human behaviour and the dynamic relationships between conscious and unconscious processes (Gay, 1988).

In 1881, he qualified as a Doctor of Medicine and became engaged to Martha Bernays. The main obstacles to immediate marriage were Freud's practical concerns about money, his annoyances of what he felt to be Martha's unreasonable expectations for a family home and pressure on both fronts from his future mother in law. Thus, their 5-year engagement was populated with long periods of separation and letter writing. Their endearment to one another is apparent in their passionate letters to one another, where Freud's terms of endearment to his fiancée have child-like, submissive characteristics; *'sweet, passionately loved child'*, *'blessed treasure'*, *'little princess'* and unsurprisingly his infantilisation of his sweetheart was tinged with controlling, possessive and jealousy to the point of absurdity behaviours. The slightest suggestion from Martha's correspondence of indecisiveness or neglect for correctness would cast shadows of doubt over the relationship, violent outbursts and unprovoked jealously. Freud's jealousy extended outside of his perceived love rivals, to people who were more attractive than himself and towards Martha's mother and brother Eli. This behaviour placed considerable strain on Martha, however, her good sense made Freud reconsider much of his unreasonable and illogical behaviours. Here we can see the emergence of Freud's thinking on emotions and reason. Freud the rational thinker was dissonant to Freud the future husband. There was a perpetual struggle between the competing needs of jealousy, possession and reason. The intensity of the base instincts must be repressed so that the powers of reasoning can win through.

Freud's relationships with his mentors and peers were similarly volatile. He would develop deep and intense friendships, but this unconditional regard would soon cool and end in overt hostility. Freud was fully aware of this tendency but explained it as a rebellious streak, which he had developed through the admiration and burning rivalry that he felt about his nephew John, an intimate friend and hated enemy.

Freud's competitiveness, his need to assert and his ambition to make a universally significant discovery were constant preoccupations, but when he experimented with cocaine in 1884 on his friend Ernst von Fleischl-Marxow, the consequences resulted in death and justifiably bitter criticism. Fleischl-Marxow was a brilliant and talented doctor who had accidentally cut his right thumb with a scalpel while researching with a cadaver. The wound would not heal; it became infected and required amputation, but the second wound also failed to heal. Neuromata, which are nerve tissue growths that can cause excruciating pain, formed and to manage his distress, Fleischl-Marxow self-medicated with morphine eventually becoming an addict.

Freud was convinced he could cure Fleischl-Marxow with cocaine. It was a time of optimism about cocaine; there was no great concern about its use and it was commonplace in drinks such as the tonic wine Vin Mariani and Coca-Cola. That year Freud published his monograph on cocaine, *Über Coca*, quickly becoming the authority on the drug. Freud's understanding was however limited. As a young doctor, the drug was financially beyond his reach. He managed some minor uneventful self-experimentation, including sending his fiancée, Martha Bernays, a gift to *'give her cheeks a red colour'*, before becoming her regular supplier. Freud was fully aware of the pain-killing properties of cocaine but had failed to report on its analgesic properties. For a man in search of notoriety, this was something of an own goal because the critical acclaim went to the ophthalmologist Carl Koller who introduced it as a local aesthetic for eyes surgery, ending decades of suffering.

Über Coca had not brought Freud the acclaim he had hoped for, but he was certain cocaine would cure Fleischl-Marxow's unbearable neuralgia. Fleischl-Marxow was, however, suffering from morphine poisoning and his protracted agony elicited stronger and stronger doses of cocaine from Freud, until death finally followed. As cases of cocaine addiction began to spread across Europe, Freud faced bitter criticism. He was labelled a public menace, and by 1887 Freud was advising the abandonment of injected cocaine in the treatment of nervous or medical disorders. Both Freud and Martha, however, continued to take cocaine in small quantities with no reported adverse effects or addiction. Fortunately, Freud's fortunes began to change. When backed by Brücke, he secured a position at Theodor Meynert's laboratory of brain anatomy, where he began to examine what would become his passion, psychiatry. He won a scholarship that allowed him to study under Jean-Martin Charcot at the Salpêtrière in Paris.

Charcot greatly influenced Freud. They shared a love of history and art and Charcot was a brilliantly lucid writer who, like Freud, spoke several languages. At the laboratory, Charcot was a defiant character who trained Freud in the controversial use of hypnosis to treat hysteria and 'dispel' paralysis by suggestion and demonstrated that hysteria is more common in men than women.

Even before working with Charcot, Freud was fascinated with hypnosis and its capacity for the study of the unconscious and this collaboration reinforced Freud's attitude that the scientist must have the courage to explore even the most unlikely scientific methods. His work in this area met with persistent resistance. His account to the Society of Medicine in Berlin on male hysteria was met with scepticism:

> *One of them, an old surgeon, actually broke out with the exclamation: 'But, my dear sir, how can you talk such nonsense? Hysteron (sic) means the uterus. So how can a man be hysterical?' I objected in vain that what I wanted was not to have my diagnosis approved, but to have the case put at my disposal. At length, outside the hospital, I came upon a case of classical hysterical hemianaesthesia in a man and demonstrated it before the 'Gesellschaft der Aerzte' [1886]. This time I was applauded, but no further interest was taken in me. The impression that the high authorities had rejected my innovations remained unshaken; and, with my hysteria in men and my production of hysterical paralyses by suggestion, I found myself forced into the Opposition. As I was soon afterwards excluded from the laboratory of cerebral anatomy and for terms on end had nowhere to deliver my lectures, I withdrew from academic life and ceased to attend the learned societies.*
> Sigmund Freud (1925, p. 15)

The typical Freudian response was that society was not ready for his work because it had taken a direction which was in opposition to the prevailing culture of observation of the physical, chemical or anatomical. The unobservable was not worthy of scientific investigation. Always the rebel, Freud hunkered down with the descending ranks. We can also see, however, the footprints of contemporary codes of ethics in Freud's attitudes for he felt passionately that if individuals were to make a profit from the distress of others, then they ought to be able to do something to help them. As it stood, the prevailing medical model did nothing more than assigning a variant of pathological symptoms to conditions which, in many cases, would have had underlying causes. The treatments of which included purging with toxic antimony, 'vapouring' with mercury, or hydrotherapy of the uterus.

On returning from Paris, Freud opened a private practice specialising in nervous diseases and was appointed Director of the Neurological Section of the Max Kassowitz Institute for Children's Diseases, and he was finally able to marry Martha Bernays. To further develop his skills in hypnosis, Freud travelled to Nancy to work with the French physician and neurologist Hyppolite Bernheim and the now ageing physician Ambroise-Auguste Liébeault. The dedication and generosity of time that Liébeault gave to his patients and Bernheim's experimental rigour were formative to the development of Freud's professional practice. Freud began to recognise the limitations of hypnosis as a therapeutic technique and the advantages of free talk. He continued to treat his patients by hypnosis between 1889 and 1895 but began to turn his attention to a method introduced to him by the Viennese physician Josef Breuer. Breuer had treated several patients diagnosed with hysteria and found that when he encouraged them to talk freely about the earliest occurrence of their symptoms, the latter often declined.

Freud further developed Breuer's thinking on free-talk by suggesting that many phobias and hysterical symptoms originated from long-forgotten traumatic experiences, and Freud sought to bring such experiences into conscious awareness and then systematically confront them; thus distress would disappear. Their mutual study of this topic was circulated in the renowned *Studies in Hysteria* (1895), which consists of a joint introduction, flowed by five case studies including Anna O, a theoretical essay by Breuer and a practice-oriented piece by Freud (the text first appeared in English in 1936).

For Freud, Bertha Pappenheim (Anna O was Freud and Breuer's pseudonym) was a fascination which led him to make significant theoretical assumptions regarding the symptoms and causes of hysteria, leading to the conclusion that early childhood events have substantial impact on our adult personality and lives. Traumatic experiences may remain hidden from consciousness and that the 'inability to remember' is supported through powerful mechanisms of self-deception. This is where the terms 'repression' and 'transference' emerge in the Freudian lexicon, during a time period described by Freud, as the 'groping' years, when the struggle towards his goal was anything but strident. Sometimes his clinical work confirmed his assumptions, and sometimes it did not. As was a predictable pattern in Freud's male relationships, Breuer and Freud parted company. Breuer considered Freud's emphasis on the sexual origin and content of many neuroses as both excessive and unjustifiable.

Freud, however, was now committed to the idea that the cases he had examined were caused by childhood sexual trauma and that early sexuality is a component of the child's personality, but he had difficulty reconciling that those traumas were caused by perverted adult acts. The commonality of hysteria would suggest that the unconscious could make no hard and fast distinction between real events and fiction. Therefore, instincts and desires for such fantasies must exist.

By 1891, the Freuds had three children, Mathilde (b. 1887), Jean-Martin (b. 1889), Oliver (b. 1891) and had moved to an apartment in the newly erected Berggasse 19, where Martha gave birth to Ernst (b. 1892), Sophie (b. 1893), and Anna (b. 1895) to whom Freud became closely attached.

Freud began to nurture a small group of intellectual elite friends, including Alfred Adler, Wilhelm Stekel, Max Kahane and Rudolf Reitler, and founded the Wednesday Psychological Society (re-established as the Vienna Psychoanalytic Society), now the oldest psychoanalysis society in the world. Again, it was not long before fractions occurred between Freud and members of the group.

Alfred Alder eventually left and founded his own Society for Psychoanalytic Research, later called the Society for Individual Psychology, but the disagreements persisted, this time with Wilhelm Stekel about the editorial committee of the journal *Zentralblatt für Psychoanalyse*. Freud founded his own psychoanalytical journal devoted to interdisciplinary research in mental life, but Stekel responded by resigning from the Vienna Psychoanalytic Society.

The most well-known friendship-estrangement cycle was Freud's relationship with the Swizz psychiatrist and psychoanalyst Carl Gustav Jung. Correspondence between the two began in 1906 when Jung sent Freud a copy of his published works. This triggered 6 years of correspondence between the two. Freud saw Jung as a kind of protégé and heir apparent to psychoanalysis; they travelled together delivering lectures, visiting retreats, hunting and fishing. During a visit to Freud in 1907, Minna Bernays, Martha's younger sister, confessed to Jung that she was engaged in a very intimate relationship with Freud. A secrete which Jung claims to have agonised over. There is, however, very little additional, corroborating evidence. Minna was living with the Freuds soon after the birth of Anna and Freud, but in letters to his friend Wilhelm Fliess Freud had declared that his sex life was over.

Towards the end of their relationship, Jung had diverged from the Freudian perspective of sexual drives towards a new conception of libido. He also felt that Freud's thinking on the unconscious was unnecessarily dark and that he tended to treat his followers as patients. Freud felt that Jung's exploration and interest in religion and myths as unscientific, and that Jung himself had little insight into his own neurosis. In 1913, Freud published *Totem and Taboo*, partly as a riposte to Jung's interest in mythology. In the end, their ideological differences were all-consuming and, by 1912, their personal relationship was abandoned. Freud remained convinced that Jung harboured anti-Semitic feelings and death wishes towards him, suffering fainting fits in Jung's presence on two separate occasions. Jung's response was to apologise to Freud for the difficulties in their relationship, while Freud's response was to write to Ernst Jones describing his fainting spell as an 'unruly homosexual feeling'. Jung was furious at what he perceived as a subtle put-down by Freud and a trivialisation of his libido theory.

Freud's early response to the outbreak of world war was animated, but this soon turned to disillusionment about the nature of humans and their state. In his essay, 'Thoughts for the Times on War and Death' (1915), he argued that civilised nations knew so little of one another that their primitive instincts meant that they could turn easily against each other with hate and loathing. Freud's entire fortune invested in Austrian State Bonds was lost. His patients were in a similar reduced state, and he struggled to make a living. Temporary assistance came from Anton von Freund, a Budapest manufacturer, but inflation was so high, the money was rapidly consumed. After the war, Freud spent less time in clinical observation, focusing on the application of what would eventually become his 'grand theory' applied to art, literature, anthropology, war and history.

By 1919 Freud, a long-time smoker, presented with the first signs of oral cancer. He was seen by the Austrian stomatologist Hans Pichler for a painful swelling in this left palate, which had persisted for over a week. Between 1923 and 1938, Freud went under some 25 surgeries. Many of these surgeries were successful, but recovery was difficult and he could barely endure the prosthesis he was eventually fitted with.

By the 1930s, psychoanalysis had a firm foothold as the 'talking therapy' that offered a powerful treatment to a range of psychological disorders. Freud was world famous, treating an array of famous and colourful characters: Princess Marie Bonaparte, who in a bid to cure her frigidity, asked Freud whether she should sleep with her own son; Princess

Alice, who Freud believed could be cured of her religious delusions by X-raying her ovaries in order to kill her libido; and the American Poetess Hilda Doolittle, who documented her experiences with Freud in such detail that we have an almost complete account of Freud's methods. Freud's work was now of such importance that the Nazi regime was reluctant to destroy his practice. Freud was similarly reluctant to leave. In 1933, his books were burned along with other works considered to contain un-German ideas (Einstein, Marx, Heine). When Freud heard the news, he dryly quipped '*What progress we are making. In the Middle Age's they would have burned me. Now they are content with burning my books*'. By 1938 however, the Nazis were no longer content with book burning, and they seized his money and property.

Princess Marie Bonaparte, Napoleon's great-granddaughter, whose wealth and patronage supported the advancement of the popularly of psychoanalysis, brokered a deal with the Nazis that permitted Freud to salvage his couch, sculpture collection and library and travel to London. Freud's travel was permitted on the condition that he wrote a statement swearing they had treated him well. Freud wrote wryly: '*I can most highly recommend the Gestapo to everyone*'.

Freud died the following year from a verrucous carcinoma, known as Ackerman's tumour. He had suffered from this tumour for 16 years and had more than 30 surgical procedures and endured primitive radium therapy. Despite his illness, Freud wrote 20 books and articles and directed the international advancement of his field. When the time was right, Freud's personal doctor Max Schur gave him 21 milligrams of morphine and Freud died within hours. Freud's sisters were not so fortunate. Mitzie (81) and Paula (78) were murdered in the Maly Trostients extermination camp in 1942. Dolfi Freud (82) died in Theresienstadt from advanced starvation and Rosa (82) was killed at Treblinka.

Freud's theoretical work

Freud advanced the medical perspective on psychology much further than his contemporaries by demonstrating how the science of medicine could be extended to the problems of the unconscious mind in a humane and comprehensible way. To Freud, the symptoms of problematic behaviour were attempts to manage unconscious forces and desires, the analyst would then work to restore balance to the patient's struggles by creating awareness, which would help them keep their struggles under control. The id is the Freudian structure of personality that consists of drives; it has no contact with reality and is driven by the pleasure principle, always seeking pleasure and avoiding pain. The ego is a structure that develops during childhood as the developing individual must manage the constraints of reality. The ego is the executive branch of personality because it coordinates and mediates, making rational decisions to bring an individual's pleasures into the boundaries of what is real and acceptable. For example, the id may be driven towards aggressive or sexual statements. Humour and wit enable these forbidden expressions to be placed into common conversation in socially sanctioned ways. The id and ego have no sense of morality. The superego considers whether something is right or wrong.

How does the ego resolve the conflict between its demands for reality, the wishes of the id, and the constraints of the superego? Through defence mechanisms: unconscious methods used by the ego to distort reality thereby protecting the person from anxiety. In Freud's view, the conflicting demands of the personality structures produce anxiety. The anxiety alerts the ego to resolve the conflict by means of defence mechanisms. The process of psychoanalysis also involves the patient expressing their thoughts, in an uncensored way, using free associations and describing fantasies and dreams which the therapists infer unconscious conflicts which are causing the patients symptoms, often confronting the patient's pathological defences with the aim of increasing insight and improvement. Repression is the most powerful and pervasive defence mechanism. It works to push unacceptable id impulses out of awareness and back into the unconscious mind. Repression was to Freud both a general construct and one which is also the foundation from which all other defence mechanisms work.

Other important defence mechanisms are displacement – the defence mechanism that occurs when feelings are shifted from one object to another; projection – the defence mechanism used to attribute our own shortcomings, problems and faults to others; and sublimation – the defence mechanism that occurs when an individual replaces a socially distasteful course of action with a socially acceptable one.

Freud's theory suggests that development of the person is associated with an orderly progression through five psychosexual or libidinal stages: oral, anal, phallic, latency and genital. These are referred to as psychosexual or libidinal stages because of the primacy of the different erogenous zones during the development of the child. The adult personality is thought to be determined by the way conflicts between the early sources of pleasure – the mouth, the anus and then the genitals – and the demands of reality are resolved. When these conflicts are not resolved, the individual may become fixated at a specific stage of development. Fixation is a defence mechanism that occurs when an individual remains locked into an earlier developmental stage because needs are either under- or over-gratified. For example, The Oedipus complex is a hypothetical construct which proposes that the young child develops an intense desire to replace the parent of the same sex and enjoy the affections of the opposite sexed parent. How is the Oedipus complex resolved? At about 5 to 6 years of age, children recognise that their same-sex parent might punish them for their incestuous desires. To reduce this conflict, the child identifies with the same-sex parent. If the conflict is not resolved, the theory predicts that the individual may become fixated at the phallic stage as illustrated by an adult whose personality is characterised by self-assured recklessness, vanity and exhibitionism.

The healthy person is characterised by a dynamic balance between the forces of the ego, concerned with reality and largely conscious; the superego, dealing with morality; and the id, the storehouse of drives and unacceptable repressed wishes and entirely unconscious. Neurotic individuals are thought to be ruled by their superegos. Psychotic individuals have had their ego defences penetrated and are ruled by their id. Thus, in the case of psychotics, the aim of therapy is to replace id activity with that of the ego.

Psychoanalytic theory embraces every aspect of the human mind and seeks to explain every aspect of human behaviour. All aspects of human behaviour, no matter how small or trivial, have meaning. Therefore, psychoanalysis is both a collection of theories and a therapeutic method. A process whereby clinical experience is cross-referenced back to clinical theory, and thus his work was constantly in a state of evolution. As we have learned more about the structure and function of the brain and its diseases, there has been considerable backlash against the Freudian unconscious.

Hans Eysenck, one of the most vociferous critics, argued that Freud's work had a baleful influence on the progress of psychological science not least because many concepts cannot be defined in ways that allow them to be measured. In fact, some, particularly those relating to the unconscious, are so formulated that they can never be measured. Moreover, the theory makes very few accurate predictions about how someone will behave but always claims to provide a satisfactory explanation for everything a person has done in the past. Others have argued, however, that the current medical perspective does little to understand the everyday life of individuals, and the role that power plays in our lives. Until Freud, every sick woman was neurotic and every masturbating child, a sexual deviant.

At the time of his death, Freud was regarded as one of the major scientific thinkers of his age receiving 13 Nobel prize nominations. His work continues to be developed throughout the world. Its continuing popularity may be due in part to the fact that its core ideas appear to be widely perceived to concur with everyday human experience and to offer the promise of a coherent explanation that cannot be matched by more mainstream psychological frameworks. For example, much of the language of psychoanalysis has become the dominant idiom in which most of us explain why we think, feel and behave as we do. However, Freud never believed that psychoanalysis was the last word in psychological explanation and he assessed its shelf-life to be limited by the rate of progress in biochemistry which, he considered, would provide a level of explanation of human behaviour to which psychoanalysis could hardly begin to aspire.

Sigmund Freud's major writings

Freud, S. (1925). *An autobiographical study* (J. Strachey, Ed. 1963). New York: W.W. Norton & Co.

Freud, S. (1966). *The standard edition of the complete psychological works of Sigmund Freud.* London: Hogarth Press and the Institute of Psychoanalysis.

Further reading

Appignanesi, L., & Forrester, J. (2000). *Freud's women.* London: Penguin.

Ellenberger, H. F. (1981). *The discovery of the unconscious: The history and evolution of dynamic psychiatry.* New York: Basic Books.

Gay, P. (1988). *Freud: A life for our time* (1st ed., p. 106). New York and London: W.W. Norton & Company. ISBN 0-393-02517-9.

Grünbaum, A. (1988). The foundations of psychoanalysis: A philosophical critique. *Journal of the American Psychoanalytic Association, 36*(2), 521–528.

Hall, C. S. (1999). *A primer of Freudian psychology.* New York: New American Library.

18 Francis Galton (February 16, 1822–January 17, 1911)

Galton pioneered the study of differences between individuals and developed a theory that explained individual differences with reference to their genetic origins.

Erasmus Darwin (physician, philosopher poet and evolutionary theorist) was the grandfather of both Charles Darwin and Francis Galton. Erasmus' first wife Mary had four sons and two daughters, two of whom died in infancy. A third child, named Charles, died at the age of 30, so when their fourth child, Robert Waring Darwin, became a father he named him Charles after his late brother. He is the Charles who is now immortalised in science and the half-cousin of Francis Galton.

Mary Darwin had long suffered from ill health (probably gallstones). To manage the pain, she self-medicated with copious amounts of alcohol and opium and died from cirrhosis of the liver at the age of 30. Erasmus, having five children to care for, hurriedly employed a young nanny, Mary Parker. Parker soon became his mistress and bore him two children. They never married because by 1775, Erasmus' attentions were directed elsewhere. At the very much married Elizabeth Pole (nee Collier); a twentysomething, adventurous, humorous dark-haired beauty.

Mary was not exactly enthusiastic; Erasmus was much older than her and a rotund man. Neither Mary's reluctance nor her marital state deterred Erasmus. Unrelenting in his pursuits, he penned her love poems until in 1780; her much older husband conveniently died. Galton finally persuaded the indifferent but also pragmatic Elizabeth to become his wife. At the end of the day, Elizabeth's previous husband had been 30 years her senior, she was used to romantic hardship, but this was somewhat compensated by the fact that Galton was a very wealthy man.

Erasmus had 14 children in total (and possibly one further illegitimate daughter), eight of whom were born to Elizabeth. Her daughter,

DOI: 10.4324/9781003229179-19

Frances Ann Violetta, shared Elizabeth's beauty and personality and would go on to marry the very conservative Samuel Tertius Galton and the couple would eventually become the mother of Francis Galton.

Samuel Galton's family were wealthy Birmingham Quakers whose fortunes had been founded on gun manufacturing. Frances Ann met her husband Samuel when his family began to move its business interests away from gun manufacturing, towards banking.

Samuel and Erasmus shared both business and scientific interests; they were both members of the Birmingham Lunar Society, a dinner club and learned society for industrialists, philosophers and intellectuals, so the marriage was a good fit.

Their first four children, all daughters, had poor health. Agnes and Violetta lived only a few months and Lucy and Adele were plagued with illness. Their children's deaths and illnesses prompted a crisis in faith and the family moved away from the Quaker Church towards the Church of England. More children followed, four daughters and three sons, the youngest of which was Francis. The family was a happy and a very wealthy one, something that would later give Galton the freedom to roam and to study wherever and whatever he chose.

The young Francis was the object of devotion, most especially from his sister Adele. Isolated for large parts of her childhood because of curvature of the spine, Adele had spent long periods in bed rest strapped to a wooden board. Little Francis gave Adele the opportunity to expand the scope of her world, and she put all her time and energy into the needs of this adorable child. She proceeded to fill his world with as much information as his newly developing mind could master. By the time he was two and a half, Francis could read and write; by four he could multiply, begin to read French and Latin; by five he was reading Homer (in its original text). Despite these early achievements, Galton often complained of struggling with turning his thoughts into language throughout his life, leading some to suggest that he may have been struggling with dyslexia.

Francis was learning fast, but Adele was his main source of education. The Galton family was becoming worried about Francis' lack of friends, so he was taken to the local school. While the school offered new social opportunities, the family was stunned by what was regarded as the complete ignorance of his fellow pupils, and thus, Francis was dispatched to board at the French coastal town of Boulogne-sur-Mer. Galton hated boarding school; he endured a harsh regime, corporal punishment and loneliness. His parents were rarely inclined to present themselves in France during school holidays, so for any kind of family news, Francis had to rely on letters.

Finally, in 1832 his time in Boulogne-sur-Mer came to an end. His father brought Francis home to England, to attend a new boarding school in a more enlightened environment where he could study not only the classics but science, carpentry and sports. He studied at Reverend Atwood's School until his 13th birthday, followed by King Edward's Grammar School where he experienced the 'best' that the Victorian educational regime could offer in the way of rote learning, humiliation and punishment.

Francis stayed at boarding school until 1838 when his parents took him on a tour of Europe. On his return, he followed his mother's long-held desire that he would follow in the footsteps of Erasmus Darwin and he commenced the study of medicine at Birmingham General Hospital. Francis never qualified in medicine. In an era of no proper anaesthesia, Galton was finding that the stress of applied medicine was taking a toll on his health. He was suffering sleep deprivation, digestive problems and headaches, but like most students still managed to find time to enjoy the sophistication of London; attending nights out at the opera, evening balls and the fencing club. His training had also managed to raise suspicions about the behaviour of his devoted sister, Adele. Francis began to suspect that her spinal problems were now more of an attention-seeking device than an actual medical affliction, and he began to create distance from her.

University education was not a resounding success. Francis went to Cambridge University (1840–1843), where he read mathematics, but he performed poorly and did not obtain a degree. He was distracted by the desire to travel, and his family's wealth meant that Francis could pursue whatever interested him. His cousin Charles had just returned from his round-the-world trip on HMS Beagle and Galton wanted some action. His heart was set on a Scandinavian venture, but his father negotiated this down to a working holiday in Germany to study with Justus von Liebig, the man now widely accepted as the father of organic chemistry. Francis, however, did not care much for von Liebig's teaching methods and decided to 'make a bolt' down the Danube for Constantinople and Athens. When Francis finally returned to England in September 1840, his father took Francis' flight from Germany in good humour, complimenting him on the great deal of experience he would have gained.

Four years later, Francis' beloved father died aged 61. He had suffered from asthma throughout his life and when it finally brought death, the family was devastated. For Francis, there was an added complexity. It was his father's last wish that Francis should complete his medical career, but on his father's death there was no real need to work at all.

In the end, the decision was an easy one. A year after his father's death, Francis travelled to Egypt with the intention of following the Victorian tradition of murdering and stuffing exotic animals.

He travelled to Egypt, Sudan and across the Middle East, sailing, swimming and shooting. Returning home only in 1856 following the death of his closest aid, Ali, to dysentery. Galton was not in good spirits or health. He had a recurrent fever, probably from venereal disease, and a significant ego deficit caused by his inability to kill '*even one single hippopotamus*'. In what would be a recurring theme of buffoonery, Galton then made the calamitous decision to bring with him two monkey companions. On arrival home, the two monkeys were promptly locked in a freezing scullery by a housekeeper, and the poor animals were found dead in the morning, clinging to each other for warmth.

Undeterred, Galton was resolute in improving his hunting skills and began living primitively in a shelter on Culrain Moor in the Highlands of Scotland. He shot seals (one can presume that on land they were easier to hit than a hippo) and took some basic instruction in rock-climbing, which enabled him to raid the nests of seabirds. His intention was to bring young birds and eggs back to add to his brother's Lakeland estate. Most of these sorry animals went the same way as the monkeys. Galton had the crates containing the birds strapped to the top of a transportation railway truck, and they died of hypothermia on the way back from Scotland. Only one oystercatcher survived. It was released into his brother's estate, then during some particularly bad frost, the little bird got stuck in ice. A fox quickly dispatched the animal, and all that was left in the morning was a little pair of orange legs stuck to the ice.

Galton was well placed within an affluent social circle and could have enjoyed a sedentary Victorian existence but for the advice of a phrenologist to pursue a more active lifestyle. At that time, phrenologists were using the now-discredited practice of estimating the relative strengths of a person's mental faculties and their suitability to different careers by calculating the size of bumps on different parts of their cranium. In what sounds like a double entendre, Galton's phenologist concluded that Galton had one of the 'largest organs of causality' that he had ever seen. Unfortunately, this experience did not give Galton the blinding realisation that a career in animal welfare was not for him, because he was soon back on his travels. He joined the Royal Geographical Society on a noble 2-year trip to South West Africa applying his 'organ of causality' to the mapping of previously unexplored territories.

Galton managed to shoot a half-starved lion in the buttocks, before one of his party finished it off. On yet another blunder, he agreed that the mules and horses should be released into a canyon to feed freely.

On release, the animals were promptly devoured by a pack of delighted lions. Fortunately, the lions, replete from their feast, left the now-starving and distressed team of pioneers a few prime chunks to keep them going. All other game and grazing animals had been previously wiped out by other gung-ho Victorian adventurers.

Starvation and the consumption of their animal transportation were not the only perils the adventurers were facing. The Namibian Damara and Nama tribes who surrounded the travellers were engaged in low-level conflict since their displacement by Dutch and British colonists. The balance of power had suddenly shifted towards the Orlam people, descendants of the illegitimate children of Nama slaves and their Afrikaner masters. The Orlam were brutal, hacking off the feet of women and gouging out the eyes of infants. Galton's pressing issue, however, was not the well-being of the local women, but more to do with the Orlam Chief, Jonker Afrikaner, preventing his travel through Damaraland. With all the usual Victorian formalities and pleasantries, Galton penned an indignant letter demanding that Jonker gave passage and then waited, and waited, for a response. While he waited, he became interested in applying his most prized navigation instruments to the mapping of a different frontier; the breasts and buttocks of the local tribe's women.

Jonker remained indifferent to Galton's travel plans, and so, Galton constructed a flamboyant response. Resplendent in a scarlet coat and a hunting cap, Galton mounted an Oxon (the horses having been eaten) and charged at Jonker's hut. At the last moment, the confused animal bolted, then somehow managed to jump the moat in front of Jonker's hut, propelling itself through the air with Galton clinging to its back. The beast and Galton landed head first through the door, startling the living daylights out of Jonker, who had been quietly smoking a pipe. The sheer madness continued as Galton proceeded to give the astonished Jonker a 'piece of his mind'.

This ham-fisted intervention was a success. Junker agreed to cooperate and behave in a more peaceful way. Galton, energised by his success in peace negation's, self-appointed himself as ambassador and began travelling around all the other local villages forewarning chiefs and setting up a common moral code of conduct. Then finally, having concluded that he had solved peace in Africa, Galton continued his journey 'taking out' the odd giraffe as he went. On his return to England, he published his first book *Narrative of an Explorer in Tropical South Africa* (1853) and, for his pioneering work on mapping the Namibian interior, was awarded The Royal Geographical Societies gold medal for the encouragement and promotion of geographical science and discovery.

Francis Galton was now famous, his reputation as a geographer and explorer was established and it was time to turn his attention to marriage. We know very little about his marriage to Louisa Butler, even in his autobiography, which has an entire chapter dedicated to the topic of marriage, there is little mention of the circumstances around his relationship with his wife. They were married in 1853, honeymooned in Europe and according to Galton, led a life that their social group would envy.

By 1954, Galton was writing again; *Hints to Travellers* which was so popular that it ran to several editions. Galton expanded the text to include survival information and this revised *Art of Travel* appeared in 1855. This highly detailed book became a key survival text. It contained information about the storage and transportation of instruments, the art of surveying and the storage of specimens, but it also included such gems as what was the best way to roll up shirt sleeves so they remain in place for hours, and the burying of valuables in your arm: make an incision into your arm, pop in a jewel into the open flesh, once it heals over you will always have a pot of ready dosh for an emergency. Galton was soon giving lectures on survival to the War Office, and his work was acknowledged as contributing to saving army lives.

By 1860, the revolution, triggered by Charles Darwin had gathered energy. Social Darwinism and 'the survival of the fittest' drove arguments for all manner of reforms in the name of supremacy, and Galton was posed to consider what might happen if the subjects for improvement were human. His interest in the variation among people had been peaked in his previous geographical pursuits; he was now inspired by his cousin Charles and the philosopher Herbert Spencer. His geographical pursuits would now take an anthropological direction; the study of individual differences at a societal level and the idea that more advanced sensory acuity was related to superior intelligence (decades later, Arthur Jensen went on to show a relationship between general intelligence and measures of sensory acuity).

In what would seem to be short slightness regarding his own sensory capabilities, Galton argued that sensory superiority was a function of genetic inheritance, and thus, intelligence should run in families. Intelligent people have more superior adaptive traits, and therefore, reputation, eminence and societal superiority was a valid indicator of intelligence. This led to Francis measuring the children of accomplished individuals and comparing them to everyone else.

Galton's approach was statistical in nature, which was groundbreaking for his time. His explorations had exposed him to the ideas of the Belgian astronomer, sociologist and pioneer statistician, Adolphe

Quételet, whose methods inspired him to approach the study of intelligence in a systematic way. Quételet's work was the precursor to what we now call the bell curve: plotting, for example, the heights of a population on a chart will create a large bulge in the middle corresponding to the average height. There will be fewer people with shorter than average and greater than average on either side of the bulge.

Galton introduced the concept of 'reversion', which would later become what we now know as regression analysis. He used this technique to demonstrate what statisticians call regression to the mean. For example, when the children of very tall parents have children, their offspring are not taller, rather they tend to produce children of average height. These calculations led to the development of the first regression line, which went on to become the correlation coefficient.

By 1864, he had crafted an outline of what would go on to become the theory of eugenics, which argued that mental characteristics were, just as physical characteristics, subject to hereditary control. By 1885, he was confounding abstract ideas on the nature of intelligence and character. The Negro he argued, had impulsive passions, whereas the North American Indians were cold and melancholic. The American was tolerant of fraud and violence. The peoples of every country were characterised, even those countries he had never been to.

Galton completed the results of his study of excellence and the results were published in *Hereditary Genius* (1869). Eminent parents, who were motivated to encourage their children, had children who were more likely to have children who would make exceptional contributions to society. The government should provide funding to both scientifically pair and support superior individuals to have more children. That such decisions should be formed through the inspection of family records and that those records would eventually form a national genealogical database, which would be used to classify families and individuals.

Races did not escape Galton's new statistical enthusiasm. Negroes, he argued, were significantly less intelligent than whites. His evidence was predictably circular. He could think of no eminent Negroes; we never hear of travellers meeting tribal Chiefs who are better men, and, he had met large numbers of half-witted men on his African Travels. Australian aboriginals were, he argued, even worse.

His ideas did little to influence the policies of the British Government, although he did manage to bolster white supremacy in countries such as America and Australia. Galton's extreme views were mostly unchallenged and when they were challenged, his scientific approach to answering those questions uncovered additional differences of interest. When challenged by the French philosopher Alphonse de Candolle that environmental climate, government and a flourishing economy were every bit as important as inheritance, Galton developed what was possibly the first psychological questionnaire. He surveyed 200 of his fellow scientists at the Royal Society, asking them if they felt their scientific callings had a genetic basis. He was struck by the number of Scots who completed the questionnaire. They, however, attributed their personal success not to inheritance, but to the liberal education system they had been born into. This data persuaded Galton, softened his ideas on the importance of inheritance to intelligence, and he began to petition for the reformation of English schools.

By 1875, his fundamentally nativist position was reinforced by the publication of 'The History of Twins'. This paper was the first detailed account of the respective role of inheritance and environment, where Galton estimated the relative influence of inheritance and the environment (nature-nurture). Concluding that monozygotic or identical twins are like one another, even when they are reared apart. Conversely, non-identical (dizygotic) twins to be dissimilar even when they grow up in the same family environment.

By the late 1870s, Galton was measuring the facial features of criminals and connecting appearance with character. Murderers, burglars, fraudsters and sex offenders were organised into piles and then scanned for obvious differences and similarities. He devised a composite measure, whereby the faces could be overlaid onto one another and an average facial profile derived. The composites were of course undifferentiated, and the failure of this experiment challenged Galton's long-held perspective that the face will change in line with mentality. He realised he would have to move deeper into the psyche of the criminal. Drawing on the work of psychologists such as Wilhelm Whunt, he began to experiment with introspection and word association tasks.

First responses to such tests tended to be the same for most people but responses were often strongly psychologically significant in their pairings. For example, mother-fear would occur less often than say, father-fear. He also found that responses were also connected to the law of errors (the early bell curve) but that many of the people he considered to be most intelligent were not terribly good at forming the images required to complete the task. This work, published in *Inquiries into Human Faculty and its Development* (1883), represents the first systematic use of the word association task and the beginning of the testing movement and the first anthropometric laboratory for the study of human body measurements at London's International Health Exhibition in 1884. Over the course of about a year, Galton took a very large number of measures of 9,337 visitors, including their head size, arm span, length of the middle finger, visual acuity and so on. Such was the volume of data that full analysis did not take place until new calculating machines could handle the task. Those analyses demonstrated that people from lower socio-economic backgrounds experienced developmental progress at a rate different to the more privileged.

However, so much in love was Galton with his own ideas, he continued to pursue dead ducks and blind alleys. His 1889 book, *Natural Inheritance*, was statistically rich, but flawed. He had become so sure of his regression models that he began to reject Darwin's theory of evolution. He could not couple the randomness of nature and the gradualness of change, with the pull of monotonic improvement. Galton had, however, one more discovery to make.

His work in the anthropometric laboratory had provided an archive of rich information, and Galton was hunting the mark of superiority. He had failed at the physical profiling of criminals and held fast to the idea that character held physical manifestations when his attention was drawn to finger ridges. He began smearing ink to decipher hand and figure prints, something that Asian cultures had been using to identify for decades. The work had been pioneered by the amateur scientist William Herschel and the Scottish Doctor Henry Faulds, and Galton sought to systematically demonstrate that it would be possible to use fingerprints (hands were too messy) to identify and convict criminals.

The 1880s and 1890s were spent analysing vast numbers of fingerprints and classifying them. Galton's intention was to identify the shapes that were related to criminality. He had amassed such an indexing system that by 1893 the home office where exploring how fingerprints could be used to overhaul the system of criminal identification. Galton received the glory, and in the process promoted heavily the work of Herschel. This was much to the indignation of Fauld and a feud ensued.

The later years of Galton's life were largely unproductive; unsettled by his increasing deafness he was becoming increasingly withdrawn from society. He and Louisa were persistently troubled by ill health, but they did at least continue to travel together touring Europe. In August 1897, Louisa became ill in France. What seemed to be an upset stomach quickly advanced and she died within a few days.

A change being as good as a rest, in the autumn of 1899, Galton was in Egypt with his new nurse and companion Evelyne Biggs. He was back on top form and, following the publication of Gregor Mendel's ground-breaking work on inheritance, Galton was ready for one last scientific hurrah. In recognition of his inestimable contributions, Galton was awarded the Royal Society's Darwin Medal in 1902. The news was quickly sullied by the news that Charles Darwin had died.

The couple returned to England the following year, and Galton turned his scientific writing towards social change to improve the nation: Eugenics – its definition, scope and aims. Galton had an audience that stretched through the Sociological Society, to Karl Pearson, H.G. Wells and George Bernard Shaw. The University of London established a eugenics lab and the University of Oxford appointed their first eugenics fellow. The drive for eugenic discrimination was taking hold and all that remained were some moral obstacles. By 1907, branches of the London-based Eugenics Education Society were branching across the United Kingdom. By 1909, the now-frail Francis Galton was knighted; in Europe, he was appointed to the council of the German Eugenics Society and his work became popular across the globe.

The frail Galton penned one last fantasy propaganda book, which was rejected by publishers, and he died on January 9, 1911. To this day, the scientist and explorer Sir Francis Galton's immense achievements remain overshadowed by his eugenics work.

Francis Galton's major writings

Galton, F. (1869). *Hereditary genius*. London: Macmillan.

Galton, F. (1874). *English men of sciences: Their nature and nurture*. London: Macmillan.

Galton, F. (1877). Typical laws of heredity. *Proceedings of the Royal Institution, 8*, 282–301.

Galton, F. (1883). *Inquiries into human faculty and its development*. London: Macmillan.

Galton, F. (1886). Regression towards mediocrity in hereditary stature. *Journal of the Anthropological Institute, 15*, 246–63.

Galton, F. (1888). Co-relations and their measurement, chiefly from anthropometric data. *Proceedings of the Royal Society, 45*, 125–145.

Galton, F. (1889). *Natural inheritance*. London: Macmillan.

Galton, F. (1892). *Fingerprints*. London: Macmillan.

Further reading

Brookes, M. (2004). *Extreme measures, the dark visions and bright ideas of Francis Galton*. New York: Bloomsbury.

Galton, F. (1908). *Memories of my life*. London: Methuen.

19 Howard Gardner (July 11, 1943) – at the time of writing aged 78

'One of a kind'

Rudolph (Ralph) Gardner and Hilde Bella (née Weilheimer) Gardner were married in Nürnberg in 1932. Their first son, Eric, was born in 1935 and the family, like Jewish families written about in this book, had to flee Germany during 1938. They eventually made it to America, settling in Scranton, Pennsylvania, in 1940. When Hilde was expecting her second child, tragedy struck. Eric was playing in the snow when his sledge smashed into a stone wall, fracturing his skull. He died on January 10, 1943, at just 7 years old. Howard was born several months later, on July 11, 1943. Neither the escape from Germany nor the death of Eric was ever discussed during Howard's childhood.

Howard's parents pushed his intellectual development, but they provided very few opportunities for risky physical activities such as cycling or rough sports. Gardner describes discovering his secret Jewish history and realising that he was different from others (he is also colour blind) and that he was expected to make his mark in this new country, but that there were major obstacles to doing so. Other intellectual giants had escaped their German and Austrian origins, moving to intellectual centres in Europe; he had arrived, however, in the *'uninteresting, intellectually stagnant, and economically depressed Pennsylvania valley'* (Cited by Palmer-Cooper, Cooper & Bresler, 2001, p. 273).

He was an introverted child that enjoyed painting and music; Howard reports that despite the awful trauma behind his parents' lives, he had a very happy childhood. When he thinks of his childhood, he sees himself seated at the piano, usually next to his mother, playing Bach. His dedication to his mother continued right through his life, Howard's children describe how he provided love and tenderness until Hilde died aged 102.

Howard began to board at a local prep school where the teachers poured attention into his development and well-being. By adolescence, he had discontinued his formal pursuit of music. He claims

DOI: 10.4324/9781003229179-20

his true education did not start until he started his studies at Harvard College in September 1961 with the intention of studying law but focused more on a broader range of subjects including psychology. He graduated with a degree in social relations in 1965, before commencing his doctoral studies. He had hoped to pursue the study of cognition in the arts, but as there were no suitable supervisors he focused instead on developmental psychology. During his postdoctoral training, he spent 12 months as a Fellow at the London School of Economics, where he expanded his learning into philosophy and sociology.

This experience, he claims, was formative in his decision to become a scholar and, after graduation, Gardner began working with the cognitive and educational psychologist Jerome Bruner. Bruner's work on cognitive learning theory was momentous in directing the questions that Gardner would later explore. Burner's personal approach to his students was something that Gardner tried to eliminate throughout his career. Bruner would bring delicious food from the Cambridge delicatessens, and he and his students would all sit down and eat together. He left a lasting impression that professors should learn, work and make personal time for people just out of college.

Bruner brought Judy Krieger, from Berkeley, to study for her doctoral degree. Gardner and Krieger fell in love immediately and wanted to get married straight away. Their parents, however, were cautious and persuaded the couple to wait a while, so they did. Judy eventually obtained her doctorate and became an important cognitive developmental psychologist in her own right. The couple had three children together Kerith (DOB: 1969), Jay (DOB: 1971) and Andrew (DOB: 1976). In 1994, Judith became ill while travelling with friends. She first showed signs of illness on a trek in Nepal with friends and then passed away from an aneurism 3 weeks later in Jerusalem.

The early part of Gardner's career focused on children's development and neuropsychology, particularly symbol processing and neurological damages. He was worked with neurologist Norman Geschwind, while maintaining strong connections with Harvard. Howard was establishing himself as the Co-Director of Project Zero when he met Ellen Winner. Gardner was looking for an assistant to work with him on the psychology of art. Winner had no idea what the psychology of art was, but she had a background in the study of metaphor and Gardner offered her the job. Winner initially rejected the idea of committing to a post for 2 years but eventually felt that on balance it would improve her chances of obtaining a place to study clinical psychology. The partnership was a productive one. They were soon publishing papers together and when

Ellen eventually obtained a place at graduate school, she continued to work with Gardner at Project Zero, by then a couple, they married in 1982 and had one child together, Benjamin.

By the mid-1970s, Howard had begun to construct a theory of human intelligence, which ran counter to many of the major thinkers of the day. Gardner's model exposed its weaknesses and provided an alternative to general intelligence 'g'. For Gardner, the focus on the isolation of g overlooked the full range of possibilities that are associated with human thinking and ability.

By the early 1980s, Gardner was a leading member of the Human Potential Project. The project, funded by the Bernard van Leer Foundation, was set up to examine scientific knowledge on human potential and Gardner's contribution in 1983 was 'Frames of Mind', where he set out his theory of multiple intelligences. What was different in Gardner's approach was not a focus on test scores and correlates, rather it was the exploration of what cognitive abilities humans, in all cultures, needed to perform roles as adults. For Gardner, intelligence is like a computer that works more or less well and that individuals can be stronger in some areas (and hence intelligent) than others (less intelligent). This theory of multiple intelligences was designed to challenge assumptions and misunderstandings, particularly in education, around traditional intelligence theory. He also hoped to influence education systems, which tended to favour mathematical and linguistic abilities over other competencies.

The book was ground breaking and in part enabling Gardner to avoid tenure and shift directly to Professor of Cognition and Education at the Harvard Graduate School. Gardner argued that as many as seven separate intelligences existed that related to how individuals process information. Only three of which, however, could be identified through ability testing: linguistic/language skills, logical mathematical abilities and spatial understanding. There were, however, four further intelligences: musical ability, bodily kinaesthetic, interpersonal (understanding and relating to others) and intrapersonal (understanding oneself). In 1996, he added two further intelligences: naturalist, which is the ability to excel in matters related to topics such as biology, and existentialist, the capacity to understand the self in relation to the world and your surroundings, for example, spirituality. Individuals deemed to be intelligent would be capable of most, if not all, of the intelligences, but they also had to have the ability to resolve problems and difficulties.

Gardner argued that these separate intelligences resided in different brain areas, and his clinical observations supported this because they could be observed in isolation in prodigies, autistic savants and other exceptional populations. His reliance on applied rather than experimental evidence, however, is one of the enduring problems with Gardner's work. His theory offered a different, rich perspective about which to understand human abilities. It supported a departure from the work of Spearman, Eysenck, Jensen and others, but it was not always backed up with experimental evidence. Gardner always argued that this was not necessary. Experimental evidence was not to him appropriate for theoretical synthesis, and it often led to labelling and stigmatisation.

Psychology remains split on Gardner's work, but he has had an important influence outside of psychology, particularly in the field of education. Educators argue that multiple intelligences validate not only their everyday experience of children and their abilities but also their experiences of the gifted. It has helped them improve pedagogical practices and design curriculums that support development in all kinds of new ways. However, because Gardner (and psychology) did not pay sufficient attention to spelling out the theoretical model behind his work, it has been open to misinterpretation and abuse by teachers, independent consultants and administrators, who added their own spin to his work – with misguided educationalists reported as revisiting a topic on multiple occasions using different methods to tap into the eight different intelligences.

Gardner refused to engage in the issues surrounding the misapplication of his work, focusing instead on new work and development. It was not until1991 that he began attempting to address some of the problems his work had caused in his book *The Unschooled Mind*, where he made it clear that he believed that the role of education was to develop deep understanding and that educators should value depth in learning, over breadth. To enable this to happen children should have opportunities to work on a problem over an extended period using different approaches.

His vision was always a broad one and he updated his work to explore what it means to be intelligent in a digital age and how intelligence and morality can work together for a better world. With colleagues, in 1994 he established the Good Work Project, which aimed to determine how those at the peak of their professions can produce work that not only is exemplarily in nature but also contributes to the wider good of society. This work developed into the eventual Directorship of Project Zero, which examines fundamental questions about human expression and development.

The misunderstanding and misuse of Gardner's work has led to the theory being praised and dammed by psychologists and educationalists alike. At the time of writing, Gardner, now 76 years of age, is still involved both in the Good Work Project and Project Zero. His children describe him as an insanely hard-working father, whose dedication to his family surpasses his dedication to work. He cares deeply about everything he does including being a dad. What he doesn't care about is his personal appearance. He once turned up at an important meeting with one brown shoe and one black shoe. Marcelo Suarez-Orozco describes him as brilliant, humble, generous and deeply ethical. A man for all seasons; '*Sui generis*' (one of a kind).

Howard Gardner's major writings

Gardner, H. (1983). *Frames of mind: The theory of multiple intelligences.* New York: Basic Books.

Gardner, H. (1991). *The unschooled mind: How children think and how schools should teach.* New York: Basic Books.

Gardner, H. (1999). *Intelligence reframed: Multiple intelligences for the 21st century.* New York: Basic Books.

Further reading

Gardner, H. (1989). *To open minds: Chinese clues to the dilemma of contemporary education.* New York: Basic Books.

Palmer-Cooper, J., Cooper, D. E., & Bresler, L. (2001). *Fifty modern thinkers on education: From Piaget to the present day.* London and New York: Routledge.

20 James Jerome Gibson (January 27, 1904–December 11, 1979)

Gibson's 'ecological psychology' sought to understand the relationships between the way a person perceives the world and how they behaviour.

J.J. Gibson was born in McConnelsville and raised in the Midwest. His father, Thomas, was a railroad surveyor and his mother, Gertrude, was a teacher until her marriage to Thomas. 'Jimmy' had two younger brothers, Thomas and William. He began his undergraduate studies at Northwestern University. After a year, he transferred to Princeton, where he was influenced by Edwin B. Holt, one of the early behaviourists, and the experimental psychology Herbert S. Langfeld, who was a strong advocate of the view that consciousness does not exist in isolation from motor actions (e.g. walking, turning, lifting) and could not be studied independently of those acts. In 1928, he completed his doctoral dissertation at Princeton. His research thesis set out to test a claim made by Gestalt psychologists such as Wertheimer that memories for complex visual forms change spontaneously to memories for simpler structures in line with Gestalt principles of organisation. He demonstrated that this was not the case and showed that learning was crucially important. After completing his doctorate, he went to Smith College to take up his first academic appointment and while he was there, he encountered an English translation of Kurt Koffka's *Principles of Gestalt Psychology*, which greatly influenced his thinking and work. One of the students at Smith, Eleanor Jack, took his courses on experimental psychology. 'Jimmy' and 'Jackie' married and Jackie became his closest and most influential colleague. About their working together he wrote:

> We have collaborated on occasion, but not as a regular thing. And when we did we were not a husband-and-wife team, God knows,

DOI: 10.4324/9781003229179-21

for we argued endlessly. . . . When it is assumed that whatever one Gibson says, the other will agree, we are annoyed, for it isn't so.

They had two children, James Jerome and Jean.

The influence of Gestalt thinking is indicated in Gibson's demonstration of a tilt-induction effect, whereby observers report a vertical line as appearing to tilt in the direction opposite to surrounding context lines and so, when attempting to adjust a line to true vertical, the tendency is to err in the direction of the context lines. The phenomenon is very similar to the tilted-room effect reported by another Gestalt psychologist, Asch. During World War II, Gibson directed a psychological research unit for the Army Air Forces Aviation Psychology Program. His unit implemented a new way of constructing tests for pilot selection; they used motion pictures to present the materials they used to test their candidate pilots. While working on these tests, he began to develop the idea that there is more information available in moving than static pictures. Following the war, he returned to Smith College but moved on to Cornell where he remained for the rest of his career.

His *Perception of the Visual World* (1950) presented his 'ground theory' of space perception. The theory suggested that gradients of texture on the ground correspond to gradients on the retina, and these are the sensory basis for perceiving depth and space. In other words, the retina of the eye is sensitive to different kinds of textures in the environment and can use that textural information to estimate distances and spaces. He became dissatisfied with this theory and began to think that theories of visual perception that focus on the way of the eye and brain respond to light are formulated at an inappropriate level. A new discipline, which he called ecological optics, was needed. Ecological optics is concerned with the study of optical information at the level appropriate for understanding vision. The implication of this statement is that an adequate theory of visual perception must incorporate an analysis of how organisms look around and move around their environment. Animals move; they are not stationary organisms passively responding to whatever light impinges on their ocular sensing devices. In fact, they often change their position in order to see things better. Thus, a theory of visual perception had to incorporate a role for the movement of the organism; it should be about ambulatory vision. His new theory of visual perception and his formulation of the new discipline of ecological optics were presented in his next book *The Senses Considered as Perceptual Systems* (1966).

The concept of invariants is essential to Gibson's theory. Gibson considered perception to be an activity – a dynamic process. A perceptual invariant is a higher-order property of patterns of stimulation that remains constant during changes associated with the observer, the environment or both. Followers of Gibson's theory distinguish between two kinds of perceptual invariant: transformational and structural. Transformational invariants are patterns of change that can reveal what is happening to an object. For instance, when a car moves away from us at a constant speed its apparent size reduces. The decrease in area is proportional to the square of the distance. Wherever this relationship obtains, it means that the distance between us and the object is changing in a regular manner. Where the relationship does not hold, it must mean either that the object is accelerating or decelerating, or it is actually changing its size. Structural invariants are higher patterns of relationships that remain constant despite changes in visual stimulation. For instance, when two cars of an identical make are parked at different distances, it is easy for us to tell that they are the same size. They will usually be viewed against a scene containing a visible horizon, and it can be shown that the ratio of an object's height to the distance between its base and the horizon is invariant across all distances from the viewer.

Another essential and novel part of Gibson's theory is the concept of affordances. The notion of affordance defines a relationship between a perceiving organism and its environment.

> The affordances of the environment are what it offers the animal, what it provides or furnishes, either for good or ill. The verb to afford is found in the dictionary, but the noun affordance is not. I have made it up. I mean by it something that refers to both the environment and the animal in a way that no existing term does. It implies the complementarity of the animal and the environment.
> (1979, p. 127)

Affordances are the meanings an environment has for an organism; they guide behaviour. Gibson claimed that affordances can be perceived directly, without prior synthesis or analysis. This means, for instance, that the properties of objects that reveal they can be grasped can be directly perceived from the pattern of stimulation arising from them. For example, a child who is shown a novel object can instantly tell whether that object can be grasped or not because there is enough information in the object for the child to make an appropriate deduction.

Gibson's ideas are in stark opposition to a physics-based approach to the analysis of visual perception. The physics-based approach is essentially data-driven or bottom-up because the emphasis is on understanding the effects of photons when they strike the retina. The perception of surfaces and depth, for instance, is thought to be a composition of the information provided by these atoms of visual perception. The organism perceiving an object attaches some value to it – value is attached to an object by the perceiver; it is not directly perceived. The ecological approach takes quite a different view that surfaces are directly perceived, not constructed in the perceptual system of organism out of bits of information collected at the retinas. The ecological approach also adopts the position that what these surfaces afford an animal are directly perceived as well, they are not worked out or deduced by the animal. Critics have argued that Gibson's account denies a place for information processing, or even for thinking, in the processes of visual perception. Supporters counter that his ecological theory shows how the environment augments the internal processes of the mind/brain, so that information processing can no longer be understood only in terms of factors internal to an animal. Thus, the environment provides structured information to a perceiving animal, reducing the amount of processing necessary for the perception of complex entities.

The theory of information that flows from Gibson's ecological theory of perception has been used in many areas of applied cognitive psychology. For example, the notion of perceptual affordances permeates much thinking in the psychology of design, where in practical use it has become synonymous with the idea of stimulus-response compatibility – the notion that what makes some tasks more or less difficult to perform is partly determined by the way in which individual stimuli and responses are paired with each other. To perform a task or use an object effectively, the stimulus (or object) must provide the perceiver/user with the information necessary to perform the desired action/response. Doors provide many examples of both good and poor design. Doors that provide a flat plate are clearly for pushing; however, doors with handles, though they afford pulling, should often be pushed instead. In the latter case, the design has failed.

Several criticisms have been made against Gibson's theory. First, it has been argued that the theory does not specify what is meant by 'direct perception'. It is possible to build simple models that can be seen to have two distinct motions even though the stimulus array reaching the retina does not change physically. When people view these models, they notice that the perception of orientation precedes the perception of motion, which suggests that perception of the motion of the object is not 'direct' but can be decomposed into stages. Second, Gibson argues that there are invariant properties in physical events, which afford the perception of those events. However, David Marr and others have attempted to create computer models of vision and build computers that see. These seeing computers include a role for invariant properties in physical events, but Marr has shown that the task of specifying these invariant properties is enormously more complex than Gibson supposed. This does not mean that Gibson is wrong, but it suggests that something that he considered to be relatively straightforward turns out to be extremely problematic and this indicates that part of his theory is under-elaborated. Third, Gibson considered affordances to be the most subtle forms of perceptual invariance. However, it is extremely difficult to define affordance and to predict a relationship with behaviour. For instance, if certain objects in the world 'afford' eating, what is it in the nature of the optic array that makes explicit this affordance? Related to this is the difficulty of actually finding invariants and affordances. Gibson's theory gives little guidance on how this difficulty might be overcome.

The theory of affordances is a fundamental departure from alternative theories of value and meaning, as indicated in Gibson's extension of affordances beyond the perceptual information surfaces provide to an animal. The more radical extension of his theory claims that surfaces can be directly perceived and that the use of these surfaces can also be directly perceived, even those uses which do not seem to have immediate connection with visual perception. This means, for example, that how a thing tastes can be directly perceived. This is possible because 'a unique combination of invariants, a compound invariant, is just another invariant' (1979, p. 141), and the taste of a thing is a compound invariant. However, as Gibson himself pointed out, the more radical version of his theory cannot adequately explain how misperceptions occur. If a person is aware of an illusory perception is the misinformation caused by the ambient light, or by the person's internal perceptual processes? The first possibility, that light in itself can be thought to have a false meaning, seems wholly untenable. The second possibility implies that some mechanism is dependent on the perceiver and this must account for the introduction of error – which implies that perception is not direct. Gibson's theory also runs into difficulties when called to account for learning. How does the learning of affordances not directly related to a perceiver's internal perceptual processes come about? For example, how does one person, such as an elderly man, come to learn that ambient light carrying affordances information to them is carrying the same affordances information to others, such as a toddler? The ambient light cannot carry information about the affordance an object provides to someone else. Thus, learning requires more than direct perception, which implies that some affordances are not directly perceived.

Despite these limitations and criticisms, Gibson's theory made some fundamentally important advances in the psychology of perception.

First, it placed the environment in the centre of perception research and encouraged the development of a line of investigation that used ecologically plausible or naturalistic stimuli rather than laboratory-created stimuli. Second, Gibson's concept of 'ecological optics' stimulated interest in perception in other species and thereby raised general questions about the nature of perceptual processes. His final (1979) book concluded with a plea that the terms and concepts of his theory should 'never shackle thought as the old terms and concepts have!'

James J. Gibson's major writings

Gibson, J. J. (1929). The reproduction of visually perceived forms. *Journal of Experimental Psychology, 12*, 1–39.

Gibson, J. J. (1933). Adaptation, after-effect and contrast in the perception of curved lines. *Journal of Experimental Psychology, 16*, 1–31.

Gibson, J. J. (1950). *The perception of the visual world.* Boston: Houghton Mifflin.

Gibson, J. J. (1951). What is a form? *Psychological Review, 58*(6), 403–412.

Gibson, J. J. (1961). Ecological optics. *Vision Research, 1*, 253–262.

Gibson, J. J. (1966). *The senses considered as perceptual systems.* Boston: Houghton Mifflin.

Gibson, J. J. (1979). *The ecological approach to visual perception.* New York: Erlbaum.

Gibson, J. J., & Gibson, E. J. (1955). Perceptual learning: Differentiation or enrichment? *Psychological Review, 62*(1), 32–41.

Gibson, J. J., & Mowrer, O. H. (1938). Determinants of the perceived vertical and horizontal. *Psychological Review, 45*(4), 300–323.

Further reading

MacLeod, R. B., & Pick, H. L. Jr. (1974). *Perception: Essays in honor of James J. Gibson.* Ithaca, United States: Cornell University Press.

Marr, D. (1982). *Vision.* San Francisco: Freeman.

Norman, D. (1999). *The Design of Everyday Things.* Cambridge, MA: MIT Press.

Ullman, S. (1980). Against direct perception. *Behavioral and Brain Sciences, 3*(whole issue).

21 Henry Herbert Goddard (August 14, 1866–June 18, 1957)

A psychologist and eugenicist, but also came to accept the flawed nature of such thinking. He was the first to argue that cognitive impairment should be used as a defence in criminal proceedings, and that blind, deaf and intellectually disabled children should receive special education.

Henry Herbert Goddard was born into a revivalist Quaker family. He was the fifth child of Sarah Winslow Goddard and Henry Clay. The couple had lost two of their children before Henry's birth and Henry describes himself as having all the devotion that the couple could not give to their lost children, heaped upon him, particularly from his kindly and gentle father.

Henry's childhood, however, was impoverished and isolated. During the 1850s, Henry Clay was a prosperous New England farmer, but after being gored by one of his bulls he became disabled. By the 1870s, he had lost his farm and was working as an agricultural worker. While he was ill, his mother mostly depended on her older married children for support. The Quaker society offered support under such hardships, but Sarah was reluctant to ask for help. When Henry died in 1875, Sarah found a new passion; she was awoken by the revivalist movement and soon became a lay preacher. By the time he was 6, the local community had established that Sarah was gifted in the ministry, and she went to Canada to spread the good work in jails, prisons, and reformatory institutions, and by holding public meetings. Herbert was left behind. Over the course of his life, he would become even more estranged from his mother as she travelled Europe and the Holy Land.

His education started locally with country teachers. At the age of 11, his formal education commenced when he entered the local Vassalboro academy, Oak Grove Seminary. In 1883, he began studying at Haverford College, where his poverty and his mother's religious commitment

DOI: 10.4324/9781003229179-22

prompted a Quakers scholarship for his board and tuition: 'Quaker Jail' as Herbert would go on to describe it. Herbert's studies were dominated by mathematics. One of the few subjects that were unlikely to corrupt young minds. Between meals, there were strict recitations. Students were always on duty, studying, marching, eating or in bible study. Goddard was tortured by the unrelenting nature of his Latin teacher who forbade him to read even one more book until he mastered his Latin. He did manage to make time for the school newspaper and Vice President of the Y.M.C.A. but concluded that he had no abilities, or those abilities were about as nil as could possibly be.

This was a harsh regime, but Goddard performed well, graduating sixth in his class and winning the Athenaeum Prize for Declamation and the Alumni Prize for Oratory and Composition. These achievements led some biographers to conclude that his more bitter reflections were not necessarily a lived reality, but reflections informed by his developed understanding during adulthood and a long career in education and psychometric testing. Goddard never criticised his mother; such an action would question her religious calling, but within a few years, he was giving her and her new itinerant husband Jehu Newlin, money.

Henry borrowed just enough money to get himself to California in 1887 and could find no employment, so he headed north to Oakland answering 'help wanted' ads for 3 months. Nobody wanted him. Finally, in the Spring the University of Southern California offered him a temporary position teaching history, botany, coaching the sports team (he became the first official coach of what would become the USC Trojans) and teaching the much-despised Latin. When that position ended, Henry had to borrow again to go back to Haverford to study for his MA in mathematics.

He still had no life plan when he met the strong-willed schoolteacher, Emma Florence Robbins. One week before his 23rd birthday they married and their union was a long, close and happy one. After some 40 years of marriage, the two would write as many as three letters a day to one another.

With the pressures of family life upon him, Henry had to find a position, although he still had no idea about what he was going to do in the world. Then he had a 'lucky break'. Emma taught at the Damascus Quaker school primary department and in 1899 Henry was able to take up the post of head teacher, teaching mathematics, moral and mental science and conducting prayer services. He stayed for 2 years, until an old friend Rufus Jones, offered him a post at Oak Grove, where Henry eventually became Principal.

Like many teachers of the time, Henry was inspired by the speeches of the educational reformist G. Stanley Hall, who argued that schools needed to change the focus of their practice and focus on the child; '*the school is for the child, the child is not for the school*'. Hall was a pioneering psychologist, later founding the American Psychological Society, whose work called teachers to work with him in the scientific study of child development and to work towards educational reform. Henry was hooked. He borrowed enough money to study at Clarke University where Hall was President, eventually gaining a Doctorate in Psychology in 1899.

Clarke campus was qualitatively different to anything that Henry had previously experienced. Hall had no interest in feeding the spiritual needs of its students, rather the University incorporated German ideals of freedom to teach, to learn and to develop intellectual independence. The educational environment did not dismiss the role of religion; rather, Hall was more focused on driving a wedge between psychology and philosophy. Rather, teachings focused on the systematic application of the experimental method to all things human, and as such, Henry Goddard settled on a research topic which explored the scientific evidence behind faith cures and sought to put some scientific reason into the subject. As Goddard turned more to psychology, he moved farther away from his mother's interpretation of God and the role of religion. He never entirely rejected religion but felt that he could in some way fuse the two, the advancement of Christian ideals through the study of science.

Henry's career in psychology finally commenced when in 1899 he was appointed Professor of Psychology and Pedagogy at the State Normal School, West Cheshire, Pennsylvania. By the time Henry joined State Normal, the membership of societies dedicated to the study of the child had reached 500. The environment encouraged the enthusiastic exploration of learning, through the recording of thousands of observations which would, it was hoped, help scientists understand the evolution of the child's mind. However, the movement was not without its critics. After decades of research, there was very little to show. Many argued that the movement was a fad at best, and at worst it operated in the same way as the vivisectionists. The study of the child should be performed by trained professionals, and teachers had no such special training. The German-American psychologist Hugo Münsterberg went further by dividing such amateurs into '*people who know they do not know psychology*' and those '*who don't know even that*'. Henry had an uphill battle if he wanted to set up his own society.

While arguments between psychologists and the child-study movement trundled along, the American school population was changing dramatically. Populations were becoming more urban and racially diverse. Most states now had a legal requirement for children to attend school, and the rapid increase in children overwhelmed the education system and the large numbers of children suddenly appearing in school caused waves of illness. Children who were blind, deaf, seriously ill, sickly, suffering from epilepsy, tuberculosis and cardiac conditions were lumped together in a class of 50 or more. School became synonymous with suffering, even death. Of course, the methods employed by the child-study movement didn't evolve in step with these major societal changes either.

Eventually, the school doctor movement began to get a grip on children who were clearly too ill to attend school; however, while those doctors could help with the sick, they could do nothing to help children's whose problems they did not understand. Few states had facilities to support children; where they did, they were often crammed with over 1,000 children with special needs. Elsewhere, the most that was on offer were special classes.

More enlightened institutions supported children using what was known as the principles of physiological education, the idea being that learning difficulties were caused by poor brain development. To promote brain development, children were educated by methods thought to stimulate the sensory organs: clay, wax, patterns, photographs, painting and books.

Edward Johnson, a schoolteacher at the Vineland Special Education School in New Jersey, and pioneer of such methods, invited Goddard in 1900 to visit his institution. Goddard was impressed by the institution's home-like structure and Johnsons radical different pedagogical approach. The two met again the following year at a child-study meeting and the '*Feeble-Minded Club*' was born, with the aim of bringing scientists and educators together in an attempt to help address the inadequacies in special needs education. By the standards of today, the title is distasteful, but the movement was revolutionary. The Club supported teachers to spend time in institutions where they had concentrated time to experience different degrees of learning disabilities and the interventions which could improve children's lives. While some teachers marvelled at Johnson's ability to manage the 'repulsive' children with whom he worked, others credited the team with helping to remove the stigma that came with teaching special needs education. For Goddard, Johnson's work epitomised not only the Christian spirit that ought to scaffold education but also the merits of the scientific principles of trial, error and careful observation. Goddard also became convinced that such children were no different from others. All children started out more or less the same, developmental difficulties presented themselves as the child progressed. At a time when many still believed that such children were of no value to society and that the most that could be done was to keep them comfortable until they died, these were progressive ideas.

As his thinking on the subject developed Goddard argued that far too much emphasis had been placed on mindless rote learning and memorisation. Being able to repeat without thought and understanding did not constitute intellectual growth. Develop the perception and the action, he would argue, because memory will take care of itself. However, even the Feeble-Minded Club was at the limits of what was possible when they were asked to help diagnose developmental and learning disabilities. The movement was raising more questions and fewer answers. A psychological laboratory could provide answers, but the trustees of Vineland were in opposition to such an idea. The well-known Educator and Professor, Earl Barnes, attempted to reassure that the humanitarian mission of Vineland was not in conflict with the scientific when he addressed the board of trustees in 1903, declaring that Vineland was already '*a human laboratory and garden, where unfortunate children would be cared for, protected and loved while they unconsciously whisper to us syllable by syllable the secrets of the soul's growth*'. Three years later, Vineland had their laboratory and the trustees were ready to hire a psychologist, and Henry H. Goddard set about the enormous task of diagnosing the feebleminded.

Initially, Goddard focused on medical diagnosis but soon realised that such information provided little in the way of classification because children varied extensively in appearance, medical history, behaviour and learning aptitude; some children had mental disabilities and some children had both mental and physical problems. Other children perhaps ought not to have been there at all, suffering from disabilities, injuries, deformities, paralysis or problems that merely had social stigmas attached such as speech impediments, cleft palates and other physical disfigurements. In some cases, there seemed to be nothing manifestly different about the child at all. One child had been admitted because he had been hitting other children in his class; another, in a country with limited gun control, had been brought in by his family because he had shot his sister. Educational ability ranged from 'idiot savants' to children who, despite years of schooling, made no progress. Undeterred, the doctors continued to search for patterns and clusters of symptoms shared by groups of this population.

Goddard began to gently and tactfully encourage physicians to shift the problem towards psychology. Studying what a child could not do, and what their deficits were, was futile. What use were classifications such as microcephalic and Mongolian in helping us understand better how to help children? Psychology could help explore if such children could recombine their mental processes in other ways. The job of the psychologist was to encourage fruit from a plant that is unusually slow in its growth. Medics, teachers and psychologists were dealing with a generally healthy organism that in some way lacked something, but it did not follow the child lacked so much that it could not develop at all. The feeble-minded child was trapped in a foreign land; psychology could find a way to establish communication. These striking arguments are in direct contradiction to later accusations relating to Goddard's eugenic motives and conduct.

After 2 years of exhausting work, Goddard had, however, achieved very little, and he left Vineland in search of new ideas in Europe. He travelled through France, Italy, Germany, Austria, Switzerland, Holland and Belgium seeking new ideas and inspiration from medics, teachers and psychologists. In Brussels, he had a major breakthrough, when a series of mental tests by Alfred Binet were given to him by Ovide Decroly. Decroly was a doctor and special educator and was impressed by Goddard's work which his wife had translated for him into French. Decroly had invited Goddard to meet with him and by chance mentioned the Binet tests, which rested on the idea that chronological age should be compared with mental age to how a child differed from what was usual or normal development.

Initially sceptical that intelligence could be measured, Goddard set about translating Binet's works, then trialling them on the Vineland children. He communicated regularly with Binet, exploring the findings, becoming increasingly convinced that the test was valid. The results corresponded exactly with what was being recorded through clinical judgements, and it had the advantage of being fast. Children need not be admitted into an institution for diagnosis and support.

Finally, the American Association for the Study of the Feeble-minded asked Goddard to submit a report on his findings. The report included not only his results but also his own systematic attempts to validate the results against clinical reports from institutions. This process was crude, but it convinced the panel that his results could be trusted. Institutional diagnosis became grounded in Binet's work and the diagnosis of mental deficits became reconceptualised. Goddard had established the value that psychology could bring to society, but that would not prevent 'unprincipled charlatans' from adopting the test for wider use.

Described as a gentleman, with a passion for mountain climbing, Henry Goddard undoubtedly helped popularise an alternative strategy to the study of mental ability and the diagnosis of feeble-mindedness.

Much early evidence suggests that he had humanitarian motives that were radical for the time and directly aimed at improving the lives and prospects of institutionalised children. For Goddard, it was important to discover and develop what a child could do, not segregate them on what they could not.

However, as the eugenics movement gathered pace in America, the test originally developed by Alfred Binet to support educational development began to be used as evidence to support the segregation and sterilisation of those considered defective in some way. Goddard was a strong advocate of eugenics, particularly segregation and his controversial work 'The Kallikaks' published in 1912 presented a sensational case for human degeneracy. The study claimed to provide extensive genealogical data from several generations of the same family. The book, depicting unattractive people, living in impoverished surroundings showed what social disasters would follow if genetically defected were not prevented from having children. No matter that the data was based on a combination of the Binet test, personal opinion and impression, it was an instant bestseller and the term 'moron' entered the common vernacular.

In 1913, Goddard turned his attention to the migrant population. Large numbers were arriving from Eastern Europe, and these 'New Immigrants' were considered to be quite different from the Germans and British who had emigrated during earlier periods. Jews, Poles and Italians, mostly young males, arrived in large numbers and initially had no intention of settling permanently; rather, their motivation was to make money to improve their standard of living at home. This great migration was a concern and, in an attempt, to manage the influx, the US government introduced quota policies which would prioritise the hardworking, intelligent and skilled. A testing programme was established on Ellis Island with the objective of controlling those considered inferior, unskilled and feeble-minded. Goddard arrived at Elis Island with his Binet tests, with the intention of evidencing their practical value. Once testing began, it was not long before he was reporting, unsurprisingly, that many of the emigrants had mental ages lower than 12 years old. There is some evidence that he understood that his data was likely to be impacted by the emigrant's lack of education, cultural differences, impoverishment, and, in many cases their lack of English. Similarly, he recognised that his results were not truly representative because he had only been able to test immigrants travelling in steerage. However, he concluded that he believed that many Europeans were unquestionably feebleminded and would degenerate American lineage. This was powerful propaganda. As the Immigration Act of 1924 was debated, Goddard and other principal eugenicists were called to advise Congress.

Scientifically, Goddard added very little to the nature versus nurture debate, and much of his data could have been explained equally well by both genetic and environmental influences. There is good evidence, that in later years, he recognised that many of his ideas were both unacceptable and out of date and throughout the remainder of his career he was a powerful advocator for educational reform and improved child-rearing. Despite the many controversies surrounding his work and motives, he set the scene for the American testing movement and his work was subsequentially built upon by Robert Yerks and Lewis M. Terman.

Towards the end of his life, Henry H. Goddard developed Alzheimer's disease. He died at his home in Santa Barbara in 1957, and his ashes are interred in Vineland.

Henry Herbert Goddard's major writings

Goddard, H. H. (1913). *Standard method for giving the Binet test.* NJ: Vineland.
Goddard, H. H. (1914). *Feeble-mindedness: Its causes and consequences.* New York: MacMillan.

Further reading

Zenderland, L. (1998). *Measuring minds, Henry Herbert Goddard and the origins of American intelligence testing.* Cambridge: Cambridge University Press.

22 Lewis Robert Goldberg (January 28, 1932)

Goldberg has played a central role in the development of the Big five trait model of personality (a name he gave it).

Lewis Robert Goldberg was born on January 28, 1932, at the Michael Reese Hospital in Chicago, Illinois, to Gertrude Mathis Lewis and Max Frederick Goldberg. His father was born in 1899 in Globe, Arizona, and raised in the small Midwest town of Danville, Illinois. He applied to Harvard University but was not immediately accepted and so spent his first college year at the University of Illinois, followed by 3 years at Harvard, where he was President of his college fraternity, and where he achieved his B.A. degree in 1922; from Harvard he received a law degree in 1925. He practised business-related law in the famed Rookery building on LaSalle Street in Chicago's Loop, where he was revered for his honesty and integrity. He died in 1996 at the age of 97.

Lew Goldberg's mother was born in 1907 in St. Louis, Missouri, where after high school she attended the Mary Institute. She met Max on an arranged double date during a trip to Chicago, and they were married in Chicago in 1929. She was an accomplished piano player, oil painter, and cook. She died in 2005, at the age of 98.

As a child, Lewis was called Skipper by his parents and relatives but deliberately changed his name to Lew when he entered high school. An only child, he lived with his parents in Chicago on Hyde Park Boulevard (across from the Poinsettia Hotel) between 55th and 56th streets, near the Museum of Science and Industry. He attended Bret Harte elementary school, skipping two semesters and graduating from eighth grade in 1944 near the end of World War II. Around that time, his parents moved to the northern Chicago suburb of Highland Park, where he spent a semester at its Lincoln elementary school, graduating from

DOI: 10.4324/9781003229179-23

eighth grade a second time in 1945. He graduated from the Highland Park High School in 1949.

His college years, 1949 to 1953, at Harvard were unusually happy, stimulating and even inspirational. Some years before he arrived, Harvard's famed psychology department had split in two, one retaining the name Psychology and the other (a fusion of anthropology, sociology, and personality and social psychology) called Social Relations. Lewis majored in Social Relations, in part because its lax requirements allowed him the freedom to take elementary everything else. In his junior year, faced with the decision where to go after college, he considered becoming a physicist or a lawyer like his father but eventually settled on graduate school in clinical psychology, under the illusion that such an education would be the best training for whatever he eventually decided to do.

Accepted into the PhD program in Clinical Psychology at the University of Michigan, he developed a strong friendship with his mentor, E. Lowell Kelly, who was the psychology department head and soon was elected President of the American Psychological Association (APA). Kelly and his wife were building a sailboat in the basement of their large house in Ann Arbor, Michigan, and Lewis spent hours handing them screwdrivers and other tools. When thinking of a topic for his doctoral dissertation, he elected to conduct a follow-up survey of the participants in the Veterans Administration assessment project that resulted in the classic volume, *The Prediction of Performance in Clinical Psychology* by Kelly and Fiske (1951). The resulting psychological monograph was titled *Correlates of Later Performance and Specialization in Psychology: A Follow-Up Study of the Trainees Assessed in the VA Selection Research Project* (Kelly & Goldberg, 1959).

Although this was quite rare for graduate students back in those days, Lewis published two articles in peer-reviewed APA journals, one of which on decision-making ('The Effectiveness of Clinicians' Judgments: The Diagnosis of Organic Brain Damage from the Bender-Gestalt Test' [Goldberg, 1959]) became frequently cited and introduced him to Paul J. Hoffman, the founder of Oregon Research Institute (ORI), the institution which was his scientific home throughout his career. At the very end of Lewis' stay at Michigan, he met Warren T. Norman, who was to play a pivotal role in his later scientific career.

While writing his doctoral dissertation, Lewis travelled with the Kelly family to Washington, DC, to attend the APA convention with Kelly as its president. There he was introduced by Kelly to Richard Sears, the newly installed Head of the Psychology Department at Stanford University, who offered Lewis a position as Acting Assistant Professor at Stanford to fill in for a faculty member who was on leave for a year. One year later, Kelly gave a lecture at Stanford and helped arrange for Lewis to stay there a second year in his temporary position. While teaching at Stanford, he became close friends with Albert Bandura and Jerry Wiggins, teaching an assessment course with Wiggins and developing the outline for what would eventually become the classic textbook, *Personality and Prediction: Principles of Personality Assessment* (Wiggins, 1973).

When it became time to secure a permanent faculty position, Kelly once again found Lewis a new job, this one at the University of Oregon. Upon Kelly's recommendation, Robert Leeper, the Oregon psychology department head, called Lewis to offer him a position as Assistant Professor, sight unseen. Almost immediately after that telephone call, Lewis received another, this one from Paul Hoffman, telling him about his new 'institute for basic research in the behavioral sciences' called the Oregon Research Institute. From 1960 on, the University of Oregon and ORI provided congenial homes for his scientific research (ORI) and for his undergraduate and graduate student teaching (U of O). It was at the U of O that Lewis met Dean Peabody, with whom he developed a deep friendship and eventual collaboration (Peabody & Goldberg, 1989).

In 1962, Kelly was appointed by Sargent Shriver, President John F. Kennedy's brother-in-law and the Director of the brand-new US Peace Corps, to serve as that agency's first full-time Director of Selection. Soon thereafter, Kelly contacted the President of the U of O (Arthur Fleming), asking him to release Lewis from his teaching duties in the middle of the academic quarter so that Lewis could assist Kelly in Washington, DC. Thus, began one of the most enjoyable and fascinating adventures in Lewis' lifetime, serving the Peace Corps (PC) in a consulting capacity as one of its first Field Selection Officers (FSO).

During those early years, Peace Corps aspirants were trained in colleges and universities throughout the United States, and their selection as PC volunteers took place only at the end of their typically 9-month training period. It was the FSO who made the actual selection decisions, upon the advice of a 9- to 12- person selection board, made up of persons involved in the training and assessment of the trainee cohort. Over the years between 1962 and 1965, Lewis served as the FSO for over two dozen of these training groups, most of them in the paradise-like location of Hilo, Hawaii. That permitted Lewis to fly from Oregon to Hawaii every 6 weeks, first to inform the trainees about the nature of PC selection process, then to conduct a mid-term selection board meeting, and last to conduct the final selection board, followed by intense personal interviews with all trainees who had not been selected to be PC volunteers.

Back at ORI, Lewis worked with Hoffman, Leonard Rorer, and Paul Slovic on topics related to human judgment and decision-making, and in 1967 he wrote a quasi-autobiographical account of that research. Knowing that the editor of the American Psychologist (AP) was interested in the topic, on a whim Lewis sent him a copy of the manuscript 'for his reading pleasure'. To his surprise, he immediately heard back that the manuscript was now in press in AP, and soon after was published there. The resulting article, titled 'Simple Models or Simple Processes: Some Research on Clinical Judgments' (Goldberg, 1968), was to become his first citation classic. Not long after, he published in *Psychological Bulletin* another highly cited article on decision-making, titled 'Man Versus Model of Man: A Rationale, Plus Some Evidence, for Improving on Clinical Inferences' (Goldberg, 1970).

Around 1965, the small group of research scientists at ORI at that time decided to apply to the National Institute of Mental Health for a 'program project' research grant, with Lewis as the principal investigator; the resulting large grant, called 'A Program Project in Personality Assessment', was used to support much ORI research for the next decade. During the 1966–1967 academic year, Lewis spent his first sabbatical as a Fulbright Professor at the University of Nijmegen in The Netherlands; during the summers before and after, he and his family explored Europe, from the Scandinavian countries south to Greece, Spain Portugal, Italy and France.

Loving the opportunity to spend substantial chunks of time in new and thus different places, during the 1970–1971 year he taught in the psychology department and the Institute for Personality Assessment and Research (IPAR) at the University of California, Berkeley; during 1974–1975 he was a Fulbright Professor at the University of Istanbul in Turkey (with a side-trip to visit Amos Tversky and Daniel Kahneman in Jerusalem, Israel); and in 1981–1982 he was invited to be a Fellow in the Center for Advanced Study in the Behavioral Sciences (NIAS) near the Hague in The Netherlands. During that last period, Lewis spent countless hours with his new PhD student Oliver John commuting between NIAS, Groningen, in The Netherlands (home of esteemed colleagues Willem K. B. Hofstee and Frank Brokken), and Bielefeld in Germany, where John was finishing an advanced degree. It was also during this period when Lewis and John met Sarah E. Hampson, who was soon to join them at ORI.

From 1960 to 1975, ORI was a fabulous place to conduct research, but over the last 5 years tension developed between Paul Hoffman, its founder and its permanent director, and the scientists whose research grants funded the institute; in 1975, all of the scientific staff elected to leave the institute, and many of them formed their own smaller institutes. Lewis founded the Institute for the Measurement of Personality (IMP), associated with the Wright Institute in Berkeley, California; IMP was housed along with Decision Research (DR), founded by Paul Slovic, Baruch Fischhoff and Sarah Lichtenstein, above a bank in downtown Eugene.

Lewis was fortunate to have his research funded by US government agencies, primarily by the National Institutes of Health, throughout his scientific career, the only exception being a 3-year period during the Reagan administration when funds for research in the behavioural sciences were out of favour. With no research funding, IMP could pay no rent to DR, but Paul Slovic in an extraordinary act of generosity insisted that Lewis and his research team stay rent-free in DR's offices, because he 'liked having them around'.

At the U of O, Lewis worked with about 20 PhD students over the years, with four of them – William Chaplin, Tina Rosolack (later Traxler), Oliver John and Gerard Saucier – becoming virtual members of his family. Lewis had been elected to the exclusive Society of Multivariate Experimental Psychology (SMEP) during the mid-1960s, and he was elected President of SMEP a decade later. Chaplin, John and Saucier followed him as elected SMEP members, and some of Lewis' most important publications were co-authored with one or more of that trio.

From roughly 1980 throughout the rest of his life, Lewis was occupied with what he considered the single most important problem in the field of personality: the quest for a scientifically compelling structural model for organising the myriad trait-descriptive terms in the English language (e.g. energetic, warm, responsible, nervous, smart) and eventually in all of the diverse languages of the world. At first, he assumed that this scientific problem would be far too difficult for him to solve, but he continuously collected self and peer descriptions from students in his university classes and used factor analysis as a methodological technique for examining the structure of the relations among the many hundreds of personality terms to which they had responded. By the end of the 1980s, Lewis thought that he had learned enough from these analyses to settle on a provisional taxonomic structure, one that he had earlier dubbed the 'Big Five' factors. The article reporting these analyses and findings was titled 'An Alternative "Description of Personality": The Big-Five Factor Structure' (Goldberg, 1990). That influential article became his most frequently cited publication, with well over 6,000 citations by 2018.

During the years when Lewis served as a consultant to the Peace Corps, Lewis became friends with a SMEP colleague, John (Jack) Digman, who was teaching at the University of Hawaii. When Digman ended up living near Eugene, Oregon, he elected to join Lewis at ORI, where the two had daily lunches together. From 1959 to 1967, Digman had persuaded 88 elementary-school teachers to describe each of the students in her class at the very end of an academic year, using various samples of trait-descriptive adjectives. Sarah Hampson suggested that Digman try to obtain a research grant to locate those children 40 years later, now as middle-aged adults, so as to be able to relate his extraordinarily rich collection of child personality descriptions to adult outcomes.

Soon after he was notified that the grant 'Personality and Health: A Longitudinal Study' had been funded, Digman passed away, and Lewis was asked to fill in as the principal investigator. Lewis served as the leader of this project for two 5-year periods, with Hampson serving in this role for the next two funding cycles; the present PI of what has been called the 'Hawaii' grant is Grant Edmonds. During the 21 years of the Hawaii project, the vast majority of the children have been located, and most of them have participated as adults in half-day medical-clinic visits and they have responded to a wide assortment of questionnaire surveys. The project has been extraordinarily productive, and its many publications are becoming highly cited.

For most of his career, Lewis had been interested in measures of personality traits, and he wrote a rather detailed account of their historical development (Goldberg, 1971). He was particularly intrigued by the different methods used to measure traits, and he sought to compare these methods empirically. Eventually, he was able to empirically compare the validity of 11 commercial inventories against behavioural acts, informant reports and clinical indicators in a sort of Consumers Reports format (Grucza & Goldberg, 2007).

Historically, developers of multiscale personality inventories, such as the MMPI and CPI, have used them as profit-making enterprises to be sold by commercial test publishers who deny users the right to modify the inventory in any way. Lewis had long felt that this historical practice served to stifle scientific progress. Ironically, one of the most popular recent proprietary inventories, the NEO-PI-R, was developed by individuals who worked for the US National Institute on Aging, and it achieved its fame from studies carried out in and paid for by that federal agency. Lewis had long felt that measures developed with taxpayers' money should be available to all, and he began to implement a public-domain website providing freely available personality measures, called the International Personality Item Pool (IPIP: http://ipip.ori.org/).

Over the years, the IPIP site has been widely used for scientific studies throughout the world, becoming especially useful to students and young scientists with no funds to purchase proprietary measures. It has come to provide well over 3,000 items, and over 450 scales, which in turn have been translated into at least 40 languages, and its measures have been used in studies described in over a thousand publications. The contents of a presidential symposium on the IPIP at a meeting of the Association for Research in Personality was synthesised for publication by the IPIP consultant, John A. Johnson; the resulting article, entitled 'The International Personality Item Pool and the Future of Public-Domain Personality Measures' (Goldberg et al., 2006), has achieved well over 2,500 citations.

Lewis married Ruby Vera Montgomery (called Robin) while in graduate school in 1956, and they had three children: Timothy Duncan (Tim), Holly Lynn and Randall Monte (Randy). Robin had been a Wave in the US Navy, serving in the stressful role of an aviation tower operator. Tim was a businessman; Holly was a noted Hollywood scriptwriter and film director, who eventually became an acclaimed writer of young adult fiction; and Randy was a monk in Europe and India, eventually becoming an alternative medical provider. Robin and Lewis were divorced in 1978, the same year that he married his present wife, Janice Crider May (Jan). Jan had two daughters from a previous marriage: Laura Marie and Kirsten Ann, whom Lewis helped raise while Jan attended law school and later served as a partner in a business-oriented law firm, specialising in employment law. Jan and Lewis presently live on San Juan Island, north of Seattle in the state of Washington, where Lewis happily carries out scientific work most mornings and works in their forest most afternoons, an extraordinarily wondrous blend of intellectual and physical activities.

Lewis Robert Goldberg's major writings

Goldberg, L. R. (1959). The effectiveness of clinicians' judgments: The diagnosis of organic brain damage from the Bender-Gestalt Test. *Journal of Consulting Psychology*, *23*(1), 25–33.

Goldberg, L. R. (1968). Simple models or simple processes? Some research on clinical judgments. *American Psychologist*, *23*(7), 483–496.

Goldberg, L. R. (1970). Man versus model of man: A rationale, plus some evidence, for a method of improving on clinical inferences. *Psychological Bulletin*, *73*(6), 422–432.

Goldberg, L. R. (1971). A historical survey of personality scales and inventories. In P. McReynolds (Ed.), *Advances in psychological assessment* (Vol. 2, pp. 293–336). Palo Alto, CA: Science and Behavior Books.

Goldberg, L. R. (1974). Objective diagnostic tests and measures. In M. R. Rosenzweig & L. W. Porter (Eds.), *Annual review of psychology* (Vol. 25, pp. 343–366). Palo Alto, CA: Annual Reviews, Inc. Retrieved from https://projects.ori.org/lrg/PDFs_papers/Goldberg_1974_ARP.pdf

148   *Lewis Robert Goldberg*

Goldberg, L. R. (1990). An alternative "description of personality": The Big-Five factor structure. *Journal of Personality and Social Psychology, 59*(6), 1216–1229. https://doi.org/10.1037/0022-3514.59.6.1216

Goldberg, L. R. (1991). Human mind versus regression equation: Five contrasts. In D. Cicchetti & W. M. Grove (Eds.), *Thinking clearly about psychology: Essays in honor of Paul E. Meehl* (Vol. 1: Matters of Public Interest, pp. 173–184). Minneapolis, MN: University of Minnesota Press. Retrieved from https://projects.ori.org/lrg/PDFs_papers/Human.mind.vs.pdf

Goldberg, L. R. (1992). The social psychology of personality. *Psychological Inquiry, 3*, 89–94. Retrieved from https://projects.ori.org/lrg/PDFs_papers/SocPsy_ofPersonality_1992.pdf

Goldberg, L. R. (1993). The structure of phenotypic personality traits. *American Psychologist, 48*, 26–34. Retrieved from https://projects.ori.org/lrg/PDFs_papers/Goldberg.Am.Psych.1993.pdf

Goldberg, L. R. (1999). A broad-bandwidth, public-domain, personality inventory measuring the lower-level facets of several five-factor models. In I. Mervielde, I. Deary, F. De Fruyt, & F. Ostendorf (Eds.), *Personality psychology in Europe* (Vol. 7, pp. 7–28). Tilburg, The Netherlands: Tilburg University Press. Retrieved from https://projects.ori.org/lrg/PDFs_papers/A%20broad-bandwidth%20inventory.pdf

Goldberg, L. R., Johnson, J. A., Eber, H. W., Hogan, R., Ashton, M. C., Cloninger, C. R., & Gough, H. C. (2006). The International Personality Item Pool and the future of public-domain personality measures. *Journal of Research in Personality, 40*, 84–96.

Goldberg, L. R. (2009). How to win a career achievement award in five easy lessons. *Journal of Personality Assessment, 91*, 506–517. Retrieved from https://projects.ori.org/lrg/PDFs_papers/Goldberg_2009_How%20to%20Win%20a%20Career%20Achievement%20Award%20in%20Five%20Easy%20Lessons.pdf

Further reading

Grucza, R. A., & Goldberg, L. R. (2007). The comparative validity of 11 modern personality inventories: Predictions of behavioral acts, informant reports, and clinical indicators. *Journal of Personality Assessment, 89*, 167–187.

Kelly, E. L., & Fiske, D. W. (1951). *The prediction of performance in clinical psychology.* The University of Michigan Press.

Kelly, E. L., & Goldberg, L. R. (1959). Correlates of later performance and specialization in psychology: A follow-up study of the trainees assessed in the VA Selection Research Project. *Psychological Monographs: General and Applied, 73*(12), 1.

Peabody, D., & Goldberg, L. R. (1989). Some determinants of factor structures from personality-trait descriptors. *Journal of Personality and Social Psychology, 57*(3), 552–567. https://doi.org/10.1037/0022-3514.57.3.552

Wiggins, J. S. (1973). *Personality and prediction: Principles of personality assessment.* Reading, Mass: Addison-Wesley Pub. Co.

23 Daniel Goleman (March 7, 1946) – at the time of writing aged 75

Just as the great intelligence debate seemed to be running out of steam, Daniel Goleman's emotional intelligence kick-started an entirely new debate. Our capacity to read the emotions of others matters more than our IQ.

Daniel's parents, Irving and Fay, were both born to immigrant parents. Both worked as professors at San Joaquin Delta Community College; Irving was teaching in the humanities, and Fay was a social worker who taught in the sociology department. Irving, a baby-boomer, thinks he was probably conceived around Victory in Europe day, towards the end of World War I. The family was settled in Stockton, California.

Daniel performed well at school, becoming high school president, and then attaining a leadership scholarship to attend Amherst College, Massachusetts, to study anthropology. He went to Amherst because his friend had been so enthusiastic about it, but Daniel had never been to the College before his first day of term. Daniel found it difficult to settle, and his academic performance suffered. Eventually, he managed to transfer to Berkeley for the majority of his degree, only returning to Amherst to complete his honours project on mental health on the historical, anthropological and social perspectives of mental health.

David graduated magna cum laude (the equivalent of 1st Class Degree in the United Kingdom system), which he considered to be a miracle, given his poor early performance. A scholarship to Harvard from the Ford Foundation secured him a place on the clinical psychology programme. What was then the Department of Social Relations at Harvard was a good fit for David. It was known for its dynamic interdisciplinary culture, where anthropology, sociology and psychology created an environment for students to explore the human mind through multiple perspectives. Daniel's supervisor David McClelland was instrumental in supporting Daniel's interdisciplinary interests and with the award of a

DOI: 10.4324/9781003229179-24

travel fellowship, Daniel was able to travel to India to study the religious practices of the Asiatic Religions and the function of ancient systems of psychology in those cultures. These experiences shaped Daniels PhD towards mediation as an intervention in stress arousal and eventually led to Daniel's first book, *The Meditative Mind*.

His first position came at the magazine *Psychology Today*. When the *New York Times* recruited him in 1984, his career as a scientific journalist was secured. He spent the next 12 years, immersed in the science of journalism. The *New York Times* offered much in the way of media presence, but Daniel was increasingly finding that the requirements for newspaper writing conflicted with the exploration of ideas that Daniel wanted to pursue.

During 1990, he had stumbled across the framework contributed by John Mayer and Peter Salovey, which addressed the role of accurate emotional appraisal in the self and others as the mechanism to a functioning life and good mental health. Mayer and Salovey offered a new way of thinking about what contributed to success. Mayer and Salovey were the architects of emotional intelligence, but it was Goleman who brought it to the public's attention; he also did some tweaking along the way.

Daniel had been writing about emotions and the brain and was convinced that the topic needed a book. He left the *New York Times* to dedicate his time to *Emotional Intelligence*, and to his surprise, it became the number one bestseller in 1995.

Goleman's theory was that emotional intelligence mattered more than intelligence in the cognitive ability sense. Emotions are there to keep us regulated, whether it be loss or love, frustration or fear; our emotions help us to manage tasks that are too important to leave to intellect alone. When those emotions are not adequately managed, intelligence is of little use, which means that emotional intelligence is more critical to success than ability and, to secure the future success of our students, schools ought to teach emotional intelligence as part of the curriculum.

Before the book came to press, Daniel was already pursuing the idea of emotional learning in schools with a group of educators and researchers, forming CASEL, the Collaborative for Academic, Social, and Emotional Learning, in 1993 with the venture philanthropist Eileen Growald and activist Tim Shriver (who went on to become the chair of the Special Olympics). The group worked to expand the scope of life skill development in schools around the world. Research and evaluations suggested that these interventions were having a wide-ranging impact on children's lives. Incidents of violence, substance abuse and unwanted pregnancies reduced, and children were more engaged in their learning, improving performance by as much as 15%.

The uptake in the business community was no less impressive, and by 1998 Daniel had published *Working with Emotional Intelligence*. His research led him to explore the competencies of high performers across industry and government departments; the best leaders had the components of emotional intelligence in large quantities. Self-awareness, regulation, motivation, empathy and social 'skill-can' are traits that go beyond self-control and getting on with the job. These ingredients enable good leaders to understand themselves and others to move people together in the same direction for a common purpose.

Educators enthusiastically adopted the concept across the world. Thousands of schools began providing social, emotional learning programmes, and by 2007, the pull towards Daniel Goleman's EI brand brought together 75 global leaders in education, including George Lucas, to scrutinise the latest scientific findings behind EI. However, some of Goleman's claims were becoming problematic for the academic community. In particular, when the contribution of technical skills, ability and emotional intelligence to performance was calculated, emotional intelligence was twice as valuable as any other variable, for all jobs at all levels. Ninety per cent of the difference between star performers and more average members of a team was attributed to emotional intelligence over cognitive ability.

This analysis overlooked the fact that top performers will all have above-average cognitive ability scores; the range is restricted and at his 2008 speech to the American Psychological Association, Peter Salovey, now Dean at Yale, slammed Goleman's statements as outrageous. Salovey continued on an openly critical assault in the American Psychologist, arguing that Goleman's journalistic accounts of EI were raising unrealised ideas that were in no way supported by research. Goleman had in fact changed and extended the framework of EI, which was driving inflated ideas about what EI could achieve. Mayer and Salovey were setting themselves apart from Goleman's work, publishing their own EI books aimed at non-academics, the EI instrument – the Mayer-Salovey-Caruso-Emotional-Intelligence Test – and making it clear that other models were available.

There are three major EI models: Mayer and Salovey, Bar-On and Goleman, of which Goleman was the most recent; Bar-On was the first to discuss what he described as 'Emotional Quotient', his doctoral dissertation of 1985. These three approaches diverge in how EI is constructed and framed, but three models have commonality in the aim of understanding how emotions impact on human effectiveness. Bar-On, Salovey and Mayer are undoubtedly the original pioneers of *Emotional Intelligence*, but it was Daniel Goleman's best-selling book and the initiatives that followed, that successfully piqued the interest of the public, academics and industry. This attention created a new wave of research which could examine legitimate EI questions. Not just questions about the nature of EI but questions that examine how, if at all, EI can be developed. If indeed EI is a skill, then there are moral and ethical issues about its development, which require more careful thought and study because the enthusiasm for the pro-social advantages of EI has obscured its darker side.

Daniel Goleman is married to the psychotherapist and educator Tara Bennett-Goleman. He has two children from his first marriage to Anasuya Theresa Matthews, Govinddass and Hanuman.

Daniel Goleman's major writings

Goleman, D. (1995). *Emotional intelligence.* New York: Bantam Books, Inc.
Goleman, D. (1998). *Working with emotional intelligence.* New York: Bantam Books.

Further reading

Ashton, S. G., & Goldberg, L. R. (1973). In response to Jackson's challenge: The comparative validity of personality scales constructed by the external (empirical) strategy and scales developed intuitively by experts, novices, and laymen. *Journal of Research in Personality, 7,* 1–20.
Bar-On, R. (2006). The Bar-On model of emotional-social intelligence (ESI). *Psicothema, 18,* 13–25.
Salovey, P., & Mayer, J. D. (1990). Emotional intelligence. *Imagination, Cognition and Personality, 9*(3), 185–211.

24 Richard L. Gregory (July 24, 1923–May 17, 2010)

Gregory's work reflects a lifelong interest in studying illusions for what they can reveal about how the brain makes sense of the information it receives about the world.

Richard Gregory's father, Christopher C. L. Gregory, was the first Director of the University of London Observatory. Richard was born in London, educated at King Alfred School, Hampstead (1931–1940) and served in the RAF (1941–1947) during World War II. Following military service, he read Moral Sciences (Philosophy and Experimental Psychology) at Downing College Cambridge, where his interest in perceptual processes was nurtured through contact with Bartlett and the neuropsychologist Oliver Zangwill. After graduating, he spent 2 years working on escape methods from submarines and was then appointed to a lectureship at Cambridge and gained a Fellowship at Corpus Christi College. He started the Special Sense Laboratory and worked on a variety of topics, including recovery of sight after blindness from infancy, visual distortion illusions and perceptual problems of moon landing and docking in space for the US Air Force. During this period, he invented a number of research instruments: a telescopic camera to minimise the effects of atmospheric turbulence for planetary and lunar landing photographs, an optical depth scanning microscope and a three-dimensional drawing machine. He left Cambridge in 1967 and moved to the University of Edinburgh, where he co-founded, with Donald Michie and Christopher Longuet-Higgins, the Department of Machine Intelligence and Perception at the University of Edinburgh. It was there that he built 'Freddie', one of the first intelligent robots, capable of recognising objects as well as handling and manipulating them. Although the work attracted considerable international recognition, failure of government funding for work on artificial intelligence

DOI: 10.4324/9781003229179-25

prompted a move to the University of Bristol. There he established the Brain and Perception Laboratory to investigate processes in vision and hearing, with an emphasis on medical applications, and founded and directed the Bristol Exploratory Science and Technology Centre. Broadly speaking, there are three types of theory of human perception: inferential (associated with Helmholtz), organisational (such as that pursued by Wertheimer and others of the Gestalt school) and ecological (such as that developed by Gibson). Gregory takes as his model of human perception the perceiver-as-scientist. In this regard he follows Helmholtz, who proposed that the core of perception is based on processes involving unconscious inference, and demurs from Gibson's ecological optics:

> Current sensory data (or 'stimuli') are simply not adequate to control behaviour directly in familiar situations. Behaviour can continue through quite long gaps in sensory data and remain appropriate though there is no sensory input. . . . In engineering terminology, we cannot monitor the characteristics of objects which must be known for behaviour to be appropriate. This implies that these characteristics are inferred, from the past. The related highly suggestive – indeed dominating – fact is that perception is predictive.
>
> (1974, p. xix)

Thus, for Gregory a central problem of visual perception is understanding how the brain interprets the patterns detected by the eye as external objects. This is important because perception involves much more than simply detecting patterns, it involves seeing objects in space and time. The act of perceiving is a dynamic process involving the brain's search for the best interpretation of the information that is being presented. The best interpretation takes the form of a 'perceptual hypothesis' or prediction which, when it is incorrect, results in a visual illusion. In other words, visual illusions are caused by the brain making incorrect calculations about how the world looks. Ambiguous pictures – pictures showing objects that look like one thing and then another – reveal that the perceptual system sometimes uses rival hypotheses about how the world looks. However, these rival hypotheses are more than mistakes; they are the inevitable consequences of the ordinary perceptual processes involved in sensing the environment around us. Gregory's work reflects a lifelong interest in studying illusions – to describe them as perceptual 'anomalies' is a misnomer because they are a product of normal perceptual processes – and in understanding the lessons to be learned from studying them. He has written on a wide range of illusions including the Ponzo illusion (sometimes referred to as the railway track illusion, whereby parallel lines appear to converge in the distance) and the Moon illusion (whereby the moon looks larger when it is positioned low on the horizon and small when it is at its zenith). He has explained a considerable number of illusions in terms of a general perspective-constancy hypothesis. The hypothesis states that in certain contexts portions of illusory figures are perceived as two-dimensional projections of three-dimensional shapes in depth. In other words, the brain normally uses a size constancy mechanism to work out that an object (e.g. a football) 2 metres away is the same size as an identical object 50 metres away. When presented with some kinds of images, the brain wrongly calculates that the parts of the figure in the image that are furthest away are larger. The perspective-constancy hypothesis explains many illusions very well, but not every illusion. For example, when some illusions are inverted the illusion does not disappear, as would be predicted by the perspective-constancy hypothesis. This has prompted some theorists to contend that some illusions depend on the age and culture of the perceiver. However, Gregory's general approach is based on the claim that visual illusions are caused by information-processing mechanisms that are normally adaptive.

Gregory's view of the perceiver as a scientist or problem solver is attractive although it can be argued that in some respects it takes too much for granted and leaves some issues unexplained. For example, it begs the questions: How do we manage to recognise anything as being the kind of object it is? How do we know that the object before us is a table and not something else? In order to understand how we recognise the patterns detected by the eye as objects, it is first necessary to explain how we recognise patterns. To recognise something as a pattern requires much the same apparatus as required to recognise a particular thing as an object, namely the possession of some appropriate categories of patterns and the ability to recognise instances as falling into one or other of them. Thus, at a fundamental level the perceiver appears to require a priori or innate knowledge of the world in their interpretation of what they see – but this account does not indicate where this a priori knowledge comes from other than to imply that it must be innate.

Gregory's account of perception suggests that in seeing something, a person relates their immediate perceptual experiences to earlier experiences and to knowledge accumulated through learning, but it says relatively little about how this might be done in a way that makes sense to others. For example, no two people have precisely the same set of experiences, but if what we perceive is influenced by our experiences how can we be sure that people see the world in similar ways? This criticism is not specific to Gregory's position – it is germane to every 'top-down' account of perception, where the perceiver is thought to be actively engaging in constructing and imposing meaning on sensory information rather than simply passively responding to sensory stimulation. How is it that people make the same interpretation of what is potentially an infinitely ambiguous visual scene? The assumption in Gregory's theory is that the range of interpretations is constrained or determined by the environment, genetic factors or a combination of both. However, there is another possibility, namely that perceptual categories are at least partly socially contrived – they are negotiated agreements and as such a social phenomenon. For example, during the 1930s Luria and Vygotsky conducted a series of studies among non-literate Uzbekistanis that demonstrated that these people either could not or would not categorise some kinds of perceptual stimuli as similar. For example, they would not classify a triangle drawn as a series of short, dotted lines with an equivalent triangle with a solid line perimeter. Instead, they categorised on the basis of the objects they thought they could see in or associate with the forms. For instance, the triangle with the solid line perimeter might be classified as a spearhead whereas the triangle constructed of short, dotted lines might be classified as a kind of tree.

Gregory made ground-breaking advances in other areas of perception too. His studies of motion perception led to the identification and description of two interdependent systems: the image-retina movement system and the eye-head movement system. In the image-retina system, successive stimuli of adjacent retinal loci provide signals regarding the movement of an object. Information from the eye-head system is used to differentiate movements of the observer from that given by the image-retina system. These systems allow observers to distinguish between movements of the retinal image caused by eye movements and movement of the retinal image caused by physical movement of objects in relation to their background. However, there is little doubting the fact that Gregory is best known for his work on visual illusions, a reputation due in no small part to his talent for popularising and making accessible complex concepts in psychology and vision science.

Gregory died following a stroke in 2010; he is survived by his partner Priscilla Heard and children, Mark and Romilly.

Richard Gregory's major writings

Gregory, R. L. (1966). *Eye and brain* (4th ed.). London: Weidenfeld & Nicholson,
Gregory, R. L. (1970). *The intelligent eye*. London: Duckworth.
Gregory, R. L. (1974). *Concepts and mechanisms of perception*. London: Duckworth.

Gregory, R. L. (1981). *Mind in science*. London: Weidenfeld & Nicholson.
Gregory, R. L. (1986). *Odd perceptions*. London: Methuen.
Gregory, R. L., Gombrich, E. H., & Blakemore, C. (1970). *Illusion in nature and art*. New York: Scribner.

Further reading

Prinzmetal, W., & Beck, D. M. (2001). The tilt-constancy theory of visual illusions. *Journal of Experimental Psychology: Human Perception and Performance, 27*, 206–217.
Robinson, J. O. (1998). *The psychology of visual illusion*. New York: Dover.

25 Starke Rosecrans Hathaway (August 22, 1903–July 4, 1984)

Author of the Minnesota Multiphasic Personality Inventory, 'The Minnesota Normals' and substantive contributor to the early development of the field of clinical psychology.

Martin Walter Hathaway and Bertha Belle Rosecrans married in the Shaker Settlement in Union Village, Darby County Ohio, in 1900. Three years later, they had moved 6 hours north to Central Lake Michigan where Starke Rosecrans was born, before they moved south again to the industrial town of Marysville where Martin could obtain work as a labourer at the Every Day Milk Plant (later bought over by Nestle).

In this heavily industrialised town, Starke grew up around machinery and loved to tinker. When he was 8 years old, his family let him set up his own workshop in a crate in the backyard. Here he could experiment with electronic equipment, building everything from bicycles to electronic circuit boards. This passion stayed with him throughout his life. As an adult, he would invent a device that would automatically open his garage door; when his car arrived. He fitted a rain detection device to his patio awning; he created his own television set and even made jewellery. When the University of Minnesota was improving its psychiatric facility to reduce injury and suicide, Starke constructed a complex system of buzzers and sound-carrying conduits that would enable staff to summon emergency help.

At high school, Starke set up the boy's science club, which brought together local kids once a week to study Elisha Gray's 1900 book *Electricity and Magnetism*. This was an exciting time for children interested in science; rural Ohio was growing fast and electricity and telephone lines were reaching the rural communities. Gray had also been embroiled in a drawn-out patient war with Alexander Graham Bell. They had both invented the telephone independently and had both lodged their patents

DOI: 10.4324/9781003229179-26

on the same day, Bell filed his patent later than Gray, and there were accusations of fraud, theft and bribes which were still being revived and circulated for some time after Gray's death. Elish Gray's book is still in press today.

Starke enrolled in Ohio University to study electrical engineering but quickly changed his major to focus on mathematics and psychology. He was particularly interested in the physiological aspects of psychology, and this provided him with the opportunity to set up a workshop dedicated to the development of experimental apparatus, which included the psychogalvanometer which was the forerunner to polygraph/lie-detecting equipment and used it to assist the local law enforcement on a murder case. By 1926, Starke had become President of the Psychology Club. The organisation aimed to promote research within the student body and membership was offered to those who had obtained advanced standing within the Ohio psychology department.

Stark graduated in 1928 with a master's from Ohio State in Psychology. He was making enough money from his inventions to marry Virginia Riddle until 2 years later he accepted an Assistant Professor position at the University of Minnesota. Minnesota was establishing itself as a centre for applied psychology, particularly behaviourism. Starke spent his entire career at Minnesota, initially teaching anatomy and studying neurophysiology, gaining his PhD in 1932. He was promoted to Assistant Professor in 1937, then Full Professor in 1947.

Starke is described as someone who was always deeply engaged in thinking about something 'else'. A serious man, keenly intelligent, Starke would frequently forget the names of his students and colleagues, he would wear shoes that didn't match, forget to put a coat on in the freezing Minnesota winters and frequently turn up to class covered in grease and oil from his inventions. He was also fiercely independent and sceptical of authority.

It was while working in the University's psychiatric department that Starke had the realisation that psychology was not really considered to provide anything of use to the treatment of mental health. He realised that his peers in psychiatry were seldom interested in a psychological approach. The medics and psychiatrists were not interested in his insights. The best tools he had to offer were crude personality and intelligence tests, but neither did he feel that medicine and psychiatry had much to offer. The best options were highly dangerous insulin coma therapy or electroshock treatment.

One pressing problem was that there was no systematic system for mental illness classification and anything that did exist was wholly inadequate, with questions that elicited superficial responses and inaccurate diagnoses and could not control for the very human tendency not to be completely honest with the test administrator.

Starke joined forces with the neuropsychologist J. Charnley McKinley, and they began to collaborate, trawling the scientific literature and other personality tests, and documenting the variety of signs and symptoms of mental illness. When they finally settled on a cluster of test items, they did something which had never been done before; they let the test takers decide. Hathaway and McKinley did not assume that they knew what abnormal was, rather, the data would speak for itself. This was a revolutionary idea. For example, test items designed to tap mental illness in tests such as the Bernreuter Personality Inventory had frequently been found to be associated with normal behaviour rather than mental illness. For Hathaway and McKinley, the data should be able to speak for itself.

Breakthroughs in statistical analysis, which enabled the handling of large datasets, had triggered the idea of the comparative norm. That abnormality could be better explored as statistical infrequency, but to understand what was infrequent it was first necessary to fully understand what the full range of normal behaviour was. The approach was a-theoretical in nature. The test itself would be free from the prevailing theories of mental health and psychiatric of that time. The patients, however, were not free of those dogmas and were labelled and treated accordingly. A reality which would have undoubtedly influenced the way in which they thought about themselves and explained their symptoms.

While Hathaway had unfettered access to abnormal populations, normal participants were more problematic, until he had the idea to use the families of those patients attending the psychiatric clinic. What was to come about was a data set that would define normality for the decades to come.

Hathaway's population were all white. Most were of Scandinavian Protestant descent, married with children who were either farmers, blue-collar workers or housewives and educated, on average, to age 14. They became known as the Minnesota Normal's. Once he had the data from 'the normal's' and the 'abnormal's' in place, the question items that discriminated between each of the groups could be identified.

The first test was published in 1943 and was an odd mix of test items that probed (at McKinley's insistence) medical problems, '*I have never had any black, tarry-looking bowel movements*'; '*once a week, or more, I suddenly get hot all over for no reason*'. Sexual preferences and concerns, '*there is something wrong with my sex organs*', '*when I get bored I like to stir up some excitement*', as well as items on religion and the devil, and questions that measured normal behaviour and others that seemed wholly judgmental, if not in fact offensive. The test contained 566 true-false items and it took almost an hour to complete. Rather than commit an answer to writing, test takers would sort the questions into true and false piles. Hathaway had the idea that removing any requirements to commit an answer to paper, would encourage users to respond more honestly. It also contained the first deception scale, a series of times that would indicate if the user was faking good on their test responses. The Minnesota Multiphasic Personality Inventory (MMPI) was cumbersome, but revolutionary.

After initially struggling to secure a publishing agreement for the test, the Minnesota Press agreed to co-publish. McKinley and Hathaway were required to find a sponsor to provide 50% of the funds. At a time when mental health practitioners were keen to move away from the vagaries of the Rorschach inkblot test, the MMPI offered new prospects for more reliable diagnosis across a range of psychopathological problems. The tests following quickly grew and by the mid-century were being written about in *Time Magazine*. The market for the MMPI began to exceed supply. The Minnesota Press could not keep up and by 1947 a new publisher had to be found. The Psychological corporation took over the publication of what had become the world's most widely used psychological test.

McKinley however was ill. He suffered a stroke in 1946, becoming partially disabled. Hathaway and McKinley had an agreement that if anything happened to either of them, they would facilitate each other's suicide. Starke did not have the heart to go through with it, so McKinley tried and failed to cut his own throat. McKinley died 4 years later.

The test was also not doing so well. The predicted clear categories that Hathaway and McKinley had expected to see from the data were becoming less evident. The data suggested that those with psychiatric problems were elevated on several scales, but so were those considered to be normal. Hathaway was becoming increasingly reluctant to discuss the test. He disapproved of the testing culture that was forming around it. His former students, still enthusiastic about the test, suggested that these patterns were indicative of complex syndromes. Individuals could be more than the sum of a cluster of specific items; rather what the test was doing was profiling a combination of conditions that the individual in question was experiencing, important ideas which served to bring psychologists, psychiatrists and neurologists closer together.

The test continued to gather momentum with a new population. Before his death, Hathaway and McKinley had already begun discussing the social applications of the test. Organisations were becoming increasingly interested in the possibility that the MMPI could be used to identify personality traits in the normal population, screening for jobs, applied in court cases, army recruitment and even high schools. A test originally designed to pinpoint extremes in behaviour was being applied in areas where behaviour varied in much more subtle ways. To expedite the process, the more complex diagnostic dimensions had been reduced to Scale 1, Scale 2 and so on. The new test barely resembled its parent, and it was applied in unsystematic and heavy-handed ways.

With McCarthyism past its peak, an argument ensued between the testing movement and the American Government. The public were rejecting the conformity that such tests imposed on its citizens. The test was considered at best intrusive, at worst immoral. A series of correctional hearings followed with the intention of banning or at least seriously limiting the use of psychological tests in government.

The testers fought back, implying the ignorance of those in opposition. That their rejection of the test was simply evidence of underlying maladaptive personality constructs. Hathaway, who was normally quiet on the subject, wrote an impassioned letter insisting that his motivations were not to pry into the lives of individuals. His work was serious science, and this explained why it was not possible to alter in any way any of the test items. Decades of data would be rendered useless.

The testers won the battle and the argument dissipated. By the 1990s, the MMPI and its occupational hybrids were being used by many major organisations as a principal method of selection and development. When a series of successful lawsuits followed against organisations that used the MMPI and other intrusive personality tests, the pay-out, which in cases were in the millions, did little to curb testing fever. Hathaway actively discouraged the use of his test in such contexts, calling it a personality cult. The test he had developed was becoming a 'stone age axe' and he became dismayed that psychology had failed to progress in this area and even began to wonder if true assessment of personality was possible at all.

Starke Hathaway held the position of Director at the division of clinical psychology with the University of Minnesota medical school from 1951 until his retirement in 1970.

Criticisms about the blind empiricism behind the MMPI are difficult to counter, but Hathaway was a pioneer and a visionary. He was the first to construct a systematic measurement process and the first comprehensive structured interview, which was self-directed and self-administered, the nature of which made it difficult for the test administrator to influence the result.

Outside of the development of the MMPI, he had an accomplished career in Clinical Psychology and deviant behaviour and often lamented that interest in the MMPI overshadowed his other work. He died on July 4, 1984, after a long illness.

Starke Rosecrans Hathaway's major writings

Hathaway, S. R. (1939). The personality inventory as an aid in the diagnosis of psychopathic inferiors. *Journal of Consulting Psychology, 3*, 112–117.

Hathaway, S. R. (1942). *Physiological psychology*. New York and London: D. Appleton Century Co.

Hathaway, S. R. (1964). MMPI: Professional use by professional people. *American Psychologist, 19*, 204–211.

Hathaway, S. R., & McKinley, J. C. (1940). A multiphasic personality schedule: I. Construction of the schedule. *Journal of Psychology, 10*, 249–254.

26 Donald Olding Hebb (1904–1985)

Hebb encouraged psychologists to think anew about how the brain functions and reawakened an interest in the neurological basis of behaviour.

Both of Hebb's parents were practising physicians, and he spent his childhood in Chester, Nova Scotia. He was a largely indifferent student, both as a child and an undergraduate. After graduating from Dalhousie, he had intended to make a living as a writer, as indeed did Skinner, but pragmatic considerations directed him to an early career in teaching. While a school principal in Quebec, he began reading Freud, James and Wundt, but his poor academic record de-barred him from direct entry to any of the regular university programs. A dispensation was granted that allowed him to enrol part-time on the psychology program at McGill. This provided his first serious introduction to Pavlov's psychology of learning, something which was not to his liking. His MA thesis was a theoretical elaboration of a radical environmentalist account of how animals learn, namely that skeletal reflexes, such as the knee-jerk reflex, are not innate but the result of learning in the womb. His thesis examiner, the neurologist Boris Babkin, encouraged him to gain more laboratory experience and introduced him to Leonid Andreyev who had joined McGill from Pavlov's laboratory. After a tough year following the death of his wife in a car accident, he left McGill in 1934 with his PhD still not completed. Robert Yerkes offered him a position at Yale, but on Babkin's recommendation he went instead to work with the neurologist Karl Lashley in Chicago. It was there that he encountered the ideas and work of the comparative neurologist C. Judson Herrick and the developmental neurobiologist Paul A. Weiss. After a year, Lashley moved to Harvard and Hebb followed. Lashley's influence was important because it diverted Hebb away from mainstream debates about the relative merits of one learning theory over another and towards an analysis

DOI: 10.4324/9781003229179-27

of whether an animal's capacity to perceive its environment is determined by genetic or environmental factors. After completing his PhD at Harvard – he examined the role of innate factors in the organisation of visual perception in the rat – he returned to Montreal to work with the neurologist Wilder Penfield. With Penfield, he examined the impact of brain injury on human intelligence and behaviour. These investigations demonstrated that surgical removal or accidental destruction of large amounts of brain tissue might have relatively little impact on memory and intelligence, which suggested to him that these processes may be widely distributed throughout the brain and are not located in a specific area. He also devised a series of human and animal tests of intelligence, including the Hebb-Williams' maze, a procedure that was widely used to quantify the relative intelligence of different species. His studies of intelligence led him to the conclusion that experience played a greater role than was generally assumed although he was a strong interactionist – the view that behaviour is the product of a complex interplay of genetic and environmental influences.

In 1942, Hebb rejoined Lashley, who was then director of the Yerkes Laboratory of Primate Biology in Florida, and worked on emotion in the chimpanzee. There he came across the work of the neurologist Rafael Lorente de Nó, which pointed to the pervasiveness of closed circuits (also called reverberatory circuits) in the organisation of the brain. Lorente de Nó suggested that these circuits could account for the persistence in memory of a stimulus that had ceased to stimulate a sensory organ. For example, reverberatory circuits could explain how brief sight of a scene can be retained in memory after the scene ceases to stimulate the retina – the sensory image metaphorically reverberates. This in turn led Hebb to the notion of a 'cell assembly', a reverberatory circuit that could be assembled by experience. The brain is composed of neurons that are connected to one another at junctions called synapses. Hebb suggested that changes in resistance at the synapse can come about through experience – these are called Hebbian synapses. Some synapses in the brain are more affected by experience than others. The ones mostly affected by experience are to be found in an area called the hippocampus, a part of the brain that is especially important in learning, emotion and motivation. Hebb suggested that these cell assemblies are the neural equivalents of what are commonly called ideas or concepts. He introduced the term 'phase sequence' to refer to the connections that link one cell assembly to another, and by implication one idea to another. When a single assembly or a combination of assemblies fires, the entire sequence tends to fire, and this is experienced as a stream of thought. Pursuing this line of reasoning, Hebb suggested

that what we experience as 'thinking' is due to connections of neuronal activity between cell assemblies. The implication is huge: activity
within the brain that appears to involve every part of that organ can be
described as networks of neural connections.

In 1948, Hebb returned to a chair at McGill and the following year
published his classic *The Organization of Behavior: A Neuropsychological
Theory*. It appeared at a time when interest in psychophysiology and
psychobiology was in decline, and it provided a revitalising impetus by
elaborating an approach that sought to explain behaviour and thought
in terms of the organ responsible for producing them – the brain. One
of the collateral consequences of this book is that it attracted to McGill
some of the best researchers on brain-behaviour relationships and established McGill as a world centre for neuropsychology (the connection
between neurology and psychology). In that book, he defined the problem of understanding behaviour as 'the problem of understanding the
total action of the nervous system, and vice versa'(1949, p. xiv). His
retirement was spent on a small farm near his place of birth. He suffered
a similar demise to Rogers, complications following hip surgery.

Hebb's neuropsychological theory is structured around three central
postulates. The first states that connections between neurons increase
in efficacy in proportion to the strength of the association between
pre- and post-synaptic activity: 'When an axon of cell A is near enough
to excite B and repeatedly or persistently takes part in firing it, some
growth process or metabolic change takes place in one or both cells such
that A's efficiency, as one of the cells firing B, is increased' (1949, p. 62).
The second postulate states that groups of neurons that tend to fire
together form a cell assembly whose activity can persist after the triggering event or stimulus and constitutes a representation of that event. The
third postulate suggests that thinking is the sequential activation of sets
of cell assemblies. Taken together, they form the core of Hebb's theory,
which he has summarised thus:

> Any frequently repeated, particular stimulation will lead to the
> slow development of a 'cell-assembly', a diffuse structure compris-
> ing cells in the cortex and diencephalon (and also, perhaps, in the
> basal ganglia of the cerebrum), capable of acting briefly as a closed
> system, delivering facilitation to other such systems and usually
> having a specific motor facilitation. A series of such events con-
> stitutes a 'phase sequence' – the thought process. Each assembly
> action may be aroused by a preceding assembly, by a sensory event,
> or normally by both. The central facilitation from one of these
> activities on the next is the prototype of 'attention.' . . . The theory

is evidently a form of connectionism . . . though it does not deal in direct connections between afferent and efferent pathways: not an S-R psychology, if R means muscular response. . . . It does not, further, make any single nerve cell or pathway essential to any habit or perception.

(1949, p. xix)

Hebb's early research had shown that environmental factors could exert a much stronger influence on neural development than had previously been suggested. When rats (reared by his daughters at home) were raised in enriched environments, their performance on diversion and maze problems was much better than that of rats raised alone in cages with no 'toys' or other objects. He attributed this difference to sensory diversity and to how the brain is built up (in cell assemblies and phase sequences). Thus, he suggested that there are two kinds of learning: associative and cognitive. Associative learning consists of the progressive construction of cell assemblies that occurs early in life and which can be explained using stimulus-response theories. Once cell assemblies and phase sequences are developed, they can be rearranged, and it is this activity that characterises higher thought processes of complex thinking and problem-solving.

There is a good deal of evidence that Hebb's innovative use of the concept of the reverberatory circuit post-dated by more than a decade a similar use by his teacher Karl Lashley. The issue of priority, and a recognition of Hebb's indebtedness to Lashley, may well have motivated Hebb's invitation to Lashley to appear as co-author on *The Organization of Behavior*. There were conditions attached to the offer: Lashley would have to abandon his commitment to the idea of the mass action of the brain and revert to a position closer to one that regards changes at the synaptic junction as underpinning learning. Hebb appears to have been perplexed by Lashley's decision to decline the invitation and wondered whether it may have been due to what he considered to be Lashley's preoccupation with countering theoretical criticism. Lashley's decision may also have been due to a feeling that he had nothing substantial to contribute to Hebb's first draft. Orbach offers the following evaluation:

Hebb . . . brought Lashley's life-work to fruition in a remarkable book . . . that contained in it three ideas that made a great impression on the neuropsychological community of the day: the interconnection of neurons referred to today as the 'Hebb synapse'; the central autonomous process; and the cell assembly. . . . Lashley expressed great admiration for the book and, at the same time, he disapproved of it because of its empiricist and connectionist cast.

(Orbach, 1998, p. 60)

Hebb acknowledged the speculative, ill-defined nature of much of his theory and maintained that his principal objective was to present a strong case for a new type of neuropsychological theory, of which this was one instance. The existence of the Hebbian synapse is not in doubt. Other claims, such as the hypothesis that reverberatory neural activity is a kind of memory trace, are yet to be convincingly supported. Nevertheless, his ideas inspired new areas of investigation, including the role of early experience in perceptual development. Many gifted students passed through his laboratories including James Olds, who made important innovations in brain recording and brain stimulation in freely moving animals, and Ronald Melzack, whose gate control theory of pain proved to be a major breakthrough in the field of pain research and therapy. The success of James McClelland and David Rumelhart in introducing Hebb's ideas into cognitive science (an interdisciplinary approach to the way the brain processes information) during the 1980s ensured that Hebb's ideas continued to figure prominently in computational representations of thought processes and language.

The history of psychology can be traced to the convergence of 19th-century philosophy and physiology. The philosophy of the associationists, who explained mental processes in terms of connections between more elementary units of mind, was particularly important. Hebb realised the potential in those ideas by providing a new kind of neural connectionism – associations among neurons in the brain – that sought to explain thought processes in terms of linkages between assemblies of neurons and larger models of those assemblies. While he believed that synaptic connections were the basis of mental associations, he went beyond the connectionism of Watson and others, who argued that an association could not be localised to a single synapse and that stimulus-response relationships could be explained by simple reflex arcs connecting sensory neurons to motor neurons. His strong opposition to radical behaviourism, as espoused by Watson and others, and the importance he attached to understanding in detail what goes on between a stimulus and a behavioural response helped clear the way for the emergence of cognitivism. (Cognitivism contends that the best way to understand human psychology is to work out the connection between what the brain does and what is experienced as thinking.) However, it did not alter his personal view that Skinner was the greatest psychologist of the century.

Donald Hebb's major writings

Hebb, D. O. (1937). The innate organization of visual activity. II. Transfer of response in the discrimination of brightness and size by rats reared in total darkness. *Journal of Comparative Psychology, 24*(2), 277–299.

Hebb, D. O. (1939). Intelligence in man after large removals of cerebral tissue: Report of four left frontal lobe cases. *Journal of General Psychology, 21,* 73–87.

Hebb, D. O. (1946). On the nature of fear. *Psychological Review, 53,* 259–76.

Hebb, D. O. (1949). *The organization of behavior; A neuropsychological theory.* New York: Wiley.

Hebb, D. O. (1968). Concerning imagery. *Psychological Review, 75*(6), 466–477.

Further reading

Glickman, S. (1996). Donald Olding Hebb: Returning the nervous system to psychology. In G. Kimble, C. Boneau, & M. Wertheimer (Eds.), *Portraits of pioneers in psychology.* New Jersey: Erlbaum.

Jusczyk, P. W., & Klein, R. M. (Eds.). (1980). *The nature of thought: Essays in honor of D. O. Hebb.* New Jersey: Erlbaum.

Orbach, J. (1998). *The neuropsychological theories of Lashley and Hebb.* Maryland: University Press of America.

27 Karen Horney (September 16, 1885–December 4, 1952)

The first woman to significantly challenge Freud's theories, in particular their relevance to woman.

Karen Clementina Theodora Danielsen was born to Clotilde Marie (Sonni) Danielsen and Berndt Henrik Wackels Danielsen in Eilbek, West Hamburg, on September 16, 1885. Sonni lost the great love of her life in the Franco-Prussian War and at 28, and fearing a life of spinsterhood, Sonni married the accomplished Norwegian Steamship Captain 'Wackels' – which possibly explains why Karen's family always believed she had been born in Blankensee, the romantic municipality to the East of Hamburg, where it was said many ship captains lived.

Wackels was one of the first to complete the Hamburg – South America route, travelling to Chile, Peru, Costa Rica and Guatemala, around the Horn and back again. He would have cut a dash with his merchant's uniform and bushy blond walrus moustache. Wackels was a man of action, a pioneer who not only had the nautical skills to pilot large ships through difficult waters but also the personal agency and charisma to command a crew of 40 men in an environment which could swing from treacherous to tedious.

The marriage was a mistake. Despite his charisma, Wackels was nearly 20 years Sonni's senior, a conventionalist, a passionate Lutheran, and, his four grown-up children from a previous marriage would frequently involve themselves in the couple's marital disagreements. Wackels would frequently spend long periods of time away from home, often up to 5 months at a time, and on his return, would make his presence felt.

Sonni probably did not help matters. She responded badly to Wackels' piety. She became a devotee of divination, communicating with the dead and fortune-telling practices. To some extent, these interests complemented a period of Victorian religious revival, a golden age of magical thinking with advances in science and technology, intertwined

DOI: 10.4324/9781003229179-28

with evangelicalism and the occult blurring together in popular thinking. In response to Karen's interests, however, Wackels would invite the local pastor to deliver fiery sermons in the family home. Sonni also seems to have found it difficult to separate herself from her biological children. She naturally favoured her two very young children, Karen and Berndt, but would often subject her children to emotional abuse, reminding them that they were her only source of happiness and if it were not for them, she might be dead. The acrid air of continual family discord, the distance of Karen's father and the obligations and guilt from her mother played out 45 years later in '*Our Inner Conflicts*', where Horney describes the consequences to children who find themselves drawn into taking sides;

> *his first attemptsto relate himself to others are determined not by his real feelings but by strategic necessities. He cannot simply like or dislike, trust or distrust, express his wishes or protest against those of others, but has automatically to devise ways to cope with people and to manipulate them with minimum damage to himself. The fundamental characteristics that evolve in this way may be summarized as an alienation from the self and others, a feeling of helplessness, a pervasive apprehensiveness, and a hostile tension in his human relations that ranges from general wariness to definite hatred.*
>
> (n.p. Horney, 1945)

These feelings of hostility and isolated, helplessness would later become what Horney termed 'basic anxiety', whereby children would come to see their social environment as unfair and unpredictable. Ultimately leading to the feeling that they had no power to influence their circumstances, developing distrusting and hostile feelings and behaviours towards others.

During her formative years, Karen avidly recorded her life experiences in her diaries. As her writings progressed, they evolve from marginally interesting 'chatter' towards an involved record of her self-scrutiny, intellectual and moral development that would later influence her theory of female personality. She would record events, expressing their meaning and reflecting on her thoughts, and feelings. A childhood crush towards her convent-school teacher, Herr Schulze, is perhaps considered a typical narrative for adolescent diary writers. Karen went further, questioning the double standards of patriarchal marriage conventions versus the reality of love: giving oneself over to a man outside marriage or over to a man in a marriage devoid of love.

> *A girl who givesherself to a man in free love stands morally way above the woman who, for pecuniary reasons or out of a desire for a home,*

marries a man she does not love. Marriage is something only external. It is bad-not theoretically-but when one comes to know how few marriages are really good ones. I know two families from our large circle of acquaintances of whom I guess this is the case. But the one couple are pretty limited people, the other very superficial.

(Diaries, Feb, 1903, cited in Horney, 1980)

Such writings are early validation of her perceptive understanding of the conflicts surrounding the female role in society, establishing herself as a progressive thinker and may also have provided an outlet for her to unburden herself about her dislike of her father who would at

'every turn every additional penny he has to spend for me 10 times in his fingers' (Diaries, Jan 18th 1901), before spending it on her education. *'I can't respect that man who makes us all unhappy with his dreadful hypocrisy, selfishness, crudeness and ill-breeding.'*

(ibid, p. 21)

Wackel's zealousness coalesced with his firebrand mentor and friend Pastor Nikolai Von Ruckteschell. Their combined belief that 'God the Father' was on their side pushed the limits of Karen's religious acceptance and conformity. Throughout her journaling, Horney demonstrates herself to be a developing liberal, doubting of religion and unable to experience faith. During a religious class examining Christ's appearance after his crucifixion to Paul as proof of Christ's resurrection, Horney described Paul as suffering from an overwrought nervous condition causing her beloved Herr Schulze to slam his bible shut. Karen's relationship with a literal interpretation of scripture had come to an end.

Despite the rigidity of her home life and her mother's very evident unhappiness, Karen fought for the opportunity to study at the girl's gymnasium in Hamburg and eventually secured a place at the University of Freiburg, medical school, in 1906. Her mother Sonni followed Karen to Freiburg and, in so doing, achieved what was almost unthinkable for Victorian women; she left Wackels.

Karen's conduct in Freiburg was shocking. Her mother's letters berate her for spending time with men without a chaperone and staying out all night. Karen also began a passionate affair with a fellow medical student before meeting her future husband Oskar Horney. The couple had a dynamic, intellectual friendship but the relationship may also have had more practical benefits for Karen in redirecting her mother's attention. She was progressively frustrated by her mother's constant husband hunting. Oskar was ambitious, with good prospects with the Stinnes Corporation, a coal and shipping company in Berlin. He was progressive, and in contrast to many men of that era, he was supportive of Karen having her own career, but Oskar was a man who was not unlike her father. He was authoritarian and he prized self-control.

It did not take long for cracks to appear in the marriage. Karen began to wonder about having extra-marital relationships; she was suffering from depression and her journaling peters out. When the couple started to experience sexual problems, Karen began to attend what would be life-changing sessions with Karl Abraham, the leading psychoanalysis and pupil of Freud. After their sessions, Karen realised that she has a strong desire to make a difference in the world and to work as a psychoanalyst. Abrahams seems to have been impressed enough with Horney to write to Freud about his new client, and after almost a 3-year hiatus; Karen begins journaling again. Her writing, however, is a jumble of personal anxiety over motherhood, and self-torture about her mother's sudden death from stroke, all through the lens of Freud, Jung, Adler and Rank.

In 1920, Karen became one of the founding members of the Berlin Psychoanalytical Institute. These were prosperous years. Oskar was now working with The Stinnes Corporation, a major supplier of German raw materials during World War I. However, Oskar's growing nationalist views were causing difficulties in the Horney's marriage. Then in 1923, Oskar's business failed, and he became seriously ill with meningitis. Barely recovering from his illness, Oskar became morose and quarrelsome, leading some to speculate that he may have suffered brain damage. The family was in decline financially and emotionally when Karen's brother Berndt suddenly died of pneumonia. Three years later Karen left Oskar and took their children to New York.

Horney could not identify with Freud's position that neurosis was an outgrowth of an individual's ability to cope with their sexual drivers and impulses. Horney agreed with Freud that anxiety-provoking childhood experiences could result in personality maladjustment but felt that Freud's perspective was limiting because it overlooked both the cultural and relational experiences that surround development. Horney put forward an alternative explanation which placed socialisation and culture at its centre, finally freeing psychoanalysis from its strict instinctive and mechanistic conception.

Horney argued that neurosis is an outcome of disturbed formative relationships, particularly with parents and principal caregivers. Broken relationships impacted on personality development, and it was this that caused impaired sexual functioning. Culture, to Horney, encouraged different manifestations of fear. For example, Western Individualistic cultures encouraged feelings of inferiority and fear of failure, whereas individuals from Eastern cultures were more at risk of the shame that dishonour brings. Individuals with well-developed defence mechanisms will adapt and change, but the neurotic will find this adjustment more problematic. At the centre of Horney's theoretical position is the warm, loving, consistent nature of parenting, respect and support she rarely experienced as a child. This nurturing environment supports the development of the 'real self', which is the ultimate expression of abilities and talents, the expression of which supports the individual to feel comfortable in the world and relate easily to others. Children whose environment fails them are more likely to experience multiple disturbances and are therefore more likely to develop neurosis. Such children are also more likely to rely upon defence mechanisms, which may operate to temporarily protect the child but will result in them becoming less in touch with their real feelings and thoughts. A split occurs between the real self and the idealised where they will create images of themselves that portray them as worthy, successful and perfect persons. Horny describes this as the '*Tyranny of the Shoulds*', non-negotiable standards that if met will resolve all inner conflicts and pain and anxiety will disappear.

The neurotic has the need for affection and approval at any cost, which pulls them toward others while fearing criticism, particularly from those whom they value. They can be overly dependent on others. Finding it difficult to function on their own, they rarely take risks. They do not seek mutual caring; rather, they need a more dominant partner to take over their life and may work to restrict their lives in safe and inconspicuous ways. Alternatively, the neurotic may seek to present an image of infallibility, moving away from others by seeking freedom from commitment and seeking a level of perfectionism, which will disguise their flaws and help them avoid feelings of self-loathing. The third theme is moving against others, whereby the neurotic will crave power, the exploitation of others, social recognition, prestige and admiration. Horney describes this as indiscriminate ambition. This ambition is unrealistic and results in resentment and hostility. As success is such a dominant driver, energy will be directed into retaining power balances in relationships and undermining others, the purpose of which is not necessarily the intention of increasing the chances of their own success but rather to ensure that others fail.

Horney largely agreed with Freud's defence mechanisms but argued that the neurotic also developed defences to help support their inner conflicts and disturbed relationships by externalising their feelings and shortcomings onto others. These mechanisms included blind spots, which allowed denial of constructs that were at odds with the person's ideal self. Compartmentalisation whereby incompatible needs or beliefs were separated so that they did not appear inconsistent, for example, the separation of beliefs from actions. Rationalisation would be applied to offer plausible excuses for conduct or actions, and excessive self-control or arbitrary rightness applied when individuals cannot tolerate feelings of doubt and indecision. They may adopt elusiveness or dogma to assert their rightness in all situations. Cynicism is where the individual purports to have no positive expectations and thus cannot be disappointed.

Where Horney potentially made her greatest contribution to the field was in her stance against Freud's position on the female personality. She was one of the first to point out that the assumptions of psychoanalysis were developed by men through the analysis of neurotic women, and she took exception with Freud's penis envy and the related construct of female masochism. These concepts suggested that all women feel themselves to be deficient and envious of men, and women who were in competition with men are seen to be the ultimate manifestation of penis envy. Horney contended that this was male-engendered nonsense and that what women wanted was the attributes of the dominant masculine society: freedom, respect and independence. That women's wishes to be male merely represented their desire for the same privileges that men had in society. By using terms such as penis envy, women were liberated from taking responsibility for their dysfunctional behaviours; it was easier to blame a sense of contempt towards husbands on penis envy, than deal with the sense of inferiority and self-denial that resided in many marriages. This female masochism was further fuelled by Freud's ideas that women were pre-programmed to derive satisfaction from pain, citing mensuration and childbirth as examples of satisfying experiences.

Horney argued that no woman enjoyed the pain of childbirth; rather, they redirect their attention to the joy of the birth of a child. The behaviour that Freudians describe as masochistic represents the caring roles that women have within society as they place the needs of others in front of themselves. Men have devalued this role by ascribing the term 'masochism', particularly when they themselves may envy women.

Horney's contribution was inspiring. She founded the American Psychoanalytic Institute, a platform that made her voice heard. In the introduction to her final lectures (Horney, 1987), her compelling theory of personality is described as triggering self-recognition in the reader. Her courage to stand against the mainstream view of psychoanalysis was ultimately her Dolchstoßlegende (stab-in-the-back). Freud

Fritz Wittels wrote a bitter letter in March 1940 to the society members in an attempt to have Karen removed from her position:

> *Our students cometo us because of Freud's invulnerable name expecting to be taught the result of forty years of patient psychoanalytic work. Instead, we are urgently asked to teach them a doctrine diametrically opposed to Freud's findings and rejected by probably ninety-nine percent of the experienced members of the International Psychoanalytic Association.*

Wittels was hot-headed and passionate. A disciple of Freud, but ironically also a writer of 'high-toned' violent pornography. In his book, *The Jeweller of Bagdad Wittels*, he recounts the love of Acmed, the jeweller for the beautiful Enis. He proceeds to beat and subjugate her through the entire book until she thinks on his command. Freud may well have had something to say on the connection between Wittels pornographic writing and his behaviour toward Horney, but there is also a suggestion that Wittels letter was in fact stage-crafted by the societies president Lawrence Kubie, a man described as tending to professionally seduce only to abandon. Wittles joined other disciples at the board of the educational committee, and a Freudian stronghold was dug in and ready for war. What followed was a series of deposements, threats to withhold society membership from students who had been trained by liberal analysts and blatant student intimidation, including one student being told that his behaviour was caused by *unanalysed homosexuality*.

The society took a hard stance against Karen Horney; she was singled out as a troublemaker, stripped of her status as a training analyst and removed from all teaching and supervision. Horney resigned and is recalled as walking out of the meeting, followed by five members of the faculty singing '*Go Down Moses . . . let my people go*'.

Horney and her group moved swiftly after the walk out; within weeks they had named their new institute the Association for the Advancement of Psychoanalysis and later the American Institute for Psychoanalysis, where she remained as Dean until her death from abdominal cancer, on December 4, 1952. Karen achieved what Alfred Alder and Carl Jung had failed to achieve, the first concrete split in the American Psychoanalytic Institute. So well thought of as an analyst and a teacher, her students pieced together their lecture notes, turning them into a book of final lectures.

Further reading

Horney, K. (1917). Die Technik der psychoanalytischen Therapie. *Zeitschrift für Sexualwissenschaft*, 4, 1917: The technique of psychoanalytic therapy. *American Journal of Psychoanalysis*, 28(1968), 3–12. Reprinted in the therapeutic process, 11–23.

Horney, K. (1937). *The neurotic personality of our time*. New York: Norton.
Horney, K. (1939). *New ways in psychoanalysis*. New York: Norton.
Horney, K. (1942). *Self-analysis*. New York: Norton.
Horney, K. (1945). *Our inner conflicts*. New York: Norton.
Horney, K. (1950). *Neurosis and human growth*. New York: Norton.
Horney, K. (1967). *Feminine psychology*. New York: Norton.
Horney, K. (1980). *The adolescent diaries of Karen Horney*. New York: Basic Books.

References

Horney, C. (1945). *Our inner conflicts*. New York, Norton & Company, Opensource.
Retrieved from http://creativecommons.org/licenses/by-nc-nd/3.0/us/
Horney, K. (1980). *The adolescent diaries of Karen Horney*. New York: Basic Books.
Horney, K. (1987). *Final Lectures*. D.H. Ingram (Ed.), New York: W.W. Norton.

28 William James (January 11, 1842–August 26, 1910)

Regarded as the 'father' of American psychology, James was a provocative and lucid writer who was particularly influential in shaping psychologists' thinking on the nature of consciousness and on emotion.

James's grandfather, also called William James, left Co. Cavan, Ireland, in 1789 at the age of 22 and settled in Albany, New York, where he started a small retail concern. His business acumen led to his accumulating enormous wealth, and he became a senior figure in the state of New York; his fortune was surpassed only by the German real estate magnate John Jacob Astor. He had 13 children by three wives. One son, Henry Sr., turned mystic and philosopher and became a Swedenborgian, a life choice that was to leave him largely cut-off from the family millions, but an annual stipend of $10,000 meant that he was not obliged to work for a living. Henry Sr. was a pensive, religious man with little interest in financial affairs and his marriage to Mary Robertson Walsh, also of Scottish-Irish descent, produced five children: William, the psychologist; Henry Jr., the novelist; Garth Wilkinson – 'Wilky'; Robertson – Bob, who both saw military service in the Civil War followed by failed ventures in farming and speculation; and Alice, a lifelong invalid with a radical intellectual fervour, coupled with strident anti-British/pro-Irish political sentiments.

With a modest inheritance, Henry James was able to move his family from city to city and from America to Europe and back again. This was a hugely stimulating, cosmopolitan environment, and William James showed considerable talent in art and in science. At the age of 18, he commenced a career as a promising artist and was tutored by William M. Hunt, an American painter in the romantic tradition. This was terminated after a year due to a combination of eye trouble and recognition of the dismal career prospects for an artist. Since he was an equally

DOI: 10.4324/9781003229179-29

gifted scientist, he enrolled on a pre-medicine course at Harvard. This was his first time away from home for any appreciable length of time, but it didn't last long. Poor health (which was to plague him throughout his life and lead to a fatal cardiac illness) forced him to return after a year but he went back to Harvard in 1863 in order to complete a medical degree. His studies were further interrupted by a trip to the Amazon with Harvard's naturalist Louis Agassiz; he contracted smallpox and returned home where his health further deteriorated (poor eyesight and acute back pain). The second disruption involved a trip to Germany to take courses in physiology: He attended lectures on neurology by Émil du Bois-Reymond in Berlin and Helmholtz in Heidelberg, as well as the pathologist Rudolf Virchow and the physiologist Claude Bernard. His time in Germany was punctuated by bouts of suicidal depression, and he returned to Harvard a weary man. Having graduated with a degree in medicine, he decided he was not cut out for a career as a physician. His psychological problems persisted, and he kept himself alive by reading – especially the works of the French philosopher of free will Charles Renouvire and the British associationist Alexander Bain. During 1871–72, he regularly attended 'the Metaphysical Club', a group of Harvard graduates who met in Boston to discuss the issues of the day. Its membership included the philosopher Charles S. Peirce, the jurist Oliver Wendell Holmes and the evolutionary philosopher Chauncey Wright. In 1872, he was appointed to a position in physiology at Harvard and 3 years later he started lecturing on physiological psychology (experimental psychology as it would be known today). He was provided with a couple of rooms to accommodate various pieces of apparatus for measuring reaction times and sensory acuity – the first 'laboratory' of psychology in America. Shortly before his marriage to Alice Howe Gibbens in 1878, he was contracted to write the two-volume *The Principles of Psychology* (1890), regarded then as now as one of the most provocative and lucid texts in the discipline. It took 12 years to complete, by which time James's interests had drifted from psychology, his disenchantment indicated in the final sentence of the *Principles*:

> The more sincerely one seeks to trace the actual course of psychogenesis, the steps by which as a race we have come by the mental attributes we possess, the more clearly one perceives the slowly gathering twilight close in utter night.

He moved to a position in Harvard's philosophy department, where he developed an extreme metaphysical position – 'radical empiricism' – and remained there until his retirement.

The *Principles* attracted much praise although one of its reviewers, James Sully, claimed it was too brilliant – a textbook should be less exciting, less engaging. Others criticised the somewhat unsystematic arrangement of chapters. Wundt commented: 'It is literature, it is beautiful, but it is not psychology' (Blumenthal, 1970, p. 238). Much later Skinner opined: 'William James is generally accepted as the last important figure in the history of mentalist psychology. He was a careful thinker and a charming writer but my own feeling is that those traits are to be regretted' (cited in Thorne & Henley, 2001, p. 252).

James's psychology was a full-frontal assault on German structuralism as articulated in Wundt's mission to identify the basic elements of consciousness. For James, there were no elements to consciousness but rather a stream, an idea that found its fullest literary expression in James Joyce's *Ulysses*. There are five main tenets to his position on consciousness. First, consciousness is personal – it reflects individual experiences, so any attempt to search for a population of elements common to all minds is untenable. Second, consciousness is continuous and cannot be fractionated by experimental methods. Third, consciousness is constantly changing – one can never experience the same thing twice. This is analogous to an adage coined by the Greek philosopher Heracleitus who stated that one cannot step in the same river twice. Fourth, consciousness is selective – only some of the many things entering consciousness are chosen for detailed consideration. Fifth, consciousness is functional – it exists so that a person can adapt to their environment. The implications are clear:

> For twenty years past I have mistrusted 'consciousness' as an entity; for seven or eight years past I have suggested its non-existence to my students, and tried to give them its pragmatic equivalent in realities of experience. It seems to me that the hour is ripe for it to be openly and universally discarded.
>
> (James, 1904, p. 477)

James is often described as being directly opposed to Wundt's search for the building blocks of consciousness, but that was only one of Wundt's psychologies. Lesser known is Wundt's Völkerpsychologie (which can be roughly translated as 'social psychology'), which is intellectually closer to James's position. Wundt argued that experimental methods can be used to describe and understand lower level processes, such as the perception of sensations, but appeared to be less certain about their appropriateness to the investigation of higher thinking functions such as problem-solving. He appeared to take the view that higher mental processes could only be examined indirectly using concepts from culture and language or 'Völkerpsychologie' – but this was quite different from the natural science of experimental psychology as he envisaged it. James too was happy to work with the ideas of the associationist philosophers concerning the connections or associations that are supposed to exist among sensations and ideas in the brain, but he regarded them as operating at an unconscious level, and more generally in lower animal species. However, in human beings' consciousness supervenes and selects those aspects of a situation required for reasoning in the service of survival. James was of the view that the capacity for consciousness is inherited rather than learned. Thus, objects in space are directly perceived and not deduced from colours and shapes as claimed by the empiricists. In this regard, his views are very similar to those of Immanuel Kant's philosophy of mind, which says that we come to know reality through categories of thinking. Kant considered some of these categories, for example, 'quantity', 'cause' and 'effect' to be a priori or innate. Similarly, James suggested that a great deal of behaviour, animal and human, is guided by instinct but with an important caveat: instinct-like behaviours, he called these habits, could be learned and modified through the lifetime of an organism. He proffered a neurobiological account of the formation of habits that is broadly consonant with that favoured by Pavlov. As a behaviour is repeated, neurological pathways in the brain are activated over and over again, and with time the behaviours are performed with greater ease and fluency. The functional gains to the animal include a reduction in fatigue and a diminution in the level of consciousness required to perform them. James spelled out the practical implications of this in a series of maxims to guide the acquisition of preferred habits and the elimination of others: (i) put yourself in circumstances where you are likely to perform the habits you wish to acquire; (ii) strive to avoid lapsing into behaviours that are contrary to the habits you wish to develop; (iii) engage in the performance of new habits wholeheartedly rather than piecemeal; (iv) the practice of engaging in particular behaviours will lead to the acquisition of new habits rather than any intention to perform them; (v) try to make yourself behave in ways that are advantageous to you, recognising that this may require considerable effort in the first instance – don't give up. These maxims capture the strong influence of philosophical pragmatism, a foundation of functionalism: any and every behaviour must be judged by its consequences. For James, the most important thing about consciousness is its purpose: to aid an animal in adapting to its environment. Wundt's voluntarism (which emphasised the goal-directed, purposeful operation of the mind) and Titchener's structuralism (which focused on identifying the elementary building-blocks of consciousness) had missed this crucial point. For James, this was both a personal and an intellectual matter. An awareness that his own depression must be functional – it must be for something – was almost certainly partly responsible for helping him through bouts of suicidal thinking and feeling. His personal commitment to understanding the function of behaviour was manifested in his belief that parapsychology (the study of apparently strange or anomalous psychological experiences) must have some pragmatic value, and he was a founder of the American Society for Psychical Research.

Hardly a vestige of the psychology envisaged by James survives in contemporary introductory texts, except for his theory of emotion. The philosophical implications of his view of psychology as 'the science of mental life' are more pervasive and underpin the professional branches of the discipline. Lightner Witmer, founder of the world's first 'psychological clinic' at the University of Pennsylvania in 1896, is associated with a view of clinical psychology that is qualitatively different from that of Binet or Freud and much closer to James. Witmer earned his doctorate under Wundt, but his emphasis on the practical usefulness of rigorous experimental enquiry for therapeutic interventions captures a core value in James's pragmatism that many clinical psychologists would recognise today. Similarly, Münsterberg, the successor to James's laboratory and widely regarded as the founder of industrial psychology, initiated an influential programme of applied research in organisational settings that was informed by James's philosophy. (Incidentally, the term 'industrial psychology' was first used in 1904 by the President of the American Psychological Association William Lowe Bryan who had intended to refer to 'individual psychology' but inadvertently wrote 'industrial psychology' and failed to spot the typographical error before it appeared in print.) The American phenomenologists (philosophers who emphasise the importance of detailed analysis of conscious experience) have also claimed James as a precursor. John Dewey and James R. Angell, regarded as the founders of the philosophy called functionalism, acknowledged their debt. More generally, James was influential through his founding of Harvard's psychology department and the large number of talented people he attracted. James did not formulate a new psychological framework. The significance of his influence lies in the freshness of his treatment of a range of psychological questions and is emblematic of the adage that the progress of psychology is often marked more by advances in the kinds of questions it asks than the completeness of the answers it gives.

William James' major writings

James, W. (1890). *Principles of psychology*. New York: Holt.

James, W. (1897). *The will to believe, and other essays in popular philosophy*. London: Longmans, Green & Co.

James, W. (1902). Does consciousness exist? *Journal of Philosophy, Psychology, and Scientific Methods, 1*, 477–491.

James, W. (1902). *The varieties of religious experience: A study in human nature*. London: Longmans, Green and Co.

James, W. (1904). *The Journal of Philosophy, Psychology and Scientific Methods*, 1(18), 477–491.

James, W. (1907). *Pragmatism: A new name for some old ways of thinking*. London: Longmans, Green and Co.

James, W. (1909). *A pluralistic universe: Hibbert lectures at Manchester College on the present situation in philosophy*. London: Longmans, Green and Co.

James, W. (1909). *The meaning of truth: A sequel to "pragmatism"*. London: Longmans, Green and Co.

Further reading

Blumenthal, A. L. (1970). *Language and psychology: Historical aspects of psycholinguistics*. Wiley.

Myers, G. W. (1986). *William James: His life and works*. Yale University Press.

Thorne, B. M., & Henley, T. B. (2001). *Connections in the history and systems of psychology*. San Francisco: Houghton Mifflin.

Wilshire, B. W. (1984). *William James: The essential writings*. SUNY Press.

29 Arthur Jensen (August 24, 1923–October 22, 2012)

Arthur Robert Jensen was possibly one of the most contentious figures in educational psychology. During his forty-year tenure at Berkeley, he was a prolific researcher, respected academic whose work was remarkable, but controversial. Jensen was not a natural fire-starter but in 1969 following the publication of an article in the Harvard Educational Review, Jensen became one of the most divisive figures in psychological science.

Jensen's grandfather was German and his grandmother Jewish-Polish-German. The couple's parents disapproved of their union on religious grounds, and thus the couple moved from Berlin to San Diego, California, to start a new life. Their son Arthur Alfred Jensen served in World War I before becoming a lumber and building-supplies merchant in San Diego and eventually marrying Linda Mary (née Schachtmayer). Arthur (Art) was born in 1923 and his sister Lois in Virginia the following year. Art is described as a loner with an insatiable appetite for books. Nicknamed 'the little professor' by his parents, he would often burst into an enthusiastic account of his readings at the dinner table until his sister Lois would plead for him to cease in the delivery of another one of his lectures.

Art embraced his hobbies with similar enthusiasm. Hiking, swimming, classical music and the study of amphibians and reptiles. His collection of snakes was both driven by interest and a drive for the practical: he would collect wild snakes to feed the King Cobra at San Diego Zoo. The zookeeper would trade white rats, which Art could then feed to his pet snakes.

By the age of 10, his capacity and appetite for knowledge were recognised, and his fifth-grade teacher would encourage him to study topics outside of the curriculum, which he would then discuss with the class. These talks were soon popular outside of his fifth-grade class, and Art would discuss topics ranging from Herpetology, evolution to Gandhi.

DOI: 10.4324/9781003229179-30

By the age of 17, he was an able clarinettist, playing with the San Diego Symphony. Realising, however, that practice was insufficient to produce that 'special something' that he believed was necessary for greatness, Art turned his attention to finding something he could truly excel at; *a case of you cannot put in what god left out.* Art was, however, much more concerned with facts than religion, and his interests in evolution, Gandhi and the rejection of matters of faith resulted in his expulsion from Sunday School. Arthur remained passionate about music until his death, regularly attending Operas and symphonies in Europe and San Francisco. Describing music as the only certitude in his life, Art clearly had talent to make it as a performer but, acutely aware of his own limitations, directed his focus towards the pursuit of advancing understanding in the innateness of success. This obsession of why some people make it became a lifelong interest.

Art graduated in psychology at Berkley in 1945 and began working to support himself through his MA at San Diego State College. He joined his father's business, then worked as a pharmacology technician, high school biology teacher and orchestra conductor and eventually in 1952 studied clinical and educational psychology at Columbia University's teacher's college. It was here that Art worked under the differential psychologist Percival Symonds. Symonds was an assistant of the behaviourist Edward Lee Thorndike but held tight to the psychodynamic approach and theories of free association. Jensen was a self-professed cynic and pragmatist, describing himself as having a lifelong antipathy to belief without evidence. He found Symonds interests to be of limited utility to an objective science, likening the approach to measuring ability in music or sport by asking people to name their favourite artists or players.

However, Art respected Symonds, and they published *From Adolescent to Adult* together in 1961. He also drew on his council that if he wanted to be a leader in science he ought to seek out a position with a leading academic and researcher in the field. This would help Art develop a better understanding of how leading scientists structured their lives and their priorities and perhaps begin to model his own behaviour. Later in his career, Art defined three things that created exceptionality; talent, unstinting energy, and an intense concentration and sustained interest in what they were doing (p. 29, Miele, 2002).

It was during a year's internship at the University of Maryland's Psychiatric Institute in Baltimore (1955–1956) that Art discovered the psychologist and prolific writer English psychologist Hans Jürgen Eysenck. Having read Eysenck's (1952) work, *The Scientific Study of Personality*, Art wrote to Eysenck seeking mentorship and asking to join his laboratory. Eysenck was Professor at University College London, which was established by the fathers of measurement Sir Francis Galton and Charles Spearman, and a fellowship from the National Institute of Mental Health supported Jensen to spend almost 2 years (1956–1958) working in Eysenck's Lab. A systematic worker, who would set goals for himself, reflecting and re-evaluating on his progress at each step, and he thrived in Eysenck's lab.

Art returned to California in 1958 and was appointed Assistant Professor of Educational Psychology at Berkeley. It was here that he met and married Barbara Jane DeLarme, describing marrying his wife as one of the two smartest decisions he ever made (the second was to become a professor). 'Barb . . . does so much that allows me to focus on my work and brings so many things into my life I wouldn't have without her' (p 9, Miele).

Art became Full Professor in 1966 at the Institute of Human Learning, where he developed his expertise in human learning through the study of such phenomena as reaction time and short-term memory. His work was important but uncontroversial. He established differences in memory processing for rote learning and recall, and abstract reasoning and problem-solving. Jensen was not, however, particularly interested in the pure study of reaction time; rather, he was driven to understand how responses to stimuli could inform understanding of human abilities.

His interest expanded by the mid-1960s to the exploration of the impact that cultural disadvantage had on abilities. The psychological and scientific literature on this topic was increasing rapidly and, in an attempt to synthesise the findings, Art began a comprehensive, systematic evaluation of the literature where he was struck by how easily genetic influences were rejected as a likely cause of deprivation-opportunity differences and Art could find no scientific basis for the rejection of this evidence. In 1967, he gave a speech ['How Much Can We Boost IQ and Scholastic Achievement?'] to the annual meeting of the California Advisory Council of Educational Research, where he raised important questions about the role of ability in society, genetic and non-genetic factors, and effectiveness of the educational process, given that ability was not normally distributed across society. This work was then published in the *American Educational Research Journal* (Jensen, 1968), which was a tentative account of the nature of the scientific knowledge on the genetic and environmental determinants of individual differences and how those determinants could be influenced by education. His work triggered an invited paper to the Harvard Educational Review (Jensen, 1969). On publication, Jensen who had lived '*generally quiet, cloistered existence of a scholar, burying himself with statistics, standards and students'* (Edson, 1969) found himself in a firestorm.

Jensen was given the remit of providing a clear positional statement of his position on the cause of deprivation-opportunity differences in relation to the role of social class, racial differences and intelligence, and Jensen responded by stating unequivocally that genetic factors could not be ruled out in explaining the 15-point difference in IQ between black and white Americans. How much could education improve this difference? Jensen made three key points: (1) that compensatory education was a failure. Programmes such as Head Start had failed to boost African American IQ; (2) 80% of the variance in IQ was the result of genetic factors. The remainder was due to environmental factors. Traits may run in families because of genes, and they may also run in races for the same reasons, and (3) the likelihood was that some genetic competent explained the black-white IQ difference.

The condemnation that followed was extreme: news coverage in the *New York Times, Time, Life Magazine, Fortune, US News & World Report*, much of which was inaccurate; student protests; sit-ins; acts of vandalism; and death threats overshadowed Jensen's findings resulting in his family being moved to a secret location. Art's childhood friend, Ellis Page, organised a two-page commentary in the American Psychologist (1972). Signed by 50 distinguished scientists, the piece argued for free and unencumbered research because '*human problems are best remedied by increased human knowledge*' (p 660), but the piece drew criticism that in fact the signatories were using their own political power to foster scholarly thinking (see, for example, Robinson, 1973 and other commentaries). The term 'Jensenism' to describe the belief that an individual's intelligence is largely due to heredity and racial heritage entered the common lexicon.

The challenges to Jensen's theory were moral rather more than scientific; Jensen had violated a societal taboo and tackled an area that appeared to be scientifically 'off limits'. There was a fear that racism might find a scientific footing. The MIT physicist Martin Deutsch claimed that Jensen's work was populated with errors and misstatements, which maximised the differences between blacks and whites (53 in total). So shocked at the outlandish claims, Jensen wrote to Deutsch requesting a list of the purported errors but never received a response. Edson in his nine-page commentary in the *New York Times Magazine* section describes how many of Jensen's peers found it unforgivable that a man with his formidable background should rock the boat and that the consequences of Nazi Germany were to make every liberal blind to any opinions in this area.

Other than the Deutsch affair, Jensen remained stoic in response to his critics, living as he described by the Gandhi principle of correspondence between inner thoughts and public pronouncements (Lubinski, 2013). He had respect for those who he felt held religiously different views of the world but had no respect for those who agreed with him simply because it reinforced their racist ideals; '*someone who likes what he thinks I'm saying just because it seems to agree with his own prejudices*' (p. 15, Miele, 2002). Art was driven not by racism but by trying to understand systematically what he felt to be societies greatest possession, intelligence. He was an opponent of social and racial segregation, supporting learning, regarding every individual as valuable by their own characteristics rather than their racial or ethnic background; '*We shouldn't make school a series of failures for students with lower learning abilities* (in memoriam, The University of California)'.

Jensen held a distinct lack of interest in politics, but politics it would seem was interested in Jensen. The sociologist and political advisor to Richard Nixon, Pat Moynihan, is credited with coining the term 'Jensenism'; '*The winds of Jensenism are blowing through Washington with gale force*' (cited in Miele, 2002, p. 36). Official Oval Office tapes of Richard Nixon and Pat Moynihan record both men saying that they knew '*the truth about race and IQ, but it was not something that they could admit to*', Nixon on discussion of the work of Jensen and the later work of Herrnstein: 'Nobody must know we're thinking about it, and if we do find out it's correct, we *must never tell anybody*'. Despite Jensen's work being politically damaging, Moynihan continued to keep the President up to date with Jensen's work. Jensen visited Moynihan and his 'Jensen-assistant' at the Whitehouse. Moynihan and Jensen had much in common, an interest in Erikson and a passion for Gandhi, and both men had put their necks above the parapet on issues related to race, all be it on different sides of the debate.

The furore over Jensen's work attracted eminent scientists such as James R. Flynn to debate his argument in his book *Race, IQ and Jensen* (1980). Flynn suggests that Jensen's ideas were largely influenced by studies on Negro intelligence by Audrey Shuey (work widely considered to be flawed) but that Jensen should not be dismissed because there was power and coherence in his work. Stephen Jay Gould's (1981) stand was more outspoken. Jensen describes *The Mismeasure of Man*, as a portrayal of '*vivid accounts of eminent but self-deluding, cheating and foolish scientific figures of the past*' (p. 121, 1982) with whom he was associated. Gould, he argued, had purposefully presented expressions which were false, misleading, or grossly caricatured. Gould's 'evidence' represented hand-picked examples which either predated 1950 or in almost 30%

of the time predated 1900. Such evidence was presented in such a way that the non-specialist might accept Gould's recants as unquestionably factual.

Despite the surrounding maelstrom, Jensen continued to excel, receiving every promotion, even to super-grades. His publication record was impressive. Over 400 papers in leading journals, he founded the Behaviour Genetics Association and was known as a fair and thorough peer reviewer of every article sent to him. He published several papers that demonstrated the extent to which impoverished environments impair intellectual development, work, which confirmed the 'cumulative-deficit-hypothesis' (Jensen, 1974, 1977).

In 1998, the exposé magazine *Searchlight* devoted a special to race science, whereby the social scientist Barry Mehler and his research associate Keith Hurt contended that the funding for Jensen's work was tainted by the Pioneer Fund (an organisation established for the study of heredity and difference). Mehler and Hurt argued that the organisation was '*at the cutting edge of almost every race conflict in the United States*' (Mehler & Hurt, 1998). There are, however, strong arguments from Jensen (Miele, 2002 and others) that the standards met by Pioneer-funded research were no different from those that were sponsored by other private foundations (see for example Weyher, 1998 and Lynn, 2001).

As Jensen's work moved from contemporary public opinion towards peer review, the greater it was valued. A special edition of the journal *Intelligence* collected articles from fellow scientists such as Philippe Rushton, Linda Gottfredson, Sandra Scarr and Thomas J. Bouchard. The articles were collected under the title *A King Among Men: Arthur Jensen* and argued that he ought to take his place with scientists such as Sir Francis Galton and Charles Spearman.

In 2003, Jensen won the Kistler Prize for contributions to the understanding of connections between the human genome and society and the Lifetime Achievement Award from the International Society for Intelligence Research (2006). Today the Arthur Robert Jensen memorial site supports public access to over 400 arts papers and books, as well as writings about Art. As Jensen argued in his 1999 Galton Lecture and subsequent 2002 paper, '*Science deals strictly with what is, not with what anyone thinks it ought to be*' (Jensen, 2002, p. 146). If research into the three parts of 'Jensenism' could advance without political interference, then his theory would at some point be proved mostly right or mostly wrong (Miele, 2002).

Arthur Robert Jensen died in his summer home in Kelseyville, California, from Parkinson's disease on October 22, 2012. Barbs preceded

190 Arthur Jensen

his death in 2007, and he was survived by his daughter Bobbi. The American Psychologist Obituary makes reference to a second wife Justine, who survived Art, but despite extensive ancestor searchers, her existence could not be verified at the time of writing.

Further reading

Jensen, A. R. (1968). Social class, race and genetics: Implications for education. *American Educational Research Journal*, *5*(1), 1–42. http://doi.org/10.2307/1161699

Jensen, A. (1969). How much can we boost IQ and scholastic achievement. *Harvard Educational Review*, *39*(1), 1–123.

Jensen, A. R. (1967). *How much can we boost IQ and scholastic achievement?* Note -1.7p.; Speech given before the annual meeting of the California Advisory Council of Educational Research (San Diego, October 1967). Retrieved from https://files.eric.ed.gov/fulltext/ED023722.pdf

Jensen, A. R. (1974). Cumulative deficit: A testable hypothesis? *Developmental Psychology*, *10*, 996–1019.

Jensen, A. R. (1977). Cumulative deficit in IQ of blacks in the rural South. *Developmental Psychology*, *13*, 184–191.

Jensen, A. R. (1980). Uses of sibling data in educational and psychological research. *American Educational Research Journal*, *17*(2), 153–170.

Jensen, A. R. (1980). *Straight talk about mental tests*. London: Methuen Publishing Ltd.

Jensen, A. R. (2002). Galton's legacy to research on intelligence. *Journal of Biosocial Science*, *34*, 145–172. https://doi.org/10.1017/S0021932002001451

References

Edson, L. (1969). Jensenism; The theory that IQ is largely determined by genes. *New York Times Magazine Section*, August 31st, p. 11.

Eysenck, H. J. (1952). *The scientific study of personality*. New York: Macmillan.

Flynn, J. R. (1980). *Race, IQ, and Jensen*. London: Routledge & Kegan Paul.

Jensen, A. R. (1923–2012, July–August). Obituary. *American Psychologist*, *68*(5), 396–397. Retrieved from https://my.vanderbilt.edu/smpy/files/2013/02/Lubinski-2013.pdf

Jensen, A. R. (1974). Cumulative deficit: A testable hypothesis? *Developmental Psychology*, *10*, 996–1019.

Jensen, A. R. (1977). Cumulative deficit in IQ of blacks in the rural South. *Developmental Psychology*, *13*, 184–191.

Jensen, A. R. (1982). The debunking of scientific fossils and straw persons. *Contemporary Educational Review*, *1*(2), 121–135.

Jensen, A. R. (2002). Galton's legacy to research on intelligence. *Journal of Biosocial Science*, *34*, 145–172. https://doi.org/10.1017/S0021932002001451

Lubinski, D. (2013). Obituaries, Arthur, R. Jensen (1923–2012). *American Psychologist*, *68*(5), 396–397. https://doi.org/10.1037/a0032872

Mehler, B., & Hurt, K. (1998). Race science and the Pioneer Fund. Revised version of "The funding of the science". *Searchlight*, 7 July.

Miele, F. (2002). *Intelligence, race and genetics, conversations with Arthur R. Jensen.* Oxford: Westview Press.

Page, E. B. (1972). Behavior and heredity. *American Psychologist, 27*(7), 660–661. http://doi.org/10.1037/h0038215

Robinson, D. N. (1973). The authority of reason will suffice. *American Psychologist, 28*(1), 83–84. http://doi.org/10.1037/h0038069

Weyher, H. F. (1998). Contributions to the history of psychology: CXII. Intelligence, behavior genetics, and the pioneer fund. *Psychological Reports, 82*(3, Pt 2), 1347–1374. http://doi.org/10.2466/PR0.82.3.1347-1374

30 Carl Gustav Jung (June 6, 1875–June 6, 1961)

Once regarded as Freud's heir-apparent, he disagreed with Freud on the primacy of the sex-drive and devised an alternative position that embraced the philosophical and spiritual needs of the person.

Karl Jung (he would later change his name to Carl) was born on June 6, 1875, in Kesswil, which is in the municipality in the district of Arbon in the canton of Thurgau, Switzerland. His father Paul Achilles Jung and mother Emilie were the 13th children from their respective families, something considered auspicious in Swiss culture, possibly connected to the Old Swiss Confederacy which expanded to Thirteen-Cantons, but also through the superstition that would manifest itself in the marriage through Emilie evolving eccentric behaviour. The Jungian lineage was impressive, traceable back to the 1650s, where the earliest records show Carl Jung (Dr. Med. Dr. Jur) as the Catholic physician, Lawyer and University President. His grandson (1759–1831) was a physician in charge of a field hospital during the Napoleonic wars and whose wife, Sophie Jung-Ziegler, is alleged to have had an affair with the German statesman and writer Johann Wolfgang von Goethe. This union resulted in the birth of Carl Jung's grandfather Carl Gustav.

Paul Achilles union with Emilie was not so auspicious or scandalous, nor happy for that matter. Their first child Paul had died shortly after his birth and his sister Johanna Gertrud was born when Jung was 9 years old in 1884. The Jung family lived in modest circumstances; Paul was a Lutheran pastor of limited income, in the most conservative part of Switzerland where the interfering town folks took delight in tracing their lineage back to German Roman Catholicism. Jung, in his later writings, describes Swizz society as full of resentments and defence mechanisms. He likened Swizz society to being in a chronic state of mitigated civil war, with its aggression directed inwards.

DOI: 10.4324/9781003229179-31

The Jungian marriage was a microcosm of Swizz society and not a happy one. Publicly, Paul Jung was self-effacing and quiet; in private, he was irritable and quarrelsome. Emily was depressive and unpredictable and she was eventually hospitalised when Carl was 3 years old. This environment fostered a solitary, lonely and unhappy childhood. Carl was sent to live with his aunt, the trauma of which was acute; he developed eczema, became distrustful of his mother, developed a morbid fascination with corpses, saw ghosts in the house at night and became unusually accident prone. By the age of 4, such was his state of mind that he was considered to be suffering from childhood schizophrenia triggered by the trauma of familial instability. In later life, he would attribute his destructive behaviour in infancy to an unconscious urge to accommodate death and that it was never his mother who saved him.

Financial fortunes and social opportunities improved when the family was appointed at the more prosperous parish of Laufen. There were more children of Carl's age, but his father's status in the clergy still set them apart from others, and Carl was described by a school friend as a 'social little monster' who would emerge only to stir up trouble. His relationship with his mother and his behaviour further deteriorated following the shock arrival of his baby sister. Carl carved himself a manikin 'god' from the ancient world, dressed it in a coat, hid it in the beams of their home and took secret pleasure in the fact that only he knew it was there. There are any number of interpretations of what this wooden object meant to Jung, the occult was prevalent in Swiss society during the 1880s, or it may have simply been a transitional object like a soft toy. Whatever the process, undoubtedly, the young Carl was turning in on himself and away from a loveless mother and a powerless father.

Carl was at least studious at home. His father had introduced him to Latin at an early age, triggering a lifelong passion for language. He developed a secret language to communicate with his sister Johanna, and as an adult could read most European languages and several ancient languages particularly Sanskrit. Carl's aptitude for learning and scholarship continued to develop mostly at home; he didn't enjoy school, particularly any activities which involved competition. He was unrelentingly bullied by a farmer's boy. Carl never pushed back against his tormentor; rather, he sought to distract attention through pranks or feigning illness. However, in the end this strategy failed, and he left school accomplished but feeling alienated.

His interest in ancient languages directed Jung towards archaeology but in the end, he enrolled to study medicine at the University of Basel. Jung was enormously influenced by the neurologist Richard Krafft-Ebing, an expert in forensic psychiatry and sexual pathology, and it was while working under his instruction that he settled on a career in psychiatry. His first position was in the Zurich Burghölzi Mental Hospital with Paul Eugen Bleuler, who reclassified dementia praecox as schizophrenia. Bleuler was instrumental in shaping Jung's examination of unconscious thought, as it was he who proposed that Jung used Galton's word-association techniques with people diagnosed with psychosis with a view to revealing their unconscious thought processes. Jung's first published paper, a psychological analysis of supposed occult phenomena, was the basis for his doctoral thesis.

In 1903, he received his PhD from the University of Zurich: *On the Psychology and Pathology of So-Called Occult Phenomena*'

In 1896, Jung met his future wife and co-analyst, Emma 'Sunny' Rauschenbach. She was still a schoolgirl when they met and the daughter of the industrialist and luxury Swiss watch manufacturer IWC Schaff-hausen. When married in 1903, Emma was the second-richest heiress in Switzerland. The couple went on to have five children: Agathe (1904), Gret (1906), Franz (1908), Marianne (1910) and Helene (1914).

Emma had a limited education but became central to Jung's work, acting as his assistant and eventually becoming a psychoanalyst in her own right. Their working relationship was powerful, but the marriage was a strain. Emma suffered his bouts of bad temper, boorishness and narcissism, possibly worst of all his perpetual affairs explained away by his opportune belief in polygamy.

Jung had several mistresses, one of the most notorious was the patient, then student, then lover Sabina Spielrein. Between 1908 and 1910 they had an affair, which for the largest part favoured erotic play over inter-course. Jung had been able to support a substantial improvement in Sabina who had entered the hospital in a complex, compulsive state. She clearly developed a crush, if not an obsession with Jung. He was fully aware of this and shared his insights and reflections about Sabrina's desire for him in his communications with Sigmund Freud. Sabrina improved quickly under Jung's care and within a year was able to attend university, but the two continued to communicate until the predictable happened and they became lovers. Whether the relationship went as far as the sadomasochistic affair portrayed by Fassbender and Knightly in the film *A Dangerous Method* is difficult to determine. By the standards of today, Jung would appear to have been opportunistic, if not in fact treating Speilrein as a sex object.

By 1911, Jung had turned his attention to Antonio Wolf. Another one-time patient who went on to become an analyst as his mistress. Jung belligerently refused to give up either woman, calling 'Toni' his

'Anima' or second wife. This initially caused tensions in his marriage, but eventually some sort of arrangement was reached because Jung would regularly turn up to events with both women, describing them 'affectionately' as his polygamous components. This triangle was surprisingly resilient, lasting until Emma's death, but Emma's refusal to engage in alchemy (she was Christian) remained a significant barrier to Jung's desire for polygamy bliss.

From 1906, Jung and Freud shared intense, interminable discussions. Freud's pattern of spotting talented, interesting people; developing intensive relationships with them and then cooling is most well documented in the case of Jung. Jung was a long-time admirer of Freud. They met in Vienna in 1907, and although Freud retained dominance, they had major influence on one another's work. Their friendship lasted over 13 years before Freud became increasingly detached to the point that he was convinced that Jung harboured death wishes towards him.

In this instance, however, Jung's increasing antagonism was undoubtedly the major influencing factor in the deteriorating relationship. Jung saw his role as the saviour of psychoanalysis; he wanted to ensure its lasting place as the leading psychotherapeutic method. The main source of their intellectual disagreement lay in their respective positions on the libido (a life-force energy). Alder had already left the Wednesday society through similar disagreements, and like Alder, Jung was unconvinced that libidinal energy was sexual in nature. Rather, Jung saw it as a more creative life force that embraced not only the sexual but also the spiritual needs of the individual. Freud in his later works moved closer to the Jungian perspective on life energy, but it was too late. Jung felt that Freud inhibited his scientific freedom, that he was paralysing psychoanalysis through a 'reductive interpretation' of the human psyche, and he verminy objected to any suggestion that he was in any way exhibiting neurosis.

By 1912, the relationship was at an end but both men struggled with the finality of their complicated professional relationship and firm friendship, suffering bouts of depression over the loss. Freud had seen Jung as his successor, his heir-apparent who would lead the psychoanalytical movement, but he was also frustrated by what he felt to be Jung's abnormal behaviour and his inability to accept that he had any neurosis.

The impact on Jung was acute. He was at his creative best developing his own distinctive theory of personality, but he became increasingly isolated and depressed nearly to the point of psychotic breakdown. None of which could have been helped by his now very public emotional triangle with his wife and Toni Wolf. Jung was inward-looking but perhaps not necessarily introspective.

World War I interrupted psychoanalysis as a field, and the world and Jung became focused on the apocalypse. Jung was never short on imagination and became convinced his dreams and visions were premonitions to World War I – that the key to understanding the mental condition was to decode the mythology that permeated culture and society and he began to develop his dimensional approach to psychology. He was drafted as an army doctor and given the command of an internment camp for British officers and soldiers. The camp was in neutral territory and, as such, the personnel were obliged to intern soldiers from either side of the conflict. Jung worked to improve both the physical conditions in the camp and the education of its interns.

This period of isolation lasted until 1920. He began to publish papers and, in 1921, published his most influential work *Psychological Types*, which put forward the two major attitudes or orientations of personality – extroversion and introversion and their four basic functions (thinking, feeling, sensing and intuiting), which yield eight pure personality types. Work which would be built upon by psychologists such as Hans Eysenck and Raymond Cattell.

In 1928, Jung joined the International General Medical Society for Psychotherapy – the same year as Herman Göring's cousin, Mathias Heinrich Göring. Jung was elected Vice-President in 1930 and President 3 years later. *Zentralblatt für Psychotherapie*, the society's journal, was reorganised about this time, the intention being to publish an international edition under Jung's editorship. The German version was under the management of Göring who publicly appealed for the adaptation of Hitler's *Mein Kampf* as a basic reference text and the journal carried the appeal alongside Jung's signature. This was the only source of a widely held suspicion that Jung was a Nazi sympathiser and that his presidency was part of a plan to impose a Nazi ideology on the business of the Society.

Jung had not helped himself. In his paper 'The State of Psychotherapy Today' (1934), he wrote feverishly on the difference between Jewish and Aryan psychology. That Freud did not understand the Germanic psyche, that Jewish categories should not be applied indiscriminately to Germanic and Slavic Christendom. '*The Jew was a nomad who has never created a cultural form of his own and as far as we can see never will*'. The Psyche of the German is more than '*a garbage-bin of unrealizable infantile wishes and unresolved family resentments*'. These sentiments were a melody to the shadows of racial bigotry and bias of the German therapists who sought to associate themselves as closely as possible to Jung's work.

Conversely, recent evidence suggests that Jung played for both sides during the war. He had no cosy relationship with Mathias Göring and had in fact resigned three times. Jung had been involved in a plot that would have a leading physician declare the Führer mad and had tried to help and support other Jewish psychoanalysts during the war. He played a key role in advising Washington policy towards the end of the war. That in fact, he had been recruited as a spy 'Agent 488' and that his strategy for persuading the German public to accept defeat went as far as General Dwight D. Eisenhower.

The most plausible explanation is that all these positions were true at some time or another. Jung wanted to secure a psychoanalysis position within the German Reich, but when America became involved in the war his allegiance shifted to wherever was in the best interests of the discipline.

Jung's later works became increasingly obscure and mystical. His travels took him to East Africa and India, where he sought to expand his understanding of primitive psychology by spending periods of time in culturally isolated areas. In Africa, his insights were limited by language barriers, but he was able to engage in more productive dialogue in India which helped advance his arguments for the role of symbolism in life. The trip was blighted, however, by 2 weeks of illness and delirium which resulted in hospitalisation in Calcutta and on returning home he confined his travels to Europe.

On February 11, 1944, the 68-year-old Jung fell on ice and broke his fibula. While in hospital, he developed embolisms in his leg and suffered a heart attack. He describes an out-of-body experience where only his essential self existed whereby he was told by God it was not his time. He was very troubled by the experience but largely because he reported seeing his Doctor, whose astral spirit left its body. Jung awoke from his heart attack and, in a strange coincidence, on the same day his Doctor was struck with septicaemia and died shortly afterwards. Jung was convinced that this meant that the Doctors life had been taken to restore his. Respiratory and circulatory diseases were now a permanent feature of Jung's health, but he continued to write and publish until his death on June 6, 1961.

Attempt at explaining human nature in terms of typology has its roots in ancient civilisations, but the field is probably best known through the contribution of Carl Jung. The dichotomies at the centre of Jung's theory, extraversion, introversion, sensing, intuition, thinking and feeling attempted to classify people into a small group of behavioural preferences. Jung has been recognised as one of the most influential psychologists of all time, but measures that have built on his theory have been the centre of continuing controversy. Jung himself did not approve of measurement tools, describing the attempts at personality measurement as *'nothing but a childish parlour game'* (p. xiv, 1934).

Ironically, Jung's charismatic aversion to theory building and his enthusiasm for alchemy and the paranormal has always deterred many psychologists from engaging in debates around his work. Nonetheless, Jung's approach was innovative, focusing on the way in which individuals make sense of personal existence. What gives point and purpose in their lives. His interest was firmly grounded in the present and not in past unresolved conflicts and unfulfilled desires. His method 'individualisation' focused on encouraging the patient to face their unconscious inner forces, integrate those forces into conscious awareness and develop their potential self. Jung retained the tripartite structure of the mind, wherein the ego is conscious but personal consciousness refers also to those things that are unconscious but can readily be brought to conscious awareness through attention.

The collective unconscious refers to experiences that cannot be brought to conscious awareness and cannot be directly examined. For example, primordial or ancestral memory traces. These are traces experienced by all individuals of a species and populate through universal symbols such as The Tree of Life, Hell, Time, Rebirth, Darkness, etc.; while they cannot be directly observed, they influence our actions and the actions of others. Examples that provided particularly strong evidence of its existence would be insights from déjà vu, near-death experiences.

Jung's dynamic model of the psyche has three governing principles. The principle of opposites states that every wish suggests its opposite. He regards the opposition between states (e.g. good-bad, happy-sad, love-hate) as the source of libidinal or psychic energy. The second principle is that of equivalence and refers to the degree to which one is prepared to recognise the presence of opposite states. For example, the degree to which one recognises that our children can not only be a source of unconditional love, but they can also be a source of unhappiness, and often hate. Denial or suppression of this state suppresses growth and development because it critically diverts essential psychic energy into the development of a maladaptive complex. To help diagnose a complex, Jung pioneered the use of word association in therapeutic contexts reasoning that delayed verbal responses to specific words and noticeable changes in breathing or posture were symptoms of a complex.

A third principle, entropy, refers to the tendency for oppositions to come together over time. He argued that entropy increases with age, and this accounts for reductions in libidinal or psychic energy as we get older. The goal of life is to realise the self. The self is also an archetype that represents the transcendence of all opposites so that every aspect of one's personality is expressed equally.

Jung regarded 'attitudes' and 'functions' as operating at both conscious and unconscious levels of awareness. He claimed that there are two principal attitudes: introversion and extraversion. Introversion is oriented towards subjective experience whereas extraversion is oriented towards objective experience. Jung regarded everyone as possessing both attitudes; the unconscious of the extravert is introverted and the unconscious of the introverted is extraverted. Both introverts or extroverts must deal with the inner and outer worlds, and Jung argued that this occurred through four functions: sensing, thinking, intuiting and feeling. He suggested that most people develop one or two of the functions, but the goal of personal development should be to use all four. One function may be more natural, but individuals could learn to use their opposites.

This combination of attitudes and functions provided the basis of Jung's eight psychological types. These types were subsequently developed by Katharine Briggs and her daughter, the dramatist and novelist Isabel McKelvey Myers. Jung himself did not approve of measurement tools but also recognised that his renunciations would make little difference '*everyone*' he said, '*is in love with their own ideas*'. Jung's rejection of measurement did not however prevent attempts at developing personality indicators, with the Jungian Type Index being developed as recently as 2001.

Carl Jung's major writings

Jung, C. (1923). *Psychological types.* Harcourt Brace.
Jung, C. (1928). *Contributions to analytic psychology.* Harcourt Brace.
Jung, C. (1928). Foreword to the Argentine edition. In C. Jung (Author) & G. Adler & R. Hull (Eds.), *Collected works of C.G. Jung, Volume 6: Psychological types* (pp. xiv–2).
Jung, C. (1934). *The state of psychotherapy today: Collected works.* Routledge.
Jung, C. (1946). *Essays on contemporary events.* Kegan Paul.
Jung, C. (1960). *Collected works, 1902–60* (18 Vols.). Routledge and Kegan Paul, Ltd.

Further reading

Bair, D. (2003). *Jung: A biography.* London: Little Brown and Company.
Jung, C. G., & Storr, A. (1999). *The essential Jung: Selected writings.* Princeton, NJ: Princeton University Press.

31 Daniel Kahneman (March 5, 1934) – at the time of writing aged 87

Kahneman has contributed extensively to the areas of judgment and decision-making, behavioural economics, and hedonic psychology.

Daniel Kahneman was born to Rachel and Efrayim in Tel Aviv in 1934. His parents, who were in Lithuania, had settled in Paris, France, but were visiting relatives in Mandatory Palestine (controlled by the British Government) at the time of his birth.

Daniel spent most of his early childhood in Paris, where his father was chief of research at a large chemical factory. He describes growing up in a world of voices and people, particularly voices about other people. He never really learned about nature or animals. Those things rarely existed; rather, he was surrounded by people talking and gossiping. These conversations were fascinating to him in their complexity, particularly the conversations that focused on people who were less than perfect. He also describes himself as a precocious, perhaps pompous child who developed his own book of essays entitled *What I Write of What I Think*. Academically curious, these essays were a good way of keeping himself happy and contented, and a helpful distraction from more physical endeavour. Physically inept, he even had his name blocked from the Tableau d'Honneur by his physical-education teacher on the grounds that even his extreme tolerance had limits.

Kahneman describes his parents as never being particularly secure. Whatever roots the family had managed to carve out for themselves in France were shaken following the invasion in 1940, and the subsequent occupation by Nazi Germany. On one occasion, Daniel recalls as a young boy walking home from playing with his Christian friends. He had stayed too late, past the curfew and so he turned his jumper inside out so that his yellow star would be less visible. However, he was approached by a German Solider.

DOI: 10.4324/9781003229179-32

*he beckoned me over, picked me up, and hugged me. I was terrified
that he would notice the star inside my sweater. He was speaking to me
with great emotion, in German. When he put me down, he opened his
wallet, showed me a picture of a boy, and gave me some money. I went
home more certain than ever that my mother was right: people were
endlessly complicated and interesting.*[1]

Then Daniel's father was arrested in the first raid (Rafle du Vélo-
drome d'Hiver) in May 1941, and he spent 6 weeks in Drancy internment camp awaiting deportation to the extermination camps. His
father managed to avoid deportation when his employer Eugene
Schueller (the French pharmacist and entrepreneur and founder of
L'Oréal) managed to secure his release. Schueller was virulently anti-
Semitic, but he liked Daniel's father and protected him whenever he
could. Thus, his family survived the war but were on the run or in
hiding for much of it. They first escaped to Vichy France, and then
onwards to the French Riviera. Then when the Germans arrived, they
escaped again to the centre of France. Then tragically just 6 weeks
before D-day his father died of badly managed diabetes, and thus
Daniel and his family began to wait for documentation for a return to
Palestine.

Despite the terrible loss of his father, the return to Palestine altered
Daniels's life in several positive ways. He was held back a year at school,
which mean he was no longer the weakest child in the class; he developed friendships, which gave him new happier ways to pass the time
(other than writing essays to himself). He was experiencing great intellectual excitement induced by great teachers and like-minded peers.
He was leading a normal life, and it was good not to feel exceptional
anymore.

Daniel completed his first degree at the Hebrew University in Jerusalem, majoring in psychology with a minor in mathematics. He was
heavily influenced by the works on motivation by Kurt Lewin, the
emergent area of neuropsychology and the neurosurgeon Kurt Gold-
stein. On completion of his degree in 1954, he was drafted into military service where he was drafted into the Psychology Branch of the
Israel Defense Forces. His work with the defence forces included
the psychological assessment of candidates for officer training and
leadership assessment, assessments which overall seemed to have little
relationship with the accurate evaluation of and prediction of effective
leadership. Daniel describes this as his first experience of a cognitive
illusion, specifically the illusion of validity. That somehow it was possible to make the most spurious and far reaching of predictions about

human behaviour based on the most limited samples of behaviour. Influenced by the work of Edwin Ghiselli and Paul Meehl, Daniel set about improving the measurement and prediction of performance process. Triggering new ways of working and inspiring interventions that would remain in use for many decades. In fact, 20 years later Daniel and Amos published their thinking on the subject (see Kahneman & Tversky, 1973).

In 1956, Daniel, was offered a PhD scholarship to study psychology abroad. The Hebrew University felt some polish would help Daniel before he had to face the wider world. As such he and his wife Irah travelled to Berkeley to start their graduate studies. With eclectic interests, Daniel embraced topics from subliminal perception, ophthalmology, programming to psychoanalysis, eventually writing his dissertation on statistical and experimental analysis of adjectives in the semantic differential. He loved teaching undergraduates; it was a gratifying experience particularly because the highly competitive nature of the university meant that most students were sound PhD candidates. This also gave him fertile ground to explore what was emerging as his passion, the exploration of erroneous thinking and judgement under uncertainty.

1968 saw the start of his lifelong friendship and collaboration with Amos Tversky. Amos was a younger peer and Daniel asked him to give a talk to his class about the field of judgement in decision-making. The following year, when Daniel was researching at the Applied Research Unit at Cambridge University, Amos who was visiting took a questionnaire that Daniel was developing to a meeting of the Mathematical Psychology Association. Amos collected data and the pair met up in Jerusalem some weeks later to work on the results and write a paper together. The pair found they had an uncanny sense of direction together; they shared not only intellectual pursuits but also humour quickly, becoming a collaborative team, who knew each other's minds, and building a relationship that would stand the test of time. For example, during their peak years, the pair published eight journal articles between 1971–1981 of which five had been cited more than a thousand times by the end of 2002.

These peak years produced the 1974 paper addressing the rationality debate, where the concepts of heuristics of judgement were reviewed (representativeness, availability and anchoring) eventually resulting in the published 'Science' paper that soon became the standard reference against the rational-agent model. This paper was never designed to be a direct attack on the rational model (the idea that individuals always make decisions that provide them with the highest amount of personal utility); rather, readers drew those inferences themselves. It was the paper's indirectness that created the right circumstances for proponents to be receptive to their message and thus triggered the subsequent spawn of new thinking and research in philosophy, economics and psychology.

Following the success of the 'Science' paper, Amos and Daniel began working on prospect theory, which analyses the weights that individuals place on gains. Losses carry a greater emotional burden than gains and can thus call errors in evaluating the probability of risk. When they were ready to publish their thinking on research on the subject, they deliberately chose a meaningless name 'prospect theory' reasoning that this would be an advantage. This title was distinctive (an advantage if this theory became well known). Which was great foresight on their part because in 2002 Daniel Kahneman was awarded the Nobel Memorial Prize in Economics for prospect theory. Had he been alive, Amos Tversky would also have received the prize as part of this partnership (he died in 1996).

Kahneman said of Amos

> *What kept us at it was a phrase that Amos often used: 'Let's do it right'. There was never any hurry, any thought of compromising quality for speed. We could do it because Amos said the work was important, and you could trust him when he said that. We could also do it because the process was so intensely enjoyable.*

(June 5th, 1996)

Daniel Kahneman was married to the educational psychologist Irah Kahneman. They have two children. He married Anne Treisman in 1978 until her death in 2018 and he now resides with Barbara Tversky, the widow of his long-time collaborator and friend Amos Tversky.

Note

1 Kahneman, D. (2003). Maps of bounded rationality: A perspective on intuitive judgment and choice. In T. Frangsmyr (Ed.), *Les Prix Nobel 2002* [Nobel Prizes 2002]. Stockholm, Sweden: Almquist & Wiksell International.

Daniel Kahneman's major writings

Kahneman, D. (1973). *Attention and effort*. Englewood Cliffs, NJ: Prentice-Hall.
Kahneman, D. (2003). A perspective on judgment and choice: Mapping bounded rationality. *American Psychologist, 58*, 697–720.

204   *Daniel Kahneman*

Kahneman, D., Diener, E., & Schwarz, N. (Eds.). (1999). *Well-being: The foundations of hedonic psychology*. New York: Russell Sage Foundation.

Kahneman, D., Knetsch, J. L., & Thaler, R. H. (1990). Experimental tests of the endowment effect and the Coase theorem. *Journal of Political Economy, 98*, 1325–1348.

Kahneman, D., & Lovallo, D. (1993). Timid choices and bold forecasts: A cognitive perspective on risk-taking. *Management Science, 39*, 17–31.

Kahneman, D., & Miller, D. T. (1986). Norm theory: Comparing reality to its alternatives. *Psychological Review, 93*, 136–153.

Kahneman, D., Slovic, P., & Tversky, A. (1982). *Judgment under uncertainty: Heuristics and biases*. New York: Cambridge University Press.

Kahneman, D., & Tversky, A. (1973). On the psychology of prediction. *Psychological Review, 80*, 237–251.

Kahneman, D., & Tversky, A. (1979). Prospect theory: An analysis of decisions under risk. *Econometrica, 47*, 313–327.

Kahneman, D., & Tversky, A. (1984). Choices, values and frames. *American Psychologist, 39*, 341–350.

Kahneman, D., & Tversky, A. (1996). On the reality of cognitive illusions. *Psychological Review, 103*, 582–591.

Kahneman, D., & Tversky, A. (Eds.). (2000). *Choices, values and frames*. New York: Cambridge University Press.

Tversky, A., & Kahneman, D. (1974). Judgment under uncertainty: Heuristics and biases. *Science, 185*(4157), 1124–1131.

Further reading

Kahneman, D. (2007). Daniel Kahneman. In G. Lindzey & W. M. Runyan (Eds.), *A history of psychology in autobiography* (Vol. IX, pp. 155–197). Washington, DC: American Psychological Association.

32 George Alexander Kelly (April 28, 1905–March 6, 1967)

The father of cognitive clinical psychology, a therapist and educator, best known for his personal construct psychology

George Alexander was born in the American Midwest to Theodore Vincent Kelly and Elfleda Merriam Perth, Kansas. This was an impoverished community whose ideals were a double-distilled grafted product of American individualism, idealism and intolerance. Farming was a struggle. Settlers had initially tried to replicate techniques developed in the East, growing corn and raising pigs, but these failed due to lack of water. Wheat eventually proved resilient, but export prices to Europe were widely unpredictable. Combined with tornadoes, blizzards, grasshopper plagues, hail, floods or dust bowl conditions, farmers were constantly living on the knife-edge of ruination.

George's parents were deeply religious. His mother Elfleda was born in Barbados, where her father had taken the family after his trading sailing ship went out of business because of the introduction of steam. Elfleda's father became an Indian agent in South Dakota. It was at the border town of Brown's Valley that Elfleda met Theodore, a Presbyterian Minister, who abandoned his religious career not long after George was born and took the family by covered wagon in search of free land in Colorado. This was one of a number of frequent movements which resulted in a sketchy early education for George, where he was largely homeschooled.

The trip to Colorado failed because no water could be found. The family returned to Kansas. Francella argues that these early experiences helped forge the young Georges imagination. If you could not imagine something in Kansas, then there would not be anything much at all. Vision and curiosity were the only way to see the world as full of possibilities. Georges Grandfather, fortunately, was able to supply stories of

DOI: 10.4324/9781003229179-33

sea adventures, the fingerprints of which can be seen in the many sailing analogies used throughout Kelly's extensive writings.

George compensated quickly for his poor education at the Quaker Institution, the Friends University in Wichita, followed by a year at Park College, where he graduated with a degree in physics and mathematics. All the while supporting himself by teaching classes at organisations such as the American Bankers association or working with prospective American citizens. He briefly enrolled at the University of Minnesota for postgraduate study but found he could not pay the fees. Applying frantically for jobs, he found there were none to be had so he moved to Minneapolis and began working at three different schools. Finally, in 1927 he found a more stable teaching job at a local college, which is where he met his future wife, Gladys Thompson. Later in his career, his students would recount how he would delight in telling of his nomadic career as a penniless scholar.

With a little more security in place, George began studying as a postgraduate. Having developed his ancestor's wanderlust, he travelled to Edinburgh to study for a degree in Education, which he completed in 1930 before returning once again to Iowa to study for his PhD on reading and speech problems with Carl Seashore. After graduation, George promptly married Gladys Thompson, a language teacher, and started seeking a position that would support family life. Gladys set about compiling the many papers he had already written in an attempt to encourage him to publish, and George began building their family home, quite literally with his bare hands.

Kelly finally started his psychological career at Fort Hays State University, where he started a clinic to support children in rural Kansas at a time when America was in the grip of the worst economic depression. It was here that he started to realise that the prevailing theories of Sigmund Freud, psychoanalysis and behaviourism worked for some patients, but for many they failed. He found behaviourism particularly objectionable as it reduced people to being nothing more than passive receptacles to life's events. The families he was supporting were paralysed by poverty, and the prevailing theories offered any mechanism by which they could make sense of their world. Psychoanalysis was ignoring the obvious; people wanted to make sense of their lives so that they could develop the capacity to predict what might happen next, and what they could reasonably do about it. Patients needed something more relevant to the circumstances they were facing, a constructive alternative, and he began experimenting with bi-polar adjectives to determine if there was something that he could use to help understand how people went about making decisions for their lives.

Before George could develop his thinking further, America entered World War II and George Kelly moved to work for the Civil Aeronautics Administration working on methods to select air cadets. He spent 5 years in the services, entering as an unknown, leaving with a series of publications which established him as a respected psychologist. After the war, George spent a period of 12 months at the University of Maryland, before being appointed in 1945, to a professorship at Ohio State University. He stayed at Ohio as Director of Clinical Psychology until 1965, before his final move to Brandeis University as Distinguished Chair.

It was the publication of his personal construct theory in 1955 that changed George Kelly's life forever. He went from virtual obscurity to being one of the most widely known presence in psychology. He had initially been ambivalent about the publication of his work, believing his ideas as too radical to be readily accepted. Kelly was passionately committed to his theory, believing that if it was indeed going to be accepted, it would have to survive the scrutiny of his British peers. For his theory to succeed, the British would have to like it, and in 1961, he set about a world tour to convince the psychological community.

Kelly was open in identifying the philosophical works of Alfred Korzybski and the psychologist, educationalist and religious thinker John Dewey as influential to his theory of personal constructs. But we can also see the fingerprint of Alfred Alder's work and his psychology of the 'undivided whole'. Personal construct theory is principally a theory of human action, whereby the individual acts as a scientist, attempting to interpret and control the environment, thereby creating some sense of expectation about what will happen in the future. No two people share the exact same world view. Each person's impressions are based on their experiences, their culture and values, and for that reason, to effect change, it was key to understand how the individual saw their world. Those different perspectives empowered individuals to explore and test out different ideas to solve their problems and could explain how people were capable of generating novel and creative solutions that were not simply based on past experiences.

This constructive alternativism moved psychological support from what was often simply a description of what was wrong with someone, or their life, and the belief that there was only one way of behaving, towards the capacity of patients being an agent of one's own destiny. Personality development within construct theory was achieved through the development of systems that support knowledge development about the world. We use these constructs to make sense and make decisions when the world bombards us with information and events. The more communality there is between our personal constructs, the easier it is for us to predict our behaviour and make sense of the behaviours of others. We continually interpret and reinterpret the world until we reach the most accurate perception possible. During infancy and adolescence, this system is forming, there is little certainty about the world and the possibilities afforded to us. As we develop experience of the world, we are able to weed out inappropriate options and grow more certain of options most likely to succeed. Through this dynamic process, we test out and reject our constructs of the world; our constructs become more focused until we are able to take control of situations and maximise our chances of a desired outcome. For Kelly, your personality is your personal construct, and personal construct theory is as much a philosophy as a psychological theory.

The theory had major implications for clinical psychology because it provided the psychologist release from the stranglehold of psychoanalysis. Patients were no longer pushed by unconscious drives; rather, they were making choices based on their world view which was shaped by their appraisals of the outcomes of their previous actions. The role of the therapist was to help clients with reframing of the constructs that they were using to understand their world. For example, patients would often think and behave in a way that suggested their ideas about something were true in reality, rather than simply that their ideas were just one of a number of possible interpretations. The therapist would explore that individual's world view, understand how they had developed those constructs, then prepare the patient for change. In this way, patients are encouraged to become actors in their lives, not reactors. By recognising that they have freedom of choice between courses of action, they can then begin to give up victimhood.

Central to this process was the idea that the patient should feel entirely accepted by the therapist. In a non-judgemental, intimate therapeutic environment, patients would feel safe to explore and analyse their personal constructs, to experiment with new possibilities and ultimately put aside maladaptive constructs, replacing them with new ways of thinking. In the days before diversity and equality, these were radical new ideas which would drive progress towards equitable and respectful psychological practice which would become the foundation of the therapeutic alliance.

Criticised heavily and also highly lorded, visiting appointments at various universities in the USA, Europe, Russia, South America and Asia soon followed the book's release. But after the initial furry, things quickly died down. There was still some modest interest within the United Kingdom, but generally the work was being quickly forgotten and replaced with the humanism of Carl Rogers. Kelly retained ambitions that construct theory would be a formative contribution to psychological theory. His work would reconnect psychologists to the wonders of people and the truth of human relationships. He was also, however, ambivalent to many aspects of his work, arguing that the publication of his book had been a mistake. Jokingly, he proposed an additional chapter, entitled 'Apologies for the Book'.

What concerned Kelly most was his development of the construct repertory test, now commonly called the rep grid. This technique affords self-discovery by enabling the exploration of opposing constructs. The rep process gives the therapist an overview of their client's personal reality, which can then be used to support further self-discovery. Kelly was perhaps correct in his concern that the rep test obscured his theoretical work. The test ultimately became more well-known than the rest of his work, particularly in the field of individual differences and industrial psychology. Yet it is because the agile rep grid technique contributed so much to the therapeutic process and also to psychological research that people were brought once again to Kelly's personal construct theory. By the cognitive revolution of the 1980s, people were ready to fully understand and appreciate Kelly's personal construct theory and over two decades after Kelly had published his seminal text, his student, Walter Mischel, appointed George Kelly as the architect of modern cognitive psychology. With his breadth of vision, Kelly was a prophet; he knew where psychology travel in the future, before anyone else.

> *a very deep, original, refreshing voice was always evident to all who knew him well. What has surprised me was not the brilliance with which he first spoke but the accuracy with which he anticipated the directions into which psychology would move two decades later.*
>
> (Mischel, 1980, p. 85)

But not all of Kelly's students have such fond memories of him; '*If, one to pull away Kelly's mask, one would find Mephistopheles*' (student cited in Francella, 1997, p. 27). Kelly's style with his students is well documented as problematic. There are many reports of the distress he caused. Kelly had a habit of 'slot-ratting', which is a psychological term from Kelly's own theory that explains someone who will suddenly switch from cold to warm, excited to aloof to the point that nobody really knows where they stood with him. Kelly instilled both admiration and dread. Excited and creative, he would welcome them into his world, cancelling all appointments and giving them his devoted attention, but then he would suddenly switch back to a more rule-bound, rigidity and aloofness. He would be sweet, then salty, or merely polite. He was no supporter of psychoanalytical theory but would draw shrewdly on Freud in ways that would undermine and humiliate his students. He would also use non-verbal tactics to get his message across. One student described the awful silence that would indicate that you knew you had done something wrong. If he was delighted, he would blow air from his mouth and grin. If you said something he disagreed with in some way, with some theatre, he would remove his glasses and drop his head to the ground.

Kelly had control over their fates and had on at least one occasion quickly dispatched a number of students deemed not to be making the grade. To carry out this unfortunate task, he arrived dressed in farming clothes, remarking to the students that when you have to clean the manure out of the barn, you must be dressed for the occasion.

What was odd about this behaviour was that it was very far aligned from the psychologist he described in his theoretical works, but he did try to change. So high were the levels of anxiety around Kelly, that in one unfortunate situation, a student was rendered silent. Once Kelly realised what the problem was, he was horrified. He seemed to have had no idea of the impact he was having on his students. He went home and promptly re-wrote his role as director. At the top of the list was 'resign as director', followed by 'move out of the office', followed by, always have your office door open and coffee for students who happen to pop by.

George Alexander Kelly died unexpectedly while compiling a new book on March 6, 1967. He was survived by his wife Gladys and two children, Jacqueline and Joseph. He was the architect of one of the most powerful theories to analyse what it means to be human, a man of caustic wit and breadth of vision. Creative and adventurous, and someone who never settled for the pervading answers to difficult questions, the scope of Kelly's thinking continues to impact on psychology today. He was also a non-conformist, requesting that on his death all his papers be destroyed. As Francella insightfully observes, there were two George Kellys, the visionary and the one who did not want to be known at all.

George Alexander Kelly's major writings

Kelly, G. A. (1955). *The psychology of personal constructs*. New York: Norton.
Kelly, G. A. (1969). *Clinical psychology and personality: The selected papers of George Kelly*. New York: John Wiley & Sons.

Further reading

Fransella, F. (1995). *George Kelly*. London: Sage.
Mischel, W. (1980). George Kelly's anticipation of psychology. In M. J. Mahoney (Ed.), *Psychotherapy process: Current issues and future directions* (pp. 85–87). New York: Plenum.

33 Elizabeth Loftus track in red (October 16, 1944)

Review of general psychology describes Loftus as the most influential female psychologist of the 20th century. Her work triggered a paradigm shift away from archival models of memory towards a dynamic system which could be shaped through emotion and language. The application of her work has been significant in legal cases to prevent injustice

Elizabeth was born in Los Angeles, California, in 1944 to Sydney and Rebecca Fishman. Sydney was a doctor, and her mother Rebecca was a librarian. Liz's father was rather cold, and her mother developed depression later in her life. However, the pages of here diaries were imbued with happiness, friendship and the fun she felt in her life. She was a happy and popular child spending weekends at the beach with friends, swimming in pools and being described as lovable comical or irresistible in the middle school popularity poll.

When Elizabeth was 13, her mother spent became depressed and shortly after her discharge from a psychiatric unit she was was found dead in their swimming pool. '*Today, July 10, 1959, was the most tragic day. We woke up this morning and found her gone*', she wrote.

Rebecca's death was ruled accidental, but her father felt that she had in fact committed suicide. What followed was something of a collective silence, whereby her sibling's avoided discussion of what had taken place, preferring to ignore their father's perspective on what had taken place. Elizabeth's life soon defaulted to what she described as 'happyville'. However, she and her siblings retained a lifelong struggle to explain, describe and articulate who their mother Rebecca was. Her brother Robert described her as an empty canvas with no adjective or noun to describe her. These early experiences became a driving force in Elizabeth's decision to explore the role that language and emotion plays in memory.

DOI: 10.4324/9781003229179-34

Her father largely decided that Elizabeth should attend University in California as a resident; the terms for student fees were more favourable. She rejected a few campuses as being too agricultural or having 'too many hippies', eventually settling on UCLA, but living less than a mile from campus meant that she never had that special college experience of living away. A competent maths student, excelling and enjoying algebra, geometry and trigonometry, Elizabeth had ambitions to become a maths teacher. Maths was also something that connected her closely to her father. By now her father had remarried, his wife had a family of her own and the dynamic between the existing family and the new was complex. Maths was about the only thing remaining that Elizabeth could easily talk to her father about.

Elizabeth began as a maths major but found that she was not enjoying calculus so much. She took an elective in psychology, loved it, and then ended up taking more psychology courses, eventually graduating in 1966 with a double major in maths and psychology. She then attended Stanford University between 1966 and 1970, studying for first her MA in mathematical psychology and then her PhD. Her doctoral thesis was entitled: 'An Analysis of the Structural Variables That Determine Problem-Solving Difficulty on a Computer-Based Teletype'. During this period, she met and married fellow psychologist Geoffrey Loftus. They remained married for 23 years but divorced in 1991.

Initially, her career focused on the field of verbal learning, specifically the coding and retrieval of words within semantic networks using the construct of 'spreading activation'. Through the publication of over two dozen papers during the late 1960s and early 1970s, she quickly established her reputation as a hard-nosed experimental psychologist.

However, Loftus had not always been particularly enthused by mathematical psychology, finding that a bit dull and unrelated to psychology in the real world. In search of something more applied, she began examining witness recordings describing what they remembered from car crashes. Her investigations expanded into a series of studies, analysing what influences what people remember. For example, when asked to recall the speed of travel, participants tended to inflate the recalled speed when highly emotive adjectives such as 'smashed' were used over less biased words (e.g. hit). When shown a simulated accident, for example, a car travelling through an intersection with a stop sign, participants could be made to recall something different just by asking them a leading question about what they saw. She was able to demonstrate that by feeding participants misinformation about experiences that never happened, it was possible to reconstruct memories of events. Her contribution to our understanding of how language and emotion distort our reality has had significant impact in the field of eyewitness testimony.

In 1974, Loftus published her findings in a magazine called *Psychology Today*. The paper was reprinted in Jurimetrics (the American Bar Association) the following year. This was a seminal piece that quite literally changed the direction of memory research. Up until this, there was very little to challenge the widespread belief that eyewitness accounts were immutable. Loftus demonstrated that memory is highly flexible and that it can become distorted and contaminated with new information, ideas and thoughts. Leading questions, in particular, can trigger a confabulating effect, whereby witnesses can presuppose facts and thus their testimony becomes distorted.

Elizabeth was soon being consulted about memory reconstruction by Lawyers, setting legal precedent in 1975 at Washington State's first expert testimony and evaluating the reliability of eyewitness memory. She has since testified or consulted on numerous cases, including many high-profile cases such as the Bosnian war trials at the Hague, the Oklahoma City Bombing and the Duke lacrosse case. Her work was critical in changing the ways in which recovered memories are used at trial, but her work has also left her vulnerable to harassment, physical attacks and abuse. This is perhaps in part because Loftus has never shied away from discussing the reliability of recovered memories, for example, the extent to which trauma remembered through therapy can be relied upon.

Elizabeth' believes that the malleability of such memories lends such poor reliability to the evidence as to render it of questionable value, and therefore inadmissible in a court of law. This stance positioned her as the enemy of social movement groups addressing the history of trauma, particularly groups that were involved in feminist activities urging people to believe women. As such Loftus has become a divisive character, the enemy of trauma survivors who are not believed, the champion of those who are accused of actions they did not commit. Providing hope to those who are still seeking answers, and she remains a challenge to the academic community who are both in admiration of her brilliant body of work and horrified at the subject matter: Elizabeth has been called to testify in the defence of Ted Bundy, George Franklin, and most recently Harvey Weinstein.

Elizabeth Loftus is Distinguished Professor at the University of California, Irvine. In addition to many other awards and recognitions, Loftus was awarded the Gold Medal Award for Life Achievement in the Science of Psychology from the American Psychological Foundation (2013) and the Association for Psychological Science's Distinguished

Scientific Award. She has also been honoured with numerous honorary doctorates, and election to the National Academy of Sciences.

Elizabeth Loftus's major writings

Davis, D., & Loftus, E. F. (2020) Recovered memories and false memories. In J. R. Geddes, N. C. Andreasen, & G. M. Goodwin (Eds.), *New Oxford textbook of psychiatry* (3rd ed., pp. 884–893). Oxford, UK: Oxford University Press.

Loftus, E. F. (1974). Leading questions and the eyewitness report. *Cognitive Psychology, 7*(4), 560–572.

Loftus, E. F. (1993). The reality of repressed memories. *American Psychologist, 48,* 518–537.

Loftus, E. F. (2017). Eavesdropping on Memory. *Annual Review of Psychology, 68,* 1–18.

Loftus, E. F., & Ketcham, K. (1991). *Witness for the defense: The accused, the eyewitness, and the expert who puts memory on trial.* St Martin's Press.

Further reading

Aviv, R. (2021). How Elizabeth Loftus changed the meaning of memory. *The New Yorker*, April 5th.

Neimark, J. (1996). The diva of disclosure, memory researcher Elizabeth Loftus, 29. *Psychology Today*, 1, p. 48.

34 Eleanor Emmons Maccoby (May 15, 1917–December 11, 2018)

Maccoby made fundamental contributions to our understanding of the role of the parent-child relationship for social development and the origins of gender differences.

Eleanor Maccoby was the second daughter in a family of four girls. She was born in Tacoma, Washington, and spent her childhood there. Her father was a farm boy from a poor family background who took pride in doing well in school and working his way to an engineering degree from Purdue University. Her mother was one of seven children. Her father established a small millwork business manufacturing cabinets, doors and windows. In an autobiographical essay, she recounted that her parents were probably disappointed not to have had a son and cast her in a role as tomboy: she had a boy's nickname and wore a short boyish haircut – she was an authentic tomboy. Her parents joined the Theological Society when she was about 9 and with other parents from the Society established a Theosophical summer camp, where the family spent their summers from the time she was about 10. A strong teenage culture existed at the camp, and their intellectual interests were welcomed as part of the adult discussion groups. These groups dealt with a variety of political and philosophical issues, and she was to develop intense political interests associated with the social and economic unrest of the time.

Maccoby took her first psychology course at Reed College, Portland, Oregon. It was given by William Griffith, a former student of Edwin Guthrie and an ardent behaviourist. Intrigued with the behaviourist perspective, she went to the University of Washington, where, to cover her tuition fees, she worked as a secretary for one of the psychology faculty members and spent nearly all her free time at the department. There she met Nathan Maccoby, a graduate student in social psychology.

DOI: 10.4324/9781003229179-35

They married in her senior year (and later had three children) and in 1940 moved to Washington, DC, where Nathan took a job with the US Civil Service Commission. She joined the staff of Rensis Likert's Division of Program Surveys at the Department of Agriculture and came in contact with Bruner, among others. When Likert moved his organisation to the University of Michigan, the Maccobys moved too. In the year she completed her doctoral dissertation on conditioning in pigeons – made possible in part by Skinner giving access to his automated data-recording equipment in his Harvard lab – she joined the developmental social psychologist Robert Sears at Harvard. At that time Sears was arguing for a focus away from the analysis of individuals in a social setting and towards interpersonal behaviour and the importance of the dyad (two persons in interaction with one another) as a unit of analysis. There she worked as part of a team examining child-rearing practises that led to *Patterns of Child Rearing* (1957), with Sears and Levin. With Bruner and Raymond A. Bauer, she co-taught a course on public opinion. Although a productive researcher, gender discrimination prevented Maccoby from advancing beyond the level of lecturer at Harvard, and in 1958 she moved to Stanford where she was appointed at the associate professor level.

Her interactions with the developmental psychologist John Flavell led to a shift in interest from a behavioural perspective to a cognitive-developmental framework. She was particularly influenced by ideas and evidence that children can actively select, process and organise stimuli within their environment and came to the view that the central task for developmental psychology is to understand sequences of development, including regularities and variations. She was also aware of Broadbent's novel work on the role of attention in perception and that there was little by way of developmental analysis in Broadbent's approach. She and some colleagues embarked on a series of studies of developmental aspects of selective perception that allowed them to trace age changes in both the ability to attend to one message while excluding another and the ability to divide attention and process more than one message at a time.

Helen Thompson Woolley carried out the first major psychological research concerned with gender differences, including differences in visual-spatial tasks, but it is Maccoby who drew all of the early work together and in so doing became the leading psychological thinker on gender differentiation in childhood. In her role as a member of the Social Sciences Research Council Committee on Socialization, she edited, with Carol Jacklin, a book on sex differences, *The Psychology of Sex Differences* (1974), in which some 1,600 studies of gender differences were reviewed. Reactions to the book were mixed. Some considered that their list of gender differences was overly selective and too brief, whereas others suggested that the emphasis on gender differences under-valued the considerable volume of work that pointed to gender similarities. Some critics considered that the book placed too great a reliance on biological factors in accounting for gender differences, whereas others contended that environmental factors were given too great a priority. However, there was general agreement that the research evidence they had surveyed pointed to four unambiguous differences between the sexes: verbal ability is superior in females, visual-spatial ability is superior in males, males show stronger mathematical ability, and males are more aggressive than females. Some of the debates sparked by their *Sex Differences* were shaped by readers wrongly inferring that if environmental factors could not account for observed gender differences, then biological factors should be taken as the default explanation. In fact, Maccoby and Jacklin were very much concerned with pressing a third, cognitive-developmental explanation based on the concept of self-socialisation. Drawing on the idea that children are active agents in their own development they used self-socialisation to refer to the active process whereby children make judgments about the gender relevance of various roles and activities available to them. For example, Maccoby showed that the most sex-typed parents do not have the most gender-typed children: there is no relationship between the division of household labour, parental attitudes to sex-typing, their sex-typing activities and the degree to which their children express sex-typed preferences and behaviours. Children's developmental trajectories vary because they are capable of acquiring stereotypes which they might, or might not, use to guide their own behaviour.

The magnitude of the gender differences identified by Maccoby and Jacklin over a quarter of a century ago appears to be in decline. For example, analysis of 172 studies of parents' differential socialisation of boys and girls has shown that cognitive and social characteristics are not as large as Maccoby and Jacklin initially concluded although this does not rule out the possibility that ostensibly small differences in the socialisation of 'gender appropriate' behaviour may have larger impacts in later life (Lytton & Romney, 1991). For instance, the verbal skills of boys have shown improvement in a number of studies conducted in different parts of the world while North American studies suggest there is a declining trend in gender differences in mathematics. Theoretical advances now argue for placing greater emphasis on the influence of relational processes in the emergence of gender differences, specifically on how the emotional relationship between parents and children may have a differential effect on girls and boys. Such a view is consistent with, and follows from, Maccoby's argument that understanding gender differences is best accomplished by examining relationships rather than individuals in isolation from their social networks. Notwithstanding these caveats and elaborations, *The Psychology of Sex Differences* remains a landmark in the development of psychology.

Eleanor Maccoby's major writings

Maccoby, E. E. (1951). Television: Its impact on school children. *Public Opinion Quarterly, 15*, 421–444.

Maccoby, E. E. (1966). Parents differential reactions to sons and daughters. *Journal of Personality and Social Psychology*, 237–243.

Maccoby, E. E. (1980). *Social development: Psychological growth and the parent-child relationship*. New York: Harcourt-Brace-Jovanovich.

Maccoby, E. E. (1994). The role of parents in the socialization of children: An historical overview. In R. D. Parke, P. A. Ornstein, J. J. Rieser, & C. Zahn-Waxler (Eds.), *A century of developmental psychology* (pp. 589–615). American Psychological Association.

Maccoby, E. E., & Jacklin, C. N. (1974). *The psychology of sex differences*. Redwood City: Stanford University Press.

Maccoby, E. E., & Zellner, M. (1970). *Experiments in primary education: Aspects of project follow-through*. New York: Harcourt Brace Jovanovich.

Sears, R. R., Maccoby, E. E., & Levin, H. (1957). *Patterns of child rearing*. New York: Row, Peterson and Co.

Further reading

Gold Medal Award for Life Achievement in Psychological Science: Eleanor Emmons Maccoby (1996). *American Psychologist, 51*(8), 757–759. https://doi.org/10.1037/0003-066X.51.8.757

Golombok, S., & Fivush, R. (1994). *Gender development*. Cambridge: Cambridge University Press.

Lindzey, G. (Ed.). (1989). *A history of psychology in autobiography* (Vol. 8). Redwood City: Stanford University Press.

Lytton, H., & Romney, D. M. (1991). Parent's differential socialization of boys and girls: A meta-analysis. *Psychological Bulletin, 109*, 267–296. https://doi.org/10.1037/0033-2909.109.2.267

Stevens, G., & Gardner, S. (1982). *The women of psychology: Volume 2: Expansion and refinement*. Rochester: Schenkman.

35 Abraham H. Maslow (April 1, 1908–June 8, 1970)

Maslow played a major role in pressing the case for humanistic psychology and developed a theory of motivation based on the idea that needs are organised hierarchically.

Abraham Harold Maslow was the eldest of seven children. His parents were uneducated Jewish Russian immigrants and were very concerned to ensure that their children availed of every opportunity afforded by them. Being the eldest, he was placed under a lot of pressure to be academically successful, an experience he found both stressful and lonely. His parents encouraged him to take a law degree at the City College of New York (CCNY). After three semesters, he transferred to Cornell and then returned to CCNY. Against his parents' wishes, he married Bertha Goodman, his first cousin (they later had two daughters), and they moved to Wisconsin, where Maslow completed his training in psychology. His dissertation, on dominance and sexuality in monkeys, was supervised by Harry Harlow, who made significant contributions to the understanding of the development of affectional systems in monkeys and humans. Maslow returned to New York to work with the learning theorist Thorndike at Columbia, where he became interested in research on human sexuality. Several years later, his expertise in this area brought an invitation from Alfred Kinsey to collaborate in his classic study of sexual behaviour but the partnership never materialised largely because Maslow published a critical commentary of the sampling framework and procedures underlying Kinsey's work. Two years at Columbia were followed by a teaching position at Brooklyn College that brought him into contact with other European immigrants, including Erich Fromm, Alfred Adler and Karen Horney. This was followed by a move to Brandeis University, where he remained until his early retirement was brought on by several years of poor health. Thereafter, he was appointed

DOI: 10.4324/9781003229179-36

Resident Fellow of the Laughlin Institute, California, before his death from a heart attack.

Maslow, the founder of Humanistic Psychology, was initially trained within the behavioural tradition and developed a strong interest in psychobiology. This was to inspire his study of human motivation which, he argued, should be the study of the ultimate goals or desires of people. Rather than attempting to enumerate every goal and desire, he focused on their relationships and sought to identify general structures. His astute awareness of the manner in which animals seek to satisfy their needs in order of precedence provided a guide to the delineation of general structures. For example, breathing takes precedence over drinking and drinking overeating. He identified five levels of need: physiological needs, needs relating to safety and security, the needs for affiliation and love, the need for esteem, and the need to actualise the self. More basic needs (e.g. physiological) take precedence over high-order needs (e.g. self-actualisation). (Maslow was aware of curiosity as an important motivational influence but, unsure of where to place it in the hierarchy, chose to omit it.) He used the personality syndrome – an organised, interdependent, structured group of symptoms – as his primary unit of analysis and focused on studying two particular syndromes: self-esteem and security. He considered the inverse forms of the needs motivating these syndromes to be associated with low self-esteem and inferiority complexes. In this regard, Maslow was in broad agreement with Adler's view that failure to satisfy more basic needs are at the root of many psychological problems. For example, someone whose childhood was characterised by concerns with scarcity might, in later life, manifest an obsessive neurosis with buying and storing large quantities of food. Under stressful conditions, we may regress to a concern with satisfying needs at a lower level, as when a friendship ends and we may feel an intense longing to satisfy needs of belongingness.

A crucial part of his theory concerns the distinction between lower ('deficiency') and higher ('being' or 'growth') needs, a division similar to one made by Allport between biogenic and psychogenic needs. Higher-order needs are thought to appear later, both in evolutionary terms and later in an organism's development (i.e. in adulthood rather than childhood). He also regarded them as less vital to survival – satisfying these high-order needs can be delayed – but once satisfied they are associated with a profound sense of self-fulfilment. He used Cannon's concept of homeostasis (the maintenance of physiological equilibrium) to explain how lower-order deficiency needs (D-needs) are satisfied. However, he also took the view that: (i) satisfying higher-order being needs (B-needs) can only be achieved given a relatively rare amalgamation of favourable environmental conditions and (ii) satisfying B-needs does not involve homeostasis. B-needs once satisfied or engaged are likely to become stronger and provoke an ongoing desire to continue to fulfil one's potential and to be all that you can be. He also argued that the dynamics of personal values changes as needs are fulfilled. Specifically, we tend to over-estimate the importance of those things that can satisfy the most powerful of our ungratified needs and to under-estimate the significance of the satisfiers of the less powerful ungratified needs, and the force of those needs. Conversely, we tend to under-estimate and under-value the importance of satisfiers of needs already gratified, and to under-estimate the potency of those needs.

Maslow described the self-actualising person thus:

> If one expects nothing, if one has no anticipations or apprehensions, if in a sense there is no future. . . . There can be no surprise, no disappointment. One thing is as likely as another to happen . . . and no prediction means no worry, no anxiety, no apprehension, no foreboding.
>
> (1962, p. 67)

His hope was that sustained effort to distil the core features of the self-actualising person would lead to the production of something akin to a periodic table of qualities, pathologies (he never regarded the self-actualised person as 'perfect') and solutions typical of the highest levels of human potential.

Maslow's criticism of the psychology he studied as a student was that it was too pessimistic: the person was regarded as enduring a hostile environment from without and descriptive, unconscious instincts from within. Much of the criticism against his more optimistic theoretical framework concerns the approach taken to the development of his ideas on self-actualisation. He began by identifying people he regarded as high self-actualisers and then used various combinations of interviews, biographical and autobiographical accounts to distil the core characteristics of self-actualisation. The approach was based on his method of iteration, which involved obtaining information from interviews and a variety of documentary sources, using the data to refine the concept of self-actualisation, conducting additional interviews or consulting further documentary evidence, further refining the concept and so on. The difficulty with this approach is that by deciding a priori who were and who were not self-actualisers, Maslow grounded the development of his theory on his personal impressions of self-actualised people (e.g. Albert Einstein, Eleanor Roosevelt, Walt Whitman, Ludwig

Beethoven). Maslow was aware of the problems this posed and always maintained that his approach to research was motivated principally by a concern to raise awareness of the fundamental issues involved in studying self-actualisation and demonstrating that the measurement issues were not insurmountable. A related criticism concerns the arbitrary limit Maslow imposed on the achievement of self-actualisation: he estimated that only 2% of humans achieve self-actualisation, and a list he produced in 1970 contained just nine living and nine historical figures. This contrasts with Rogers' view that self-actualisation is about what every organism strives to do: to grow and fulfil its biological fate. Thus, while Rogers regarded babies as the best examples of human self-actualisation, Maslow considered it a rarity among the young. Moreover, Maslow contends that organisms seek to satisfy lower-order biological needs before attending to self-actualisation, yet many of the finest human achievements in arts and science are attributed to people who live an impoverished lifestyle and endure physical and psychological ill health as a consequence.

Maslow's impact was partly a reaction against the prevailing mechanistic and behaviouristic Zeitgeist and offered an optimistic, holistic and even mystical account of the human condition. His approach offered the prospect of refocusing psychology away from the study of behaviour towards the analysis of the whole organism – the person. Although Maslow's theory has little empirical support with respect to the order of priority of needs, it has proved a useful descriptive model of personality and a good framework from which to investigate individual differences. An enduring feature of Maslow's psychology is its concern with well-being and the realisation of potential. His interest in understanding the constituents of psychological well-being contrasted with the traditional interest in the 'abnormal' and with psychological illness. His humanistic psychology stimulated the development of new kinds of therapies that focused on realising personal resources for growth and healing and on helping people overcome barriers to achieving this. The most famous of these was Roger's client-centred therapy. With its emphasis on personal growth and 'becoming', Maslow's theory is often described as representing a 'fulfilment' account of personality. As such, it is usually classified with other theorists labelled as 'Third Force' psychologists. 'Depth' psychologies such as psychoanalysis constituted the first force, behaviourism was the second force and humanistic psychology constituted the third force. Towards the end of his life, Maslow inaugurated what he called the 'fourth force' in psychology: The fourth force refers to transpersonal psychologies which, taking their cue from Eastern philosophies, investigate meditation and altered levels of consciousness.

Abraham Maslow's major writings

Maslow, A. H. (1943). A theory of human motivation. *Psychological Review, 50*(4), 370–396.

Maslow, A. H. (1954). *Motivation and personality.* New York: Harper and Row.

Maslow, A. H. (1959). *New knowledge in human values.* New York: Harper and Row.

Maslow, A. H. (1962). *Toward a psychology of being.* New York: Van Nostrand,

Maslow, A. H. (1964). *Religion, values and peak experiences* (lectures). Columbus: Ohio State University Press.

Maslow, A. H. (1965). *Eupsychian management: A journal.* Irwin-Dorsey Series in Behavioural Science. Homewood, IL.

Maslow, A. H. (1971). *The farther reaches of human nature.* New York: Viking.

Maslow, A. H., & Mittelmann, B. (1941). *Principles of abnormal psychology.* New York: Harper.

Maslow, A. H., & Sakoda, J. M. (1952). Volunteer-error in the Kinsey study. *The Journal of Abnormal and Social Psychology, 47*(2), 259–262.

Further reading

Goble, F. (1970). *The third force: The psychology of Abraham Maslow.* Grossman.

Hoffman, E. (1988). *The right to be human: A biography of Abraham Maslow.* St. Martins.

36 Stanley Milgram (August 15, 1933–December 20, 1984)

Milgram conducted a classic and controversial experimental study of obedience that suggests that most people are capable of heinous behaviour.

Stanley Milgram was born and raised in New York City and attended James Monroe High School – he and Zimbardo were in the 12th grade together – before entering Queen's College, where he studied political science. His interest in psychology emerged during his graduating year, so acceptance of his application to Harvard's Department of Social Relations was deferred until he completed six psychology courses during the summer of 1954. His doctoral dissertation was supervised by Allport, who pioneered the application of social psychological approaches to the study of personality. Milgram's dissertation addressed cross-cultural differences in conformity and was based on data collected in Norway and Paris. Whereas Asch had previously asked participants to judge the length of lines in circumstances where there was strong social pressure to conform to the erroneous judgement of the majority, Milgram used judgements of sound duration. He concluded that pressures for conformity were greater in the relatively small, homogenous society of Norway than in France with its greater cultural variability and stronger tradition of intellectual dissent. While teaching at Yale, Milgram directed his interests in conformity to the study of obedience to authority and thereby developed a line of enquiry initiated by Asch, under whose supervision he worked for a short time in 1959.

Milgram was fundamentally interested in social issues as people experienced them. For example, his mother-in-law wondered why the chivalrous practice of giving up one's seat for another appeared to be in decline among the users of the New York sub-way. One of his students set about testing the possibility that the citizens of New York City were

DOI: 10.4324/9781003229179-37

inured to the needs of others. The findings, Milgram concluded, indicated that New Yorkers were not callous but were socially inhibited from engaging with one another. His Jewish heritage undoubtedly contributed to his intellectual and personal concern for finding an answer to an even bigger question: 'If Hitler asked you, would you kill a stranger?' Milgram devised a research paradigm that sought to provide an answer. His research program set out to examine the degree to which ordinary people will comply with the orders of authority when those orders go against conscience. In his classic and controversial study, he created a laboratory situation that turned out to offer a very powerful way of investigating obedience. Essentially, someone taking orders from a scientist can be persuaded to deliver what they believe to be an extremely dangerous electric shock (450 volts) to someone who they understand to be an innocent victim with a heart condition. In a set of 21 experiments, Milgram found that about two-thirds of the participants were willing to administer a life-threatening electric shock to the victim. The study has been replicated in dozens of countries, and while there is some variation in the percentage of participants prepared to administer this level of shock, a fair summary is to state that about two-thirds were obedient and that figure has become a benchmark statistic. The first published commentary on this work appeared, not in a psychology journal but in a highly critical editorial of the *St. Louis Post-Dispatch*. Milgram was unaware of the piece until Robert Buckhout, a social psychologist based at St. Louis, brought it to his attention. Numerous critiques followed, many of them addressing issues regarding the ethics of using deception, the nature of informed consent, the dignity afforded to people who agree to participate in psychological experiments and the extent to which Milgram's studies should be regarded as bringing the discipline into disrepute. One of the strongest claims, first articulated by the developmental psychologist Diana Baumrind, was that Milgram's study did not meet ethical standards because participants were subjected to a research design that caused them undue psychological stress that was not resolved after the study. Milgram's response was that the study was well designed and that there was clear evidence that the participants' distress dissipated after a thorough debriefing. The level of controversy was such that his application to the American Psychological Association was delayed, pending the outcome of an investigation into the ethics of his studies. The conclusion was favourable and his membership was approved in 1963. Two years later, this work was awarded the annual socio-psychological prize of the American Association for the Advancement of Science. It is no accident, perhaps, that when translations of this work appeared, they appeared first in Hebrew and in German.

Milgram contends that everyone has the dual capacity to function as an individual: capable of exercising their own moral judgement and of taking ethical decisions based on their personal character. However, two-thirds of us – men and women alike – are capable of heinous behaviour when, in deference to authority, we allow our own moral judgements to be over-ruled. The interpretations that can be placed on Milgram's findings, together with the ethical issues they raise, are still debated. They are often explained in terms of the presence of (a) normative pressures induced by the experimenter's insistence that participants do what they are told – unlike the less pressured procedures adopted by Asch in his investigations; (b) informational influence – the tendency to allow others to reach a decision on what to do when faced with an ambiguous or crisis situation and (c) conflicting social norms – once the first shock had been administered participants placed additional pressures on themselves to continue to obey. Subsequent studies have shown that having peers model vicious behaviour towards others will increase the willingness of participants to inflict what they believe to be life-threatening shocks. However, victims who demand to be shocked elicit an opposite reaction from participants now reluctant to engage in a sado-masochistic rapport. Most participants decline the invitation.

Would Milgram find less obedience if he conducted his experiments today? Two reasons for thinking that fewer people would be obedient are that the mass media have alerted the general public to human susceptibility to obedience to authority and that the outcome of Milgram's own studies has found its way into popular culture (e.g. a popularised account of his experiments appeared in *Harper's* in 1973, and they are the subject of Peter Gabriel's 1986 song 'We do what we're told – Milgram's 37'). Moreover, whereas Milgram found that the predictions of those unfamiliar with his experimental paradigm grossly under-estimate the actual obedience rates, later studies indicate that the gap has greatly diminished (Blass, 1999). Thus, knowledge of one's vulnerability to obedience to authority might act as a protective factor against demands for compliance. However, Blass (2000), drawing on 35 years of accumulated research, examined the correlation between the year in which a study was published and the amount of obedience reported. He found no association: later studies found neither more nor less obedience than that reported in earlier investigations.

Milgram's methodological ingenuity is also revealed in his investigations of more benign forms of social influence. Since his laboratory looked out onto New York's 42nd street, he arranged for various numbers of pedestrians (all of them confederates – students or colleagues) to stop and gaze up at a sixth-floor window. Behind the window, Milgram filmed the crowd. He systematically varied the number of confederates and measured the size of the crowd that would gather. With one confederate gazing, about 45% of pedestrians stopped to look up, but with 15 confederates about 85% of the passers-by stopped. This is a different type of social force – contagion rather than obedience – but it is a powerful demonstration that as the number of sources of influence increases the intensity of their social impact seems also to increase. This is not to imply that contagion is inherently wrong: it can confer an information processing advantage because merely noticing what others are doing and imitating their actions means that people can spend less time deciding what to do – a strategy that leads to appropriate decisions most of the time (Cialdini, 1993). Milgram's work informed a generation of experimental investigations of social influence most forcefully articulated in the work of Zimbardo.

Milgram carried out studies of social processes based on a set of highly original experimental techniques, notably The Lost Letter Technique, The Small World Problem and the Cyranoid paradigm. The lost-letter technique is a procedure for investigating altruism, which involves a researcher 'losing' a number of stamped and addressed letters throughout an area. The behaviour of people finding a letter is covertly observed, and their behaviour (e.g. post it, read it, trash it) is used to indicate their altruism. In the first study, Milgram systematically changed a minor detail on the address (e.g. 'Friends of the Nazi Party' or 'Medical Research Organisation') in order to examine the impact of social and political attitudes on willingness to help. He devised the Small World Problem to test the postulate that everyone on earth is connected together in an enormous social network. The theory predicts that any two people chosen at random from anywhere in the world can be connected to one another through a surprisingly short chain of friends or associates – just six. Originally supported by anecdotal evidence and folklore, more recent studies have suggested that the phenomenon is fundamental to structures occurring throughout nature, and it appears to be an essential component in the structural evolution of the world wide web. Several attempts have been made to provide a decisive test of the 'Six Degrees of Separation' hypothesis by involving several thousand people from around the world. The findings have been inconclusive but whatever the final outcome, the answer to Milgram's small world problem will reveal a great deal about structure of social networks on the planet. The Cyranoid paradigm (named after Cyrano de Bergerac who put words in the mouth of a suitor) involves an experimental manipulation in which one of the participants in a conversation speaks, not their own thoughts, but those of a hidden observer, the thoughts being transmitted to them via a tiny radio receiver. His interests in other areas, such as his 1972 study of the mental maps of the inhabitants of Paris and New York, anticipated the emergence of the environmental psychology of the built environment.

There is no evidence that Milgram's interests in understanding obedience and his willingness to deceive research participants were a reflection of aspects of his own personality and his treatment of others. Like his own doctoral supervisor, Gordon Allport, he enjoyed a reputation as a supporting rather than a demanding mentor, and while at the Graduate Center of CUNY only one of his many doctoral students worked on the topic of obedience. The social psychologist Irwin Katz offered the following observation on the occasion of Milgram's untimely death:

> After two decades of critical scrutiny and discussion, they remain one of the most singular, most penetrating, and most disturbing enquiries into human conduct that modern psychology has produced this century. Those of us who presume to have knowledge of man are still perplexed by his findings, with their frightful implications for society.
>
> (cited in Blass, 1999)

Stanley Milgram's major writings

Milgram, S. (1961). Nationality and conformity. *Scientific American, 205*(6), 45–52.
Milgram, S. (1963). Behavioral study of obedience. *The Journal of Abnormal and Social Psychology, 67*(4), 371–378.
Milgram, S. (1965). Some conditions of obedience and disobedience to authority. *Human Relations, 18*(1), 57–76.
Milgram, S. (1967). The small world problem. *Psychology Today, 1*, 60–67.
Milgram, S. (1969). The lost letter technique. *Psychology Today, 3*, 30–33, 66–68.
Milgram, S. (1974). *Obedience to authority.* New York: Harper and Row.
Milgram, S. (1977). *The individual in a social world.* US: Addison-Wesley.

Further reading

Baumrind, D. (1964). Some thoughts on ethics of research: After reading Milgram's "Behavioral study of obedience". *American Psychologist, 19*, 421–423.
Blass, T. (1999). The Milgram paradigm after 35 years: Some things we now know about obedience to authority. *Journal of Applied Social Psychology, 29*, 955–997.
Blass, T. (Ed.). (2000). *Obedience to authority: Current perspectives on the Milgram paradigm.* Erlbaum.
Cialdini, R. B. (1993). *Influence: Science and practice* (3rd ed.). New York: Harper Collins College Publishers.

37 Walter Mischel (February 22, 1930–September 12, 2018)

Building on the work of Alfred Bandura, Walter Mischel's body of work argues that an individual's personality is influenced both by attributes of a given situation and the perceptions of that individual in that situation.

Walter Mischel was born in Vienna, close to Freud's house, on February 22, 1930. Walter was the third child of Salomon Mischel and Lola Leah Schreck. The family fled Austria in 1938. Adolf Hitler had taken direct control of the German military and Austria was annexed. 1938 was a fateful year. The beginning of the racialisation of the Nazis Jewish policy. Jewish property was being seized and Jews were being expelled from Germany or having their passports invalidated; they were arrested, sent to concentration camps or simply murdered in the streets. Vienna had high numbers of prosperous Jewish citizens, nearly 200,000, but as the Nazis were welcomed into Vienna, the cultural, economic and social lives of its citizens were systematically dismantled. Within a week, Walter went from sitting at the front of his class, to having to stand at the back, and then, to the door to the school being locked to him. Walter's father struggled to accept that the situation would not improve. In fear and denial, the family waited almost too long before exiting Vienna. They just about got of Vienna before 'Kristallnacht' when Jewish homes, synagogues and buildings all over Austria were ransacked and burned during the 'Night of the Broken Glass'.

To leave the country, Jews were forced to pay high taxes and leave everything behind. The Mischel family escaped to the United States, alive but with almost nothing. They eventually settled in Brooklyn in one of the poorest neighbourhoods. Walter reports a transformation in his parents. His father was severely withdrawn and depressed, holding on to the dream that one day they would return to Vienna. His mother Lola, however, took control of their destiny as best she could. While

DOI: 10.4324/9781003229179-38

in Vienna, Lola was neurotic and unmotivated; in America, she was transformed – working hard, taking control of the family and obtaining a waitressing job. Eventually, with the help of the Refugee Committee his father opened a five-and-dime shop.

Walter performed well at school, graduating as valedictorian (top of his class) and winning a scholarship to Columbia University at a time when only 2% of Jews were permitted (by quota) to enter university. However, just as he started at Columbia, his father had a heart attack and he had to delay for a year, to support his father's business and make deliveries between other part-time jobs that he had taken on. When his father was mostly recovered, Walter found himself unable to get himself re-admitted to Columbia, so he had to attend New York University instead. He began to study psychology but did not enjoy the subject, finding it 'ghastly'. The categorisation in particular of humans and the study of 'rats' before Skinner's work was something that did not sit well with him.

Walter shifted his focus towards literature before settling on clinical psychology, which he studied at City Colleague. At first, he was intrigued and fascinated by psychoanalysis but became increasingly frustrated by what he described as '*when questions were being asked, the response was not to answer the question, but to get into the dynamics and resistance of the question asker*'. A turning point was when he was working as an uncredentialised social worker with impoverished children in the Henry Street Settlement House, in one of the most underprivileged areas of New York. While his family had challenges, these children were living under very difficult conditions; they were very troubled. He recalls giving wisdom to these troubled children only to find that one of them had set his jacket on fire and recognising that he really needed to go to graduate school and get some proper training.

Walter settled on the University of Ohio in Columbia largely because their financial support was 50 dollars higher than other offerings and his first wife, Francis Henry, had received a budget to support her Doctoral thesis. Francis's study of the tribes in the Caribbean Islands necessitated a move to Trinidad, where Mischel found an exotic sun-drenched haven and where he could enjoy rum and Coca-Cola while exploring the local's responses to the Rorschach test. He discovered significant cultural differences in attitudes towards gratification in the local ethnic groups. The Indians felt that the blacks were unconcerned about tomorrow and their children's futures, the blacks felt that the Indians did not know how to enjoy life. Mischel found that these differences manifested themselves at school. His work in this area was the start of what we now know as temporal economics. *Do you prefer a small amount of money today or a large amount of money sometime in the future?*

Walter Mischel obtained a PhD from Ohio State University in 1956. His mentors Julian Rotter and George Kelly had the most significant influence on his work, introducing him to personal construct and social learning theories, work that would later become central to his work on personality. The two psychologists operated from quite different perspectives, but Mischel felt that between the two, there was a useful approach to the study of psychology that empowered the individual to liberate themselves from past problems and trauma. Rotter and Kelly gave Walter the signature combination that provided the context for exploration of the interaction between commitment and expectancies, with his first publications appearing in anthropological journals, marking what is often called the cognitive revolution. Later in his career, he would go on to give particular credit to George Kelly as profoundly influencing the future of cognitive psychology.

Mischel became part of the Columbia University faculty in 1956, moving to Harvard in 1958. Harvard was not a positive experience; it was an LSD '*la la land*' that showed him the kind of psychologist he did not want to be. His marriage to Francis did not survive and the couple divorced in 1959. Walter married Harriet Nerlove the following year. Their relationship lasted until 1996 and they had three children together Judith, Rebecca, and Linda.

Walter Mischel made a career studying self-control. The central focus of his work was the examination of the motivational structures behind delay of gratification in children, which formed a larger investigation into the links between self-control, achievement and well-being in later life. Ironically, Mischel had no control where cigarettes were concerned. The nicotine addiction was so strong; he worked out he was craving a cigarette every 3 minutes and smoking as many as 60 cigarettes a day. When the cigarettes ran out, he had a pipe to fall back on and when the pipe tobacco ran out, he supplemented his habit with cigars. Fully aware of the damage he was causing to his health, Walter failed repeatedly to stop, including making a pact with his 3-year-old child that he would stop sucking his pipe if she would stop sucking her thumb. It was, however, easy to explain away his habit as part of his professorial image and something that kept him calm and balanced.

Eventually, in 1962, Mischel could move to Stanford University. At Stanford, he found the pressure released from fast publishing towards slow thought and impact on important issues. He made Stanford his academic home for 21 years.

In the same year, in what he describes as a 'cry' against psychoanalytical theory, Michel published *Personality and Assessment*. There was, he argued, no connection between diagnosis and treatment under the psychoanalytical model. The method was producing high levels of reliability (everyone agreed with everyone else) but zero validity; they were all wrong. Consistency of personality was not what is intuitively assumed. The environment was being overlooked as a factor in personality and behaviour. The idea that scientists could 'do personality' more simply than 'a urine analysis' was to Mischel insane and the discipline was in crisis.

Perhaps more supported in this radically different environment, Mischel's attitude towards his smoking habit changed dramatically. When, in the late 1960s, he met a man who was suffering from lung cancer. His hair was gone, his chest was bare and he had crosses on his chest which marked the points of where the radiation would go in a final attempt to manage what had become metastasised lung cancer. He never smoked again.

The response to Mischel's work was initially highly critical. The divide between social psychology and personality psychology was widening. Mischel had hoped his work would bring the disciplines closer together; the opposite was happening. The personality psychologists felt that Mischel's work was a personal attack, whereas the social psychologists misinterpreted Mischel's work, believing that he was endorsing a purely social model, rather than a person by situation interaction. In the spirit of *don't interfere with our lovely war*, his work was vilified to the point that his friends who worked in personality research refused to speak to him.

Walter Mischel died in his New York home of pancreatic cancer on September 12, 2018. He was survived by his partner Michele Myers and three daughters. Among other accolades and honours, he held the distinguished Science Award from the Society for Experimental Social Psychologists in 2001, the Personality Award of the Society for Social and Personality Psychologists in 2005, and in 2007 he was elected President of the Association for Psychological Science.

Possibly best known for his 'marshmallow study' and work on gratification, Walter Mischel's contribution to the study of personality from an interactionist perspective is no less remarkable. The cognitive affect personality system proposed by Mischel and Shoda (1995) moved away from personality as a dichotomy by arguing that inconsistencies in behaviour are not in fact inconsistent. Personality is therefore determined by the psychological, social and physical aspects of any given situation. How individuals interact with that environment will change depending on the determinants of that situation, but it will be relatively stable.

Despite Mischel's belief that he had failed to reconcile the gap between personality and social psychology, his theory that individuals could have agency over the stimuli that were 'controlling' them was profoundly important. Mischel sparked new methods and models to study individual differences in social behaviour and opened the door to the role of cognitive-affect processing, particularly the study of the acts, dispositions and personality factors that come together to help individuals to overcome pressure and exert self-control.

Walter Mischel's major writings

Mischel, W. (1968). *Personality and assessment.* New York: Wiley.

Mischel, W. (1973). Toward a cognitive social learning reconceptualization of personality. *Psychological Review,* 80, 252–283.

Mischel, W. (2004). Toward an integrative science of the person. *Annual Review of Psychology,* 55, 1–22.

Mischel, W., & Shoda, Y. (1995). A cognitive-affective system theory of personality: Reconceptualizing situations, dispositions, dynamics, and invariance in personality structure. *Psychological Review, 102*(2), 246–268.

Further reading

Inside the Psychologist's Studio with Walter Mischel. *The American Psychological Society.* Published on December 19, 2017. Retrieved from www.psychologicalscience. org/publications/observer/obsonline/aps-past-president-walter-mischel-passes-away. html

38 Henry Alexander Murray (May 13, 1893–June 23, 1988)

An advocate for research into human personality that incorporated multiple methods to capture as many facets of an individual as possible. Murray is possibly best known for his work profiling Adolf Hitler during the second world war.

Henry Alexander Murray (Harry) was born in New York in 1893. The America that the infant Harry grew up in is one of sharp contradictions. His life was comfortable and secure. Growing up in an affluent area, close to Central Park, the children would have had little sense of the growing societal divisions. Immigration was increasing, and with it the harsh realities of low wages, exploitation and slum living.

His mother Fannie Morris Babcock was from New England with a long prosperous pedigree. She married Henry Alexander (Sr), a well-bred but financially modest Scot who worked in stocks and bonds. Through hard work, he found favour with the Babcock family, eventually winning Fannie's heart. The couple prospered and lived in a fashionable part of New York attending social clubs with the financially elite of the day.

Harry was the middle child; he had an older sister and younger brother. Harry's mother was nervous and self-absorbed; she suffered from hypochondria and was prone to meddling. Fannie made no secret of the fact that her favourite child was Virginia. She was a demanding child, a 'terrier', whose demands probably resulted in Harry's abrupt weaning at aged 2 months. Harry fared poorly afterwards. He did not eat properly for 2 years and was suffering not only from lack of nutrition but also lack of maternal love. At the age of 9, he recalls coming home from school where he was confronted with an operating theatre in the family dining room. His mother, who was obsessed with perfection, had decided he had a squint in his eye. This deviation needed adjusting and there in his home, two surgeons awaited him. The terrified

DOI: 10.4324/9781003229179-39

boy was offered the option of a general aesthetic, or he could just get on with it and she would buy him an aquarium. Not understanding fully what was about to take place, Harry opted for the aquarium. The trauma of the surgery not only resulted in Harry developing a stutter, but the surgeons overcorrected his eyes which caused Harry to suffer from a complete lack of stereoscopic vision. These experiences had a profound impact on what he would describe as his marrow of misery and melancholy, which would be counteracting disposition of sanguine and excessive buoyancy.

His relationship with his father and younger brother Cecil was better. He describes his father, as a jolly, kindly man who would take him to central park, read to him, take him fishing and on trips to Europe. Rather than protect Harry from his mother, his father's strategy was that they should all find ways to keep their distance. Harry credits his father with giving him rules for living and simple self-esteem.

After a period at private preparatory schools, Harry was sent away to board in 1906 at Groton School, an Episcopal college in Massachusetts. Harry worked and played hard at Groton, becoming a positively engaged and well-rounded adolescent. Sport was his passion, but as a result of his yet unknown eye damage, he was not particularly good at it. His physical development was still slow, he suffered bouts of scarlet fever and mumps. He needed to have adenoids removed. But generally his health was good, he would brush the illness off and bounce back quickly. As his adolescence developed, Harry would show more interests in hunting, fishing, drinking (but not excessively) and 'chorus line girls'. A pursuit he reports himself to have been quite successful in. He did well at school, emerging a stable and secure man. Not all in his cohort of 26 faired so well. Many developed drinking problems and six of his peer group took their own lives in the years to follow.

At Harvard, Harry would jest that he graduated in the three Rs; Rum, Rowing and Romance, eventually majoring, poorly, in history. He compensated for his early poor performance at Columbia University, where he studied for his MD, also receiving an MA in biology. In 1919, he graduated, took up a position as an instructor in physiology at Harvard and began studying for a PhD in biochemistry which he completed in 1928. While pursuing his medical studies, he met and married Josephine Lee Rantoul and they had a child together, also called Josephine.

In 1923, Harry met Christiana Morgan, which would change both the nature of his personal life and the trajectory of his professional career. Christina was strikingly beautiful and held many qualities that may have seemed familiar to Harry. She was married to Will O. Morgan, a graduate of Harvard and an acquaintance of Harrys. They had an infant child, from whom Christina had withdrawn, giving total care over to their nanny. Depression, anxiety and inner turmoil surrounded Christina. She was beautiful and she knew it, bold and flirtatious, but she was also destructive and the creator of drama. Harry knew she was neurotic, but he was also besotted.

It was Christina that introduced Harry to Karl Jung's major writing, *Psychological Types*. At dinner one evening, she articulately contrasted Jung's work with the writings of Freud. Perhaps to impress Christina further, or because he was sincerely interested in the topic, Harry promptly went and acquired the copy from Christina. It was a turning point; the book and Christina seemed to offer Harry direction and answers to his most scattered self. Although the relationship started out a largely intellectual exchange on Jung's work, it was not long before an instance intellectual, but non-physical affair began.

Harry was already starting to think about a route into psychology and was due to spend a year in Cambridge, England, in study. Christina persuaded Will that they should follow the Murray's to Cambridge. Jo who until this point was bending to the situation was becoming increasingly strained. Harry still loved his wife; she made him deeply happy, but Christina was becoming more overly confident in meddling between the couple. Highly critical to Harry, of his wife's inability to make allowances for this important side of Harry's psyche, Harry did little to protect his marriage. Matters started to come to a head one night after dinner. As the Morgan's left the Murray household after dinner one evening, Harry blurted out to Christina, 'you fertilize me'. Jo and Will were started, but with all the politeness of New England society in the mid-1920s said nothing. They could see what was happening, and the pain was acute but there was always the hope that it would wear itself out.

In 1925, with this slow-burning affair simmering in his personal life, Harry took himself to Zurich to meet with Karl Jung. On route, he was taken by the striking presence of a beautiful woman, Lady Winifred Gore, who was also on her way to visit a Swizz psychiatrist. Harry was convinced that he was having an anima experience, that their souls were somehow connected and that they had met before. Little came of the meeting, but when Jung was showing little interest in discussions with Harry on Psychological Types, Harry began to relay this experience and then explain in detail his relationship with Christina Morgan. Jung's interest was piqued, and he began to share his own candid detours in love. The sessions continued for 3 weeks, interspersed with sailing trips, meals and talking – followed then with Jung's mistress Antonia Wolf and his wife Emma Jung serving tea. Jung's insights helped to explain away what was happening in his personal life. To reach full creative potential, he would have to cast off his neurotic ties. He would finally abandon biology and biochemistry in favour of psychology and continually openly with both relationships.

The couples met with Jung. Christina consented to pursue therapy with Jung, then confessed all to Will and Jo. Will was hurt but stoic, and Jo felt the meeting with Jung was a complete waste of time. She concluded that Jung was nothing but a dirty old man, but his assessment that her husband's affair with Christina was base helped her accept the situation. As divorce was out of the question, Will and Jo were resolved to try and make the best of an awful situation.

On returning to the United States in 1926, Harry took up a post at Harvard University at a clinic to study abnormal psychology. He was hopelessly underqualified and worse still the department was not in the least bit interested in the teachings of Jung. He deplored the experimental focus and measurement science and quickly became known as a difficult if not, in fact, openly hostile and obnoxious member of the Harvard team. Somehow, he managed to secure directorship of the clinic in 1928. He changed the direction of the clinic to focus on understanding human nature and man and gave Christina Morgan an office in the clinic. The clinic became more of an intellectual salon, where the great artists, thinkers and psychologists of the time would come to dine and share conversation. Harry never saw the clinic as being aligned to one psychological approach or another, strongly resisting descriptions of the clinic as Freudian or Jungian. Rather all perspectives were embraced.

It was within this body of great minds, that Harry began to wrestle with the question of abnormal psychology. Rorschach and the MMPI had a foothold in the psychologist's toolbox, neither provided much in the way of understanding what manifested as abnormal personality, and both were often applied in over-zealous and high-handedly ways. Murry felt such techniques were superficial measures and, quoting the philosopher George Santayana, human imagination and fancies were more revealing to personality – what Murray liked to call 'apperception'. Others such as Francis Galton had been down this road, exploring the relationship between word associations and thought. Freud saw slips of the tongue as the means of accessing the inner self and Rorschach's inkblots attempted to explore Freud's ideas of projection.

Murray began to create techniques for use in the clinic that would enable the mind to wander and provide the psychologist with an additional route by which to understand the patient. These were highly inventive for the time and included musical stimuli, literature, art and odour. Dozens of approaches were developed but one in particular was emerging as useful on the clinics; pictures that depicted 'stories' that could be interpreted and expanded upon by the viewer. The team set about collecting large numbers of pictures from magazines, newspapers and other media resources. Those pictures were shown to students, peers and family with the aim of understanding how those considered to have normal personality functioning would interpret the pictorial messages. Henry and Christina called their test the Thematic Apperception Test (TAT). Thematic because of its capacity to elicit themes that were prevalent in the test takers life and apperception because they triggered fantasy and imagination. The test seemed to do what everyone hoped. In clinical practice, patients would share their deepest thoughts and emotions about the images and the therapist was thus able to quickly understand the patient. TAT still did little to combat the culture of high-handed testing. The testers nativity about the purpose of the instrument was essential to understanding human thought processes. As such, takers were often lied to that the test assessed intelligence or creativity. The work was not readily accepted by the scientific community, suffering a number of journal rejections before finally finding a home in the Archives of Neurology and Psychiatry in 1935, but even then, the publication was a minor achievement, mostly circulated within the clinic's promotional material.

It was 1939 before interest in the theories behind such projective techniques gathered momentum. Harry's major work on psychogenic need theory, helped to stimulate attention. The publication of *Explorations in Psychology* was based on the experience, and understanding that Harry had developed through his clinical practice. The theory examined the interaction between motivation and personality arguing that our personalities reflect behaviours which we control by our needs. Some needs are fleeting, while others are more fundamental to our nature. Primary needs are based on biological demands; food, sex and sleep. Secondary needs are psychological, for example, nurturing, achievement, love and power, and are essential for our well-being and happiness. Thus, personality was a process which was governed by the fabric of the person and their environment at that time.

Explorations also contained an overview of TAT, explaining how the test could tap into the unconscious processes that governed those needs because, in addition to using lived experience to explain the pictures, test takers would also project their own personal, emotional and psychological existence into the pictures. The test made it possible to find the 'buried self', and finally the American Press began to take notice.

The TAT would be the first projective test developed and published in the United States.

While the TAT was gathering momentum, War in Europe was looming. Keen to help the war efforts, Harry set about developing an effective officer selection technique. The test was a ground-breaking method, which could be used to select the best agents behind enemy lines to work as spies and saboteurs. Harry had yet more ground-breaking contribution to make, a psychological profile of Adolf Hitler. Commissioned by the Intelligence agencies and with the briefest of time frames, Harry carried out an extensive analysis of Hitler's speeches and writings. He studied reports from people who were in relationships with Hitler, including reports from women who had sex with him, his childhood friendships and familial connections. By 1943, Harry had produced a 227-page analysis, including predictions about this future behaviour and how the allies might deal with him once the war ended. The extreme contradictions in Hitler's personality and the galvanising ideology that compelled him to drag Europe into an abyss presented a frightening combination of insanity and sanity. Despite expressing esteem at the exceptional insights within the report, the report was quickly swallowed up by the American military establishment, and ordered to be destroyed. This was a blow, but Harry moved on quickly to other war matters. The report never saw the light of day, until in 1972 Walter Langer, published *The Mind of Adolf Hitler*. Langer had taken Harry's work and published it as his own.

Throughout the 1950s and 1960s, Murray continued to work with the CIA on the forensic applications of his work. This included a series of controversial experiments, intended to increase understanding of stress and resilience. Harvard students were subjected to intense interrogation and humiliation. One of those students, John Kaczynski, would later blame this disturbing experience as a contributing factor to his psychological state. Kaczynski spent 200 hours over 3 years in Murray's studies. The Unabomber (University and Airline Bomber), Kaczynski went on to conduct a terrorist campaign against anyone involved in modern technology.

Harry's wife Jo died suddenly of a heart attack on January 14, 1962. Despite his ongoing devotion to Christina, Murray was devastated. His relationship with Christina was also faltering. Following excruciating sympathectomy surgery, she had developed a drinking problem. Her alcoholism was now an open secret, and she was now an embarrassment to him. In an attempt to help her sober up, Harry refused to marry Christina if she continued to drink. She managed to stop briefly but was soon back drinking heavily. Christina had been drinking heavily when she drowned in shallow water on March 14, 1967. Life, however, had one more great love for Harry. At the age of 76, he married Nina Chandler Fish whom he described as the most balanced and stable of his life. The couple shared almost 20 years together before Harry died from pneumonia at the age of 95.

In addition to his lasting impact on the field of psychological profiling, Henry A. Murray's imaginative tool has perhaps had its most lasting influence in the field of advertising. The application of TAT-like methodologies in encouraging customers to talk about what they see in an advertisement is a key marketing technique in determining what customers think and feel, what they want and what they don't want. This application is some distance from the contribution that Harry might have hoped for, but they are effective in predicting how customers will behave in a marketplace.

Henry Alexander Murray's major writings

Morgan, C. D., & Murray, H. A. (1935). A method for investigating fantasies: The thematic apperception test. *Archives of Neurology & Psychiatry, 34*, 289–306.

Murray, H. A. (1938). *Explorations in personality*. Oxford, UK: Oxford University Press.

Murray, H. A. (1973). *The analysis of fantasy*. Huntington, NY: Robert E. Krieger Publishing Company.

Further reading

Novak, Jr., F. G. (Ed.). (2007). *"In old friendship": The correspondence of Lewis Mumford and Henry A. Murray, 1928–1981*. Syracuse, NY: Syracuse University Press.

Robinson, F. G. (1992). *Love's story told, a life of Henry Murray*. Cambridge, MA: Harvard University Press.

39 Ivan Petrovich Pavlov (1849–1936)

Pavlov detailed a theory of learning called classical or Pavlovian conditioning based on the analysis of the relationship between a stimulus and a behavioural response.

Ivan Pavlov was born in Ryazan, about 120 miles southeast of Moscow. The son of a village priest, Peter Dimitrievich Pavlov, he was the eldest of 11 children, six of whom died in childhood. He suffered a serious injury as a result of a fall and his entry to the Ryazan church school was delayed until he was 11. After graduating, he entered the Ryazan Ecclesiastical Seminary, expecting to follow his father's career. It was there that he encountered the work of Charles Darwin, the literary critic Dmitrii Pisarev and Ivan Sechenov, the latter regarded as the 'father of Russian physiology'. Pavlov did not complete his studies at the seminary but pursued his interests in natural science at St Petersburg University. There he encountered the ideas of Ilya F. Cyon, a staunch critic of vitalism, the view that life is more than a physical process and cannot meaningfully be reduced to such a process, under whose direction he developed his skill in vivisection and completed his first empirical studies on the physiology of circulation and digestion. He decided to make his career as a physiologist and after graduating took up a position at the Military-Medical Academy with the purpose of developing his research skills and studying for a medical degree. He lectured on physiology at the Veterinary Institute and studied the circulatory system for his MD dissertation. He was also responsible for the management of the small-animal laboratory of the Academy's clinical director Sergei Botkin, an eminent physician whose ideas on the importance of the nervous system to disease were later to influence Pavlov's own ideas on the matter. After completing his doctorate, he spent 2 years in Germany where he studied in Leipzig with Carl Ludwig and in Rudolf Heidenhain's laboratories in Breslau. At that time, Heidenhain was studying

DOI: 10.4324/9781003229179-40

canine digestion using an exteriorised section of the stomach, but Pavlov perfected the technique by overcoming the problem of maintaining the external nerve supply (a technique termed the Heidenhain-Pavlov pouch). His appointment (1890) as Professor of Pharmacology in the Military-Medical Academy coincided with his marriage to Seraphima Vasilievna Karchevskaya, a teacher and the daughter of a doctor in the Black Sea fleet. The following year, he was invited to organise a department of physiology in the newly established Institute of Experimental Medicine; he was appointed to the chair in 1895. When he was awarded the Nobel Prize (1904), he received the very substantial sum of 73,000 gold rubles, which he deposited in Nobel's Russian company. He lost it all when the Bolsheviks liquidated its stocks and bonds during the 1917 revolution. During 1921–1922, conditions were so bad in Petrograd that Pavlov requested permission from Lenin to move his laboratory abroad. The request was denied but on February 11, 1921, the newspaper *Izvestia* published a decree, signed by Lenin, which stated thus:

> In view of Academician I. P. Pavlov's outstanding scientific services, which are of tremendous importance to the working people of the world, the Council of People's Commissars decrees: To set up . . . a special commission with broad powers . . . whose task is to create, as soon as possible, the best conditions to ensure the research work of Comrade Pavlov and his associates.

The same decree authorised the printing of a deluxe edition of Pavlov's work, a doubling of rations to Pavlov and his wife and an instruction to the Petrograd Soviet 'to assure Professor Pavlov and his wife of the use for life of the flat they now occupy, and to furnish it and Academician Pavlov's laboratory with every possible facility'.

There were political pressures on Pavlov, as there were on Vygotsky, Luria and others to reconcile Marxism with their emerging intellectual positions. At first, this did not seem an intractable task because Marx regarded the human psyche as a reflection of the physical environment but with the capacity to change that context and thereby shape its own development. Pavlov's conditional reflex appeared to be the simplest physiological event linking an organism to its environment and with the creative potential required to permit an organism to change its physical context. Pavlov was less than enthusiastic not least because of his concerns about the excesses associated with the implementation of Marxist policies. A scathing attack on the Marxist thesis delivered in September 1923 attracted a commensurate riposte from Nikolai Bukharin, editor of the official Communist newspaper *Pravda* and a member of the Central Committee. After

Stalin came to power in 1924, Pavlov resigned his post in protest against the expulsion of sons of priests from the Academy. He persisted with his critique of the prevailing political ideology but later, with Russia under attack from Hitler, he moderated his criticism and like many others at that time got on with his scientific work as best he could. In 1927, he was diagnosed with liver cancer and endured several bouts of serious ill health until his death on February 17, 1936. However, the political pressures persisted beyond his death and a joint meeting of the Soviet Academy of Sciences and the Soviet Academy of Medical Sciences held in 1950 inaugurated a systematic review of teaching in psychology, medicine and cognate disciplines, with the goal of ensuring the primacy of Pavlovianism.

Pavlov's research into conditioning grew from his Nobel prize-winning work on adaptive phenomena of the digestive reflex. This focused on the mechanisms controlling the secretions of the various digestive glands and how those mechanisms were stimulated by food. His surgical skill was crucial to the success of this line of investigation – attempts at Heidenhain's laboratories had failed because the staff there lacked Pavlov's proficiency. Pavlov was able to insert food and chemical compounds on the exposed part of the gut and observe the activity of the digestive glands. His method of 'sham feeding', in which an opening is made in the animal's throat so that food entering through the mouth would not reach the stomach, allowed him to the observe the effect of food in the mouth on the secretion of digestive juices elsewhere in the gut. Using this technique, he was able to show that the taste of food in the mouth causes the release of gastric juices in the stomach.

Pavlov changed the emphasis and direction of his research, away from digestion to the analysis of conditional reflexes following the publication of a paper by two British physiologists, William Bayliss and Ernest Starling. They coined the term 'hormone' to refer to a kind of chemical signal that seemed to be crucially important in the control of the digestive system. Pavlov had assumed that signals between the mouth and the secretory glands in the stomach were controlled by the nervous system. Bayliss and Starling's work indicated that chemical messages are also involved. Work on the conditional reflex led Pavlov to the psychology of learning where, as a careful experimenter, he made basic advances to learning theory. (Pavlov's work is often quoted as the 'conditioned reflex' but the term 'conditional reflex' is a better English language translation because it conveys the importance of the contingent association between the neural stimulus and the response-evoking stimulus.) He had started work on his 'psychical secretions' about the same time that Thorndike was commencing his own studies on animal learning but Pavlov credited him with laying the necessary experimental

244 Ivan Petrovich Pavlov

groundwork: 'We may fairly regard the treatise by Thorndyke (sic), The Animal Intelligence (1898), as the starting point for systematic investigations of this kind' (Pavlov, 2010, p. 6).

The essential characteristic of Pavlovian or classical conditioning is that a previously neutral stimulus, such as the sound of a bell, can elicit a response, such as salivation, because of its association with a stimulus, such as food, that automatically produces the same or a very similar response. The food can be regarded as an unconditioned stimulus and the salivation, an unconditioned response. Presentation of the neutral stimulus, the bell, would not elicit the same response. However, if the sound of the bell is presented just before the food it will, over several trials, elicit a salivatory response. At this point, the bell is referred to as the conditioned stimulus and the salivation, the conditioned response. This simple but ingenious paradigm allowed Pavlov to explore learning mechanisms by asking, for example, whether a conditioned response could be elicited by presenting stimuli that were similar but not identical to the unconditioned stimulus. He found that it could, a process referred to as generalisation. Using the same paradigm, he explored the capacity of an animal to recognise differences between stimuli, a process referred to as discrimination, and what happens when repeated presentation of the unconditioned stimulus is not followed by the presentation of food – that the unconditioned salivatory response diminished until it completely disappeared, he referred to as the process of generalisation. Pavlov noted that the same principles could be applied to understanding human learning. For example, a child who is bitten by a dog might develop a fear response to that dog and, through a process of generalisation, acquire a fear of all dogs. However, by gradually reintroducing her to dogs that never bite, her fear would decline first through a process of discrimination – she would come to fear only the type of dog that first bit her – and finally the fear might be extinguished. During the 1930s, Pavlov began to use the concept of the conditional reflex to explicate human psychosis, which he regarded as a device by which people attempt to isolate themselves from the outside world. This led to changes in the way psychiatric patients were treated: they were placed in monotonous surroundings in order to moderate the environmental stimuli for psychosis. (Incidentally, Edwin B. Twitmeyer, a PhD student working at the University of Pennsylvania, had independently observed that the patellar or knee-jerk reflex could be conditioned to the sound of a bell. He reported his findings at the American Psychological Association convention of 1904, but the general lack of interest among delegates discouraged him from pursuing this line of work any further.)

Pavlov's identification of the conditional reflex was the impetus for an enormously productive programme of work – referred to by some as his physiology factory – which led him to postulate the existence of a complex neurophysiological system of cortical excitation and inhibition. He argued that these two fundamental processes formed the basis of all behavioural reactions. A balance was required between the two processes for an organism to behave in an adaptive manner. He went on to argue for the existence of three fundamental dimensions in neural activity: (i) the absolute strengths of excitation and inhibition, (ii) the balance between the two processes, and (iii) their susceptibility to change in a particular nervous system. These ideas, which started in his analysis of individual differences among dogs and inaugurated the field of temperament research, also informed his theory of personality types. His classification of the types of higher nervous activity, which was based on the neurological dimensions of excitation and inhibition, was mapped onto Hippocrates' four classes of temperament: Melancholic – weak in both excitatory and inhibitory processes, Choleric – dominant excitatory processes, Phlegmatic – a state of equilibrium, and Sanguine – balanced with lively external behaviour.

Pavlov's theoretical framework is essentially an anatomy and physiology of the nervous system, but it seemed to psychologists to offer the missing link between behaviour and the nervous system. Some set about incorporating his findings into their respective systems, although it was not too long before the cracks started to appear: Pavlov's purpose was to understand the nervous system, not to formulate a psychological theory based on his findings. In this regard, he differed from his contemporary and competitor Vladimir Bekhterev, who was less cautious in his approach and efforts to build a conceptual framework between psychology and physiology. Bekhterev was probably better positioned to take on the task because his training had been somewhat broader than Pavlov's and included studies with Wundt, the neurologist du Bois-Reymond and the French psychiatrist Charcot. Pavlov regarded the views espoused by Watson as oversimplified applications of his own position:

> The psychologist takes conditioning as a principle of learning, and accepting the principle as not subject to further analysis, not requiring ultimate investigation, he endeavours to apply it to everything and to explain all the individual features of learning as one and the same process.
>
> (1932)

Indeed, by the time Clark Hull was devising his mathematical representation of learning, psychologists were *de facto* pursuing an account of conditioning without reference to the nervous system.

Thorne and Henley (2001) have suggested that Pavlov's impact on psychology can be more clearly understood by structuring his influence in three phases. The first phase is associated with the impact of Pavlovian conditioning on the emergent American school of behaviourism; the second is identified with the attempts of Hull to develop a formal, mathematical model of learning; and the third phase can be discerned in the differentiation of Pavlov's classical conditioning from Thorndike's instrumental conditioning and the emergence of 'two-factor' theories of learning. These theories postulated that classical theory is teaching an animal about significant environmental events, whereas instrumental conditioning enables an animal to learn to manipulate aspects of those events. Thus, Gray concluded: 'The influence of Pavlov on the study of animal learning is stronger and more direct now than at any time in the past; and it appears to be growing' (Gray, 1979, p. 127). That his assessment was not over-stated is supported by two examples. First, R.A. Rescorla received the American Psychological Association's 1986 Distinguished Scientific Contribution award for his innovative work on Pavlovian conditioning and its relevance to the tenets of associationist philosophers. Second, Jan Strealau's studies of temperament, conducted within a Pavlovian framework, demonstrated the importance of temperamental features in regulating the stimulative value of an organism's surroundings and the role of behaviour in controlling the need for stimulation.

Ivan Pavlov's major writings

Pavlov, I. (2001). *Selected works*. Forest Grove: University Press of the Pacific.
Pavlov P. I. (2010). Conditioned reflexes: An investigation of the physiological activity of the cerebral cortex. *Annals of Neurosciences, 17*(3), 136–141. https://doi.org/10.5214/ans.0972-7531.1017309

Further reading

Catania, A. C., & Laties, V. G. (1999). Pavlov and Skinner: Two lives in science. *Journal of the Experimental Analysis of Behavior, 72,* 455–461.
Gray, J. A. (1979). *Pavlov.* London: Fontana.
Thorne, B. M., & Henley, T. B. (2001). *Connections in the history and systems of psychology.* Houghton Mifflin.
Todes, D. P. (2001). *Pavlov's physiology factory.* Johns Hopkins University Press.

40 Jean Claude Piaget (1896–1980)

Piaget pioneered the study of the development of thinking and problem solving in children based on innovative methods of enquiry that focus on the analysis of errors for what they reveal about the child's conception of the world.

Piaget was the first child of Arthur Piaget, a Professor of Medieval Literature at Neuchâtel University, and Rebecca Jackson. Born in Neuchâtel, Switzerland, his early education was based upon the system devised by Friedrich Fröbel, who developed the first age-sequenced cognitive materials for use with young children. While a pupil at Neuchâtel Latin, he developed an interest in the natural history of molluscs and in 1907 started a programme of work in collaboration with Paul Godet, Director of the Natural History Museum at Neuchâtel. Such was his reputation that in early 1912, Maurice Bedot, Director of the Natural History Museum at Geneva, offered him a position as an assistant in malacology, apparently unaware of the fact that Jean was only 15 years old. Jean explained why he had to decline the invitation but went on to study natural sciences at the University of Neuchâtel and completed his doctorate there. A semester spent at the University of Zürich, where he attended lectures by the eminent Swiss psychiatrist Eugen Bleuler and by Jung, sparked an interest in psychiatry and psychoanalysis. He left Switzerland to spend a year working in France at the Ecole de la rue de la Grange-aux-Belles, a boy's school established by Binet and later directed by Théodore Simon. While working there, he conducted his first experimental studies of children's thinking and reasoning, which he structured around the way they solved problems in Simon's new tests of mental ability. He was particularly struck by the fact that young children's answers to some of the items were qualitatively different from those of older children. A superficial interpretation of these differences would lead one to conclude that the answers given by the younger

DOI: 10.4324/9781003229179-41

children were simply wrong and that, as they matured, they would learn the right answers. However, Piaget considered otherwise and the errors made by children suggested to him that the younger ones answered the questions differently because they thought differently. This approach to understanding children's thinking was to become a core feature of his developmental theory of children's thinking processes.

In 1921, the Swiss psychologist Eduoard Claparède appointed Jean Director of Studies at the Rousseau Institute in Geneva. He married Valentine Châtenay 2 years later and they had three children: Jacqueline, Lucienne and Laurent. Drawing on his earlier experience at Grange-aux-Belles, he used a quasi-clinical method of investigation, based on careful questioning of the child during the course of a task, to study the intellectual development of his own children. His observations comprised the core of much of his empirical research. The ideas and arguments that guided the formulation of his theory of cognitive development were also vital to the founding of a new discipline called 'genetic epistemology', a term coined by the American developmental psychologist J.M. Baldwin. Although Piaget's reputation and influence stem directly from his work in child psychology, he regarded his major contribution as relating to the theory of knowledge directed upon its genesis or development (hence 'genetic epistemology'). In 1955, he founded the International Center for Genetic Epistemology and was its director until his death.

It is possible to delineate three general views on the development of thinking. One view contends that there is little 'intellectual development' and no profound underlying changes in the way a human being thinks from infancy through to adulthood. This view, as articulated by radical behaviourism, contends that it is all a matter of learning based on associations. A second school of thought can be traced to Vygotsky and the claim that humans are born with considerable intellectual abilities. Their major developmental tasks are to do with coming to terms with the cultural artefacts that permeate the environment given to them. The third is represented by Piaget who argues that for a child to come to terms with the world around them, they must acquire a repertoire of intellectual mechanisms that will allow them to organise their thoughts and experiences and make reliable predictions about what will happen in the world around them. As a genetic epistemologist, Piaget set out to answer the question 'How does knowledge grow?' His 'central argument is that if rational knowledge is a fact, its development must be at least partly rational during child development and the history of science. Piaget's research programme characterizes the sequences and mechanisms by which rational knowledge develops' (Smith, 1997,

p. 450). His explanation for the growth of knowledge contends that knowledge is a progressive construction of hierarchically embedded structures. The structures supersede one another by a process of inclusion of simpler logical modes to higher, more powerful ones. Thus, the way a child reasons about the world is initially qualitatively different from that of adults but becomes more adult-like as the child develops. His approach stresses the claim that children actively construct their own rational view of the world. The child's mind may be lacking intellectual mechanisms, but it is not a 'tabula rasa' (blank slate), as argued by philosophers such as Aristotle and Locke and radical behaviourists such as Watson. His theory uses two hypothetical constructs to describe two processes that are suggested to underlie the child's construction of the world: organisation and adaptation. To make sense of the world, a child both organises its experiences and adapts ways of thinking to new experiences. Piaget hypothesised that this process of adaptation consists of two sub-processes: assimilation and accommodation. Assimilation occurs when children incorporate new information into their existing knowledge. Accommodation occurs when children adjust the way they think about and solve problems in order to make sense of new information that challenges, and cannot be explained by, existing ways of thinking. Thinking develops through a number of qualitatively different age-related stages. It is the different way of understanding the world that makes one stage more advanced than another; knowing more information does not make a child's thinking more advanced in a Piagetian view. His theory of knowledge follows the rationalistic tradition in the importance attached to schemata, or thought structures, in determining a person's construction of reality. His books on the child's conception of space, time, cause, chance and morality reveal the influence of Kant's rationalist position on the categories of thought.

The following précis should be regarded as a sketch of a more elaborate exposition offered by Piaget. During the sensorimotor stage (0–24 months), infants construct an understanding of the world by co-ordinating sensory experiences (such as seeing and hearing) with physical, motoric actions – hence the term 'sensorimotor'. At the pre-operational stage (2–7 years), children begin to represent the world with words, images and drawings, but they lack the ability to perform mental operations. The concrete operational stage (7–11 years) is associated with the ability to perform operations, and logical reasoning replaces intuitive thought as long as reasoning can be applied to specific or concrete examples. For instance, concrete operational thinkers cannot imagine the steps necessary to complete an algebraic equation; this is too abstract for thinking at this stage of development. The formal operational stage (11–15 years) indexes a world that includes under-standing and explanation based on physical, concrete experiences but moves towards a qualitatively different way of thinking based on a capacity for high-level abstraction, theorising and a capacity for logi-cally driven problem-solving. Piaget's stages of cognitive development are sometimes wrongly depicted as a ceremonial progression with little individual variation from child to child. This is a misrepresentation of his position: knowledge is a progressive construction of hierarchically embedded structures, but there is enormous variety in the ways indi-viduals achieve that progression.

Equilibration is a mechanism used by Piaget to explain how children move from one stage of thought – one organised system of thinking – to the next. The shift occurs as children experience large amounts of cognitive conflict or a disequilibrium in trying to understand the world. Eventually, the child resolves the conflict and reaches a balance, or equi-librium of thought. Piaget suggests that there is considerable movement between states of cognitive equilibrium as assimilation and accommo-dation work together to produce cognitive change. For example, if a child believes that the amount of liquid in a bottle changes when it is poured into a container of a different shape, she might be puzzled. She might wonder how the amount of liquid could possibly have changed. In time she must resolve the puzzle through a qualitative change in the way she thinks. Conservation is Piaget's term for the consistent use of the criteria that define whether or not an instance is included within a concept. Conservation involves recognising that the length, number, mass, quantity, area, weight and volume of objects and substances do not change by transformations that alter their physical appearance. Children do not conserve all quantities or all tasks simultaneously. Empirical stud-ies indicate that the order of mastery is usually: number, length, liquid quantity, mass, weight and volume. 'Horizontal decalage' describes how similar abilities do not appear at the same time within a stage of thought development.

Piaget's theory has attracted considerable critical attention and pro-vided the impetus for rapid advances in cognitive developmental psy-chology. Some critics have focused on his view of stages as unitary, schematic structures of thought and the implication that there is a syn-chrony in cognitive development. This predicts that various aspects of a particular stage of thought development should emerge at about the same time. However, several concrete operational concepts do not appear in synchrony. For example, children do not learn to conserve at the same time they learn to cross-classify. Others have demonstrated that small changes in the procedures involved in a Piagetian problem-solving task sometimes have significant effects on a child's cognition. In other words, slight modifications in wording that appear not to substantially change the meaning of a question may prompt a child to provide significantly different answers. Clearly, this is not a fatal weakness in his theory, but it identifies one of the problems associated with any attempt to test it. More generally, it highlights the value of recognising that the intended meaning of a question may not be apparent to a child and the need to ensure that the child understands both the words used in a question and the intended meaning of those words. A third criticism points to the evidence that in some cases children who are at one cognitive stage – such as preoperational thought – can be trained to reason at a higher cognitive stage – such as concrete operational thought. This poses a problem for Piaget's theory, which suggests that such training works only on a superficial level and is ineffective unless the child is at a transitional point from one stage to the next. Possibly the greatest problem for his theory concerns his position on the causes of cognitive development. The veracity of his claim for the primacy of internal conflict as the main driver of cognitive development has yet to be established. The rate of progress on this will be contingent on the construction of an appropriate test.

Although the name Piaget is fundamentally linked with the developmental analysis of the child's way of thinking, his influence in other parts of psychology is often under-estimated. For example, the Hawthorne Effect refers to an enormously important series of studies in the area of industrial psychology. The studies were conducted between 1929 and 1932 in the Hawthorne works (Chicago) of the Western Electric Company. When the lighting was improved, production improved and when the lighting was further improved productivity was increased still further. When the lighting was worsened, the productivity gains remained or got even better. In order to understand why this could happen, the Australian psychologist Elton Mayo designed and managed a series of studies that included interviews with tens of thousands of employees. Mayo was familiar with Piaget's methods for interviewing children and transferred those to the Hawthorne industrial setting. There is a good deal of controversy surrounding Mayo's explanation for the Hawthorne effect but that should not detract from the importance of Piaget's influence in shaping the professional toolkit of industrial psychologists during the 1930s and 1940s.

Jean Piaget's major writings

Piaget, J. (1928). *Judgment and reasoning in the child* . Oxfordshire: Routledge & Kegan Paul.

Piaget, J. (1951). *Play, dreams and imitation in childhood*. London: Heinemann.

Piaget, J. (1952). *Child's conception of number*. Oxfordshire: Routledge and Kegan-Paul.

Piaget, J. (1953). *Origins of intelligence in the child*. Oxfordshire: Routledge and Kegan-Paul.

Piaget, J. (1954). *Construction of reality in the child*. Oxfordshire: Routledge and Kegan-Paul.

Piaget, J. (1958). *Growth of logical thinking*. Oxfordshire: Routledge and Kegan-Paul (with B. Inhelder).

Piaget, J. (1971). *Biology and knowledge*. Edinburgh: Edinburgh University Press.

Piaget, J. (1985). *Equilibration of cognitive structures*. Chicago: University of Chicago Press.

Piaget, J. (1989). *Psychogenesis and the history of science*. New York: Columbia University Press (with R. Garcia).

Piaget, J. (1991). *Towards a logic of meanings*. New Jersey: Erlbaum (with R. Garcia).

Piaget, J. (1995). Commentary on Vygotsky's criticisms. *New Ideas in Psychology, 13*, 325–340.

Further reading

Evans, R. (1973). *Jean Piaget, the man and his ideas*. Dutton.

Smith, L. (1996). *Critical readings on Piaget*. Routledge.

41 Jing Qicheng (March 3, 1926–September 29, 2008)

Jing Qicheng (also known as Jing, Q.C. and Ching, C.C.) was born on March 3, 1926, in Shenyang, Liaoning Province, China. As an infant, his family travelled to Japan for 2 years to study. His father finished his studies, he became a Chinese Government official (and later a wealthy banker) and in 1928 the family returned to what was then Japanese-occupied China. Qicheng's family moved farther North, settling in Beijing when Qicheng was about 4 or 5, where he completed most of his primary education. Qicheng describes himself as a boy who liked to use his hands. He had lots of hobbies that involved making and doing. As an amateur carpenter, he would not only try to create but also break apart to understand the mechanisms inside.

However, his childhood was once again interrupted by Japan's territorial expansion ambitions. Japan was increasingly dependent on oil and minerals. Shortages compounded with crippling tariffs on exports to the United States were creating a precarious economic situation. With rising unemployment and a downturn in the industry, and an eye to the abundance of minerals and oil in Northern China, Japan, who already had a firm foothold in Shandong, triggered a full-scale invasion. By 1931, they had grabbed large parts of Northern China, including the ports, then sequestered the area off from the rest of the country and created the puppet state of Manchuria.

The Chinese government in Manchuria left along with many Chinese citizens, and most refugees were moving towards rural areas in cities such as Szechuan and Yunnan provinces. Chongqing in Szechuan province became assigned as the temporary capital of wartime China and his father became stationed there, but Qicheng's parents were concerned about the impact of rural living on their children's education, so he and his sister were sent in 1938 to Hong Kong to the care of family friends. Hong Kong was a British Colony and considered relatively safe. His sister was sent to a girl's boarding school and Qicheng was sent to a

DOI: 10.4324/9781003229179-42

British boy's catholic boarding school (St. Joseph's College). The school taught and cared for a mix of Chinese, British, Portuguese-Macau and Spanish-Philippine students; it was his first multi-cultural environment and where he began to learn English. A language he found much easier to master than the native Cantonese. Speaking English enabled him to 'get along'.

On December 7, 1942, the Japanese invaded Pearl Harbour, and the following day Japanese ground forces, aeroplanes and warships began to bombard Hong Kong for 17 days. Qicheng could not get out and had to take shelter with his sister at the house of his father's friend. He recalls this as a harrowing time; people were starving, there was no water, looting was common and the Japanese military could take with impunity rings, watches and other valuables as well as committing atrocities such as summary executions, dismemberment, rape, and the sexual enslavement of women. Somehow, they managed to get out of his father's friends' home to a safe house and then onto a cargo ship, 9 days later they escaped to Shanghai. They eventually managed to join their mother in Shanghai (his father was still in Chongqing with his two younger sisters), and they moved back to Beijing to live in the Jing family's large feudal house with his grandfather, uncles, siblings and other family members. From there, he went to university at Fu Jen Catholic University, Peking (now Beijing).

Qicheng's high school education held him back briefly. He had not completed his education because of the Japanese invasion but was able to take an entrance exam in psychology. And thus, Jing Qicheng's career as a psychologist began. Fu Jen University was run by German missionaries; it had a German rector and largely German staff, which meant that the university was left largely untouched during the Japanese occupation. The psychology department was run by Joseph Goertz, a student of the experimental psychologist Johannes Lindworsky, and as such the department was well stocked with chronoscopes, memory drums and tachistoscopes. Qicheng soon developed a passion for experiments, but lack of communication between other departments in China (and the rest of the world) stilted any inroads into his later specialisms in areas such as human factors.

Qicheng graduated from the Department of Psychology Fu Jen Catholic University, Peking (now Beijing) in 1947, and he carried out his graduate work at the Institute of Anthropology. There was no graduate department for psychology at Fu Jen, so anthropology enabled him to further develop his interest in psychology. For his master's thesis, he explored the relationships between prehistoric paintings and children's drawings. The thesis ended up somewhat challenging the recapitulation theory of J.M. Baldwin who had argued that development follows a pattern of phylogenetic development towards a perspective more palatable to theology. It was after all a Catholic University, and his tutoring professor was a catholic missionary.

The following year Qicheng married Xingan Wang, who was also a psychology student. The following year, the troops of the Communist People's Liberation Army arrived in Beijing and the Peoples' Republic of China was founded. Qicheng describes himself as being 'dispatched' with a group of Fu Jen master's graduates to the Chinese Academy of Sciences on the Northwest side of the Forbidden City. Over the following months, other academics, scientists and professors joined and were assigned to the Institute of Psychology. He remained there for the rest of his career.

With broad research interests in cognition (particularly the psychology of colour), ergonomics, developmental psychology and the study of the only child, Qicheng is possibly best known for his efforts towards the ideals of international psychology. An established experimental and theoretical psychologist, Qicheng made substantive inroads towards the recovery and reform of psychology in China after the devastating blows of the cultural revolution which imposed soviet principles on the Chinese Sciences (1966–1976).

The Chinese communist party gradually indorsed only Soviet models (largely Pavlovian models) of human behaviour. The dominance of this approach was reinforced through campaigns such as 'Learning-from-the-Soviet-Union' campaign, the 'Hundred Flowers' campaign whereby citizens were encouraged to openly express their opinions, which was swiftly followed by an ideological crackdown and the 'Anti-Rightist' campaign of the 1950s. As a result, classical conditioning became the dominant, politically correct and enforced orthodoxy across most subject areas but particularly in physiology, medical science, psychology, psychiatry, animal husbandry and education.[1] Jin Qicheng was one of the first to directly challenge the Chinese unquestioning devotion to classical conditioning and the associated anti-Western attitudes which fuelled it, arguing that 'psychology is international' and that 'the blindly anti-foreign attitude can only result in a loss for us' (Ching, 1980 cited in Yun, Haosheng, & Wendeng, 2012, p. 18).

Qicheng is often described as a psychologist who was able to explore the role of culture, influencing factors and the tough challenges that it brought to international psychology in an objective and fair way.[2] By providing leadership and subject matter expertise on Chinese psychology, his work was instrumental in demonstrating that culture had a significant role to play in the acceptance and integration of psychology into any society, for example, in the case of China, that the 'harder' aspects of Western psychology (e.g. the psychophysiological) was entirely compatible with Chinese culture, but that softer aspects, such as social psychology, was much harder to transplant but of significant value.

His theoretical position was that psychology could be largely divided into two groups: where human behaviour is passive and mechanical (mechanical), or where humans are more active (humanistic). The mechanical group is closely aligned with behaviourism models; it is more applicable to the experimental method and aligned to older philosophical traditions of associationism. Whereas humanistic approaches are more connected to the nature of humans and embrace the applied fields of social, clinical and counselling psychology (areas less developed in Chinese psychology). He argued that the future was not for Western or Eastern psychology, rather that international psychology would converge into a science that would reach a consensus that learned or associated behaviour and consciousness would blend, and while culture and history might play a role, psychology was in fact a family among other disciplines, and that those disciplines also had a role to play.

By publishing widely in his native country, advocating a critical borrowing from psychology outside of China, and by publishing in international journals such as the *American Psychologist* and the *International Journal of Psychology*, Qicheng was able to both improve the psychological exchange between China and the rest of the world, increase exposure to Western psychology in China and ultimately reform Chinese psychology. One of the most significant contributions was Qicheng's capacity to articulate the development of psychology in China to an international and largely unfamiliar audience. He took the reader through a journey from the roots of Chinese psychology and its relationships with Greek philosophy, Confucian, Buddhism, Jesuit missionaries and merchants and writers such as Marco Polo, demonstrating that there was in fact a long tradition of integrating foreign ideas into Chinese culture and psychology and that Chinese psychology had many original and valuable ideas which had influenced the rest of the world. He explored the development of psychology through the early part of the People's Republic of China (1949–1957), its expediential growth and development between 1958 and 1965, then the attack on psychology by the four Chinese Communist Party officials, the 'Gang of Four', protagonists of the Cultural Revolution (between 1966–1975) and then mapped the revival of psychology in the mid-1970s. He analysed the deviations that Chinese psychology had taken from the rest of the world, and what it might still learn from abroad. His work also highlighted the priority (or lack thereof) that psychology was given in areas experiencing economic hardship. Areas with high levels of industry and agriculture, science, technology and education benefited from a psychological presence, but where the standard of living was more depressed, resources that might provide interventions to support communities and individuals would be diverted towards the improvement of basic living conditions. Psychology was seen as an unimportant and perhaps a luxury, with the result that psychologists were often carrying out challenging work with limited resources.

Qicheng was a leader of the International Union of Psychological Science; he was the leading Chinese subject matter expert on Wundt, Watson and Pavlov and during the 1960s and 1970s (driven by the Chinese desire to develop a colourised television to compete with Western devices), he conducted original research in vision function and colour perception, an area in which China remains influential today.

The extent of his many achievements and accolades are recorded in 'An Appreciation' published in the *European Psychologist* (2012): In 1998, he was awarded an honorary fellowship by the Hong Kong Psychological Society and in 1999 he received the CPS Lifetime Achievement Award Chinese Psychological Society. Jing Qicheng also attained international recognition as a distinguished visitor at La Trobe University in Australia, Henry Luce Fellow at Chicago University in the USA, Fellow of the Centre for Advanced Study in the Behavioral Sciences, Visiting Professor at the University of Michigan, and Fellow of the New York Academy of Science. He has been a member of the American Association for the Advancement of Science, International Fellow of the American Psychological Society, Fellow of the International Association of Applied Psychology, and Fellow of TWAS, the academy of sciences for the developing world. He was honoured with the titles Honorary Research Scientist by the University of Michigan and Outstanding Scientific Worker by the China Association for Science and Technology, and he received the International Honorary Award by the American Psychological Society as well as the Award for Distinguished Scientific Contributions to Child Development from the US-based Society for Research in Child Development.

Nobel Prize winner Herbert A. Simon said that as an envoy of Chinese academic exchanges, Jing Qicheng's contributions to psychology in both China and the world far outweighed his.

Notes

1 Gao, Z. (2015). Pavlovianism in China: Politics and differentiation across scientific disciplines in the Maoist era. In H. Chiang (Ed.), Special issue "Ordering the social: History of the human sciences in modern China". *History of Science, 53*(1), 57–85.
2 Yun, Z., Haosheng, Y., & Wendeng, Y. (2012). Jing Qicheng (1926–2008): An appreciation. *European Psychologist, 17*(4), 344–346. https://doi.org/10.1027/1016-9040/a000130

Further reading

Wellman, H. (2007). *SRCD oral history Interview.* Institute of Psychology in Beijing Chinese Academy of Sciences, November 12th. Retrieved from www.srcd.org/sites/default/files/file-attachments/jing_qicheng_interview.pdf
Wen-Deng, Y., & Hao-Sheng, Y. E. (2009). Jing Qicheng's thoughts and practice of international psychology. *Acta Psychologica Sinica, 41*(9), 902–910.
Yun, Z., Haosheng, Y., & Wendeng, Y. (2012). Jing Qicheng (1926–2008): An appreciation. *European Psychologist, 17*(4), 344–346. https://doi.org/10.1027/1016-9040/a000130

Qicheng Jing's major writings

Ching, C. C. (1980). Psychology in the People's Republic of China. *American Psychologist, 35*, 1084–1089.
Ching, C. C. (1981). *Exchanges are of mutual benefit* (A conversation with Professor Chicheng Ching, a psychologist from the People's Republic of China.). Michigan: LSA, University of Michigan, 4.
Jing, Q. C. (1958). *Theoretical foundation of structuralism of Wundt and Titchener.* Beijing: Science Publishers.
Jing, Q. C. (1964). The historical background of behaviorism psychology. *Journal of Psychological Science, 2*, 1–8 [In Chinese].
Jing, Q. C. (1984). Psychology and the four modernizations in China. *International Journal of Psychology, 19*, 57–63.
Jing, Q. C. (1987). Psychology in China. In R. J. Corsini (Ed.), *Concise encyclopedia of psychology.* New York: Wiley.
Jing, Q. C. (1989). Recent developments of psychology in China. *Psychology Research, 60*, 117–121 [In Japanese].
Jing, Q. C. (1990). *Developing trends of modern psychology.* Beijing, China: People's Publishing House [In Chinese].
Jing, Q. C. (2000). International psychology. In K. Pawlik & M. R. Rosenzweig (Eds.), *International handbook of psychology* (pp. 570–584). London, UK: Sage.
Jing, Q. C. (2001). Psychology in China. In W. E. Craighead & C. B. Nemeroff (Eds.), *The Corsini encyclopedia of psychology and behavioral science* (pp. 287–289). New York: Wiley.
Jing, Q. C., & Fu, X. L. (1995). Factors influencing the development of psychology in China. *International Journal of Psychology, 30*, 717–728.

Jing, Q. C., & Fu, X. L. (2001). Modern Chinese psychology: Its indigenous roots and international influences. *International Journal of Psychology, 36,* 408–418.

Jing, Q. C., & Zhang, H. C. (1998). China's reform and challenges for psychology. In J. G. Adair, D. Belanger, & K. L. Dion (Eds.), *Advances in psychological science, Vol. 1: Social, personal and cultural aspects* (pp. 59–73). Hove, UK: Psychology Press.

Yang, W. D., & Ye, H. S. (2009). Jing Qicheng's thoughts and practice of international psychology. *Acta Psychologica Sinica, 41,* 902–910 [In Chinese].

42 John Carlyle Raven (June 28, 1902–August 10, 1970)

Developer of the most widely used nonverbal test of general human intelligence and abstract reasoning in the world.

John Carlyle Raven was born in Islington, London, in 1902 to John Raven, an umbrella maker, and Jane Elizabeth Martin. The couple were married in St Matthew's church in Westminster in 1894 and went on to have three children Phoebe Jane, Sara Edith and John Carlyle. We know very little about John's early life other than he struggled at school with Dyslexia. His work was always marked highly for creativity and content, but presentation was always poor, as such his teachers discouraged further academic study.

John Carlyle disagreed with this assessment of his future, but his father died prematurely in 1923, aged 54, leaving John with the task of providing for his older sisters and mother. To resolve this problem, John worked to convert the rooms in their Islington home into rooms for lodgers and as luck would have it, one of the lodgers married his sister. This happy event at least partially released him from family responsibility; John took up a position as a teacher at St. Probus School in Salisbury (1923), and he was soon made Assistant District Commissioner. Eventually in 1928, the family was stabilised to the point that he could start a formal education in psychology with Francis Aveling at Kings College, London. Even as a postgraduate, John Carlyle had little contact with Aveling. As an undergraduate, he became friends with Charles Spearman, who introduced him to the geneticists and mathematician Lionel Penrose. Spearman asked John Carlyle to deliver a letter to Aveling, and John sold himself instead. Lionel needed an assistant to help him in the investigation of mental deficiency and, in 1928, John agreed to join his team at the Royal Eastern Counties Institution in Colchester.

DOI: 10.4324/9781003229179-43

Penrose's exploration into the genetic and environmental determinants of mental defect relied mostly on the Stanford-Binet test of intelligence and required extensive fieldwork across East Anglia testing children and adults in homes, schools and workplaces. John struggled both with the cumbersome nature of the test and the testing constraints which included noise, time pressure and the management of parents who were always keen to assist their children. Unconvinced about the theoretical basis behind the test which lumped diverse constructs together, the results were nearly impossible to interpret. The sub-scales were too short to be reliable, and the overall score disguised individual strengths and weaknesses. John Carlyle also disagreed with the testing movement. It was not, he argued, the job of psychologists to measure and put people right, rather psychologists ought to be attempting to understand people and their problems.

When the work was completed at Colchester, he set about devising a different method of psychological measurement that would be more theoretically based and easier to administer and score. A test was needed that could measure intelligence throughout life course, from early years to older adults.

To compensate for his struggles with the written word, John also had a strong preference for diagrams over words, peppering his publications with figures that continue to fascinate students of dyslexia for decades. With a preference for pictures over written word, and convinced by Spearman's two factor model of intelligence, John began developing a model which would assess the two factors of g identified by Spearman. His method for the test's development is set out in his master's dissertation. The information is not so much a literature review in the usual sense, but the set of standards that the then non-existent test should meet.

He began working closely with Mary Elizabeth Wild, who would later become his wife. The couple met accidentally when Elizabeth was looking for someone to help create a fountain in her garden and a friend suggested that '*Raven would do that*'. They married in Salisbury in 1923 and went on to have three sons together, John Jr, Barton and Martin. John's mother Jane Elizabeth also lived with the family in their new home in Tendring, Essex until her death.

Mary was also a key support for John. Helping him improve the quality of his writing, which was challenged by his dyslexia. Then with a grant from the Darwin Trust, he and his wife set about developing a test based on the principles that John had set out in his master's thesis. A test that would eventually measure the desire and the ability of individuals to make sense of '*booming, buzzing, confusion*' (Raven, 2008, p. 22) and make meaning, what he termed 'eductive' ability.

John Carlyle Raven produced the first experimental version of his Raven's Progressive Matrices test in 1936, publishing in 1938. The test methodology applies what is now known as Item Response theory and analysis, which enabled researchers to improve the analysis of test results by obtaining a measure between an individual's performance on a given item and that items level of difficulty relative to the items on the test. There were two principal components to Raven's theoretical model. The eductive aspect of mental ability, which relates to making meaning and gaining insights from disparate pieces of information. For example, to master language, children need to progress from 'mark making' through to the complex integration of motor skills co-ordination, and then learning and integrating different sounds and shapes. The reproductive aspect of mental behaviour relates to mastery, being competent at recalling and reproducing information. The two are interactive, the ability to absorb information in the first place is dependent on being able to manage ambiguity and confusion. Using item response theory, it became possible to demonstrate that while test items differ, in this regard. Test takers would be required to integrate the ambiguous, to make meaning, but also apply sets of rules which increased in difficulty. The processes involved in problem-solving were cumulative, demonstrating that individuals with higher intelligence scores have more capacity to build on previous information, which extended their performance. Intelligence was thus a continuous process, rather than a sum on a particular test.

1939 was a significant year. John Carlyle was awarded Fellowship at the London Child Guidance Clinic and became psychologist to the Child Guidance Council, but as war was declared against Europe, the Raven family moved out of central London. The family moved into Larkspur cottage near Elmstead in Essex. It had no electricity, gas, or running water, but ever the outdoor enthusiast John Carlyle set about creating a smallholding to support the family. The farm was an escape from not only the dangers of London but also the impracticalities of war. The government were encouraging families that it was the patriotic thing to do, to put down their beloved pets. Countless pets were humanely destroyed, or simply thrown in canals. Millions were destroyed within the first few weeks. For the Carlyle family, Larkspur was a new world of chickens, goats and rabbits; hundreds of rabbits in different colours, which would later become hats, gloves and bed covers. The children, who were aged between 3 and 7, would walk the billy goats gruff down the cottage lane each day, tethering them to where the sweet grass grew. Until one day, to their horror, the sweet green grass was replaced by anti-aircraft guns. The tranquil Larkspur was right under the German flight path. The Luftwaffe, running short on aviation fuel, would regularly offload their cargo in the fields around their cottage. Bombs would fall so close that the fields became peppered with craters. JR Jr. recalls the stench of burning flesh when they hit the nearby cattle barn.

John Carlyle was a Quaker and a conscientious objector, but largely because he was of the conviction that war removed autonomy and that individuals followed orders without rational thought. He was not prepared to put himself in a situation where this could happen, and he directed his cause towards using his professional skills to support the war effort. He could, however, apply his skills and knowledge towards the war effort by studying the impact of stress and injury on human behaviour by taking up a fellowship at the London Child Guidance Clinic and joining the Mill Hill Emergency hospital team.

While working with the sick and injured, John Carlyle also began to collect additional test data that would enable him to predict success on army training courses. He began directing experiments for the Royal Army Medical Corps at Beckett's Park, in Leeds. Four thousand troops were tested in the first-ever large-scale psychological investigation and testing of British Army troops. The project was a success. The test's puzzle-solving nature overcame the challenges of numeracy and literacy in the troops and the absence of language enabled the test to be used across the world. Raven's Progressive Matrices became the army's standard psychological test and Hans Eysenck later used this work as an example to evidence that a single psychological test could provide as much information about candidates as an assessment centre.

In 1944, 1 year before the war ended, John Carlyle moved his family to Dumfries in Scotland to work at the psychological department of the Crichton Royal Institution, which was a mental hospital. The family lived in a roomy lodge house in the grounds of the hospital, but gradually the boys and their father constructed a three-roomed cabin. The boys and surprised guests would often find themselves accommodated there.

In Dumfries, John Carlyle could split his time between his children, his research interests and clinical work. He continued to seek ways about thinking about and assessing the broader application of individual differences, criticising the construct of personality and lobbying psychologists and psychometricians to change their models. The department at Crichton was a research, not a clinical department, so in order to create distance between the medical model, or indeed becoming drawn into clinical work, Raven had the physical department shifted into the centre of town.

Hans Eysenck had started his anti-Freudian offensive, attacking the creditability of psychoanalysis and all who sailed in her. His role at the Maudsley meant that their clinical programme 'brand' became synonymous with science and evidence, whereas the more interdisciplinary, psychoanalytical department at Tavistock was being held back in what was described as a narrow intellectual agenda. As key psychologists at the Maudsley and Tavistock took their feud to the British Psychological Society, Raven began his own gentler offensive. Drawing on his training in the sciences, psychometrics, therapy and an appreciation of the works of George Kelly, in an attempt to reduce polarisation, he began reminding psychologists of their role as clinicians:

> It is not the clinical psychologist's function to put other people right, either by treating them therapeutically or by fitting them into appropriate social situations. By trying to understand people we also change them; at the same time, if we try to change people or even think their conduct is pathological, we are less likely to understand them. For this reason, a clinical psychologist who desires not only to understand people but also to alter them is not only in danger of being pretentious; as psychologist he is less likely to become successful.
>
> (cited in Raven, 1997, p. 20)

In response, the board began to seek out someone who would deliberately secure this distinctive feature of psychology at Crichton. While John Carlyle Ravens carried out very limited work to demonstrate that Spearman's could be used to understand the nature of eductive ability, this work was carried on after his death by his son John Jr.

John Carlyle Ravens retired in May 1964, but his retirement was brief; he died on August 10, 1970, aged 68. He was working in his beloved garden. His wife had died 2 years previously. She had been suffering from a brain tumour since 1960. JC had spent several years caring for her, driving her back and forwards from Edinburgh for brain surgery and caring for her in-between. He had a brief year of happiness when he married Irene Hunter, his hospital housekeeper. The two would often plot together to accommodate visiting students, by concealing empty beds from NHS inspectors.

John Carlye's work on item-response theory created a paradigm shift in testing that went on to influence leading statisticians such as Lord and Novick and Georg Rasch. In addition to his many contributions to psychological testing, John Carlye was also a keen naturalist, particularly in human ecology. His son John, who carried on the work of his father, believes that his most pervasive motivation in life was elegant design. He was motivated to progressively create not only through the Progressive Matrices test but also through the recreation of evolving rock gardens. A fascination which continued until his death, John Carlye's work is carried on by his son John.

Responses to the Raven's test were initially cool, but following the acceptance of the armed forces, the test soon gained widespread adoption throughout the world. Its cultural neutrality has driven educational systems in Europe, Russia, Asia and South America to embrace Raven's Progressive Matrices; it is now the most widely used test in the world.

John Carlyle Raven's major writings

Raven, J. C. (1936). *Mental tests used in genetic studies: The performances of related individuals in tests mainly educative and mainly reproductive.* M.Sc. Thesis, University of London.
Raven, J. C. (1948). The comparative assessment of intellectual ability. *British Journal of Psychology, 39,* 1219.

Further reading

Raven, J. (1997). *Scotlands greatest psychologist.* Eye on Society. Retrieved from http://eyeonsociety.co.uk/resources/jcravenandcontemporarypsycology.pdf
Raven, J. (2000). The Raven's progressive matrices: Change and stability over culture and time. *Cognitive Psychology, 41*(1), 1–48.
Raven, J. (2008). Uses and abuses of intelligence: Studies advancing Spearman and Raven's quest for non-arbitrary metrics. In *The Raven Progressive Matrices Tests: Their theoretical basis and measurement model.* Budapest: Competency Motivation Project.
For a full list of Raven's work and other related resources, John Carlye's son has put together resources at eye one society. Retrieved from www.eyeonsociety.co.uk/resources/fulllist.html

43 Carl Ransom Rogers (January 9, 1902–February 4, 1987)

A humanistic psychologist, Rogers developed a non-directive or person-centred method of therapy.

Carl Rogers was born in Oak Park, Illinois, the fourth of six children. His father was a civil engineer and his mother, a devout Christian, nurtured a closely knit religious family environment. His formal education started with entry to the second grade because he was able to read before entering kindergarten. When he was 12, his family moved to a farm 30 miles west of Chicago, and his adolescence was spent in an environment characterised by self-discipline, order and independence. His early interests in the natural sciences led him first to the study of agriculture at the University of Wisconsin. After 2 years, he decided to enter the ministry and as part of his studies he acted as a pastor in a small church in Vermont. After graduating from Wisconsin in 1924, he married Helen Elliot against his parents' wishes. Following a trip to China and the Philippines with the World Student Christian Federation, he attended Union Theological Seminary (New York City) and later transferred to Teachers College, Columbia University, where he obtained a degree in clinical and educational psychology. The development of his clinical practice drew on diverse influences, including Otto Rank and John Dewey (the latter through the influence of W.H. Kilpatrick a former student of Dewey's), and his later emphasis on theorising from experience, belief in the potential of human action and the importance of considering the human organism as a whole can be traced to some of their ideas. For example, Kilpatrick is best known for 'The Project Method', a child-centred approach to learning and teaching that is similar to Roger's notion of client-centred therapy.

As an intern at the Institute for Child Guidance, Rogers was impressed by the emphasis on eclectic psychoanalytic techniques and

DOI: 10.4324/9781003229179-44

ideas and much of his later work demonstrates this strong commitment to eclecticism. In 1928, he joined the staff of what was later to become the Rochester Guidance Center, and following a period of 9 years as its director, he accepted a professorial position at Ohio State University. In 1945, he accepted a professorship at the University of Chicago, where he directed the Counseling Center and elaborated his client-centred method of psychotherapy. His successes during this period led him to be regarded as potentially posing the most serious challenge to the psychoanalytic community's dominance in American therapeutic practice. Twelve years later he returned to his alma mater, Wisconsin, where he held positions in the departments of psychology and psychiatry. While at Wisconsin, he used his approach and techniques with people with schizophrenia but without the same level of success he had achieved with student populations while at Chicago. In 1963, he moved to La Jolla, California, where he joined the staff of the Western Behavioral Sciences Institute and later helped to found the Center for Studies of the Person. He was actively involved with the work of the Center until his death in La Jolla, California, following surgery for a broken hip.

Carl Rogers is best known for the development of a method of psychotherapy called non-directive or person-centred and for his pioneering research on the therapy process. As a theoretician, Rogers was primarily concerned with the development and growth of the person and consequently his theory of personality is not as structurally explicit as many others. Two concepts are fundamental to his theoretical framework: the organism and the self. The organism is the physical creature that actually experiences the world. The totality of experiences constitutes the organism's phenomenal field. It is impossible to know another's phenomenal field except through empathic inference. Thus, according to Rogers, behaviour is not a function of external reality or of surrounding stimuli but of the phenomenal field. Within a phenomenological framework, it is necessary to determine how people can separate fact from fiction and construct a correct representation of reality. The only way to test reality is to check the correctness of the information on which one's hypothesis about the world is based against other sources of information. In other words, the person uses sensory information to supplement information stored from previous experiences. Through experience a part of the phenomenal field becomes differentiated – this is the self. Rogers defines this as the

> organized, consistent conceptual gestalt composed of perceptions of the characteristics of the 'I' or 'me' and the perception of the

relationship between the 'I' or 'me' to others and to various aspects of life, together with the values attached to these perceptions.

(1959, p. 200)

He distinguishes between the self as it is (the self-structure) and the ideal self (what the person would like to be). The degree of congruence between the self and the organism determines maturity and psychological well-being. When the person's perceptions and interpretations reasonably reflect reality as perceived by others, the self and the organism are said to be congruent. When there is a significant discrepancy, people feel threatened and anxious and tend to think and behave in stereotypical or constricted ways. The organism is thought to have a single motivating force, the drive to self-actualisation. Two important needs that are linked with the organism's drive to maintain and enhance its self are the need for the positive regard of others and the need for self-regard. In regarding the person as oriented towards growth, self-actualisation and fulfilment, Rogers is similar to Jung and Maslow.

Roger's chief concern is with understanding how incongruence develops and how self and organism can be made more congruent. In his person-centred psychotherapy, the therapist enters an interpersonal relationship with the client rather than adopting a role of doctor (as in the doctor-patient model) or scientist (as in the scientist-subject model). Therapists are expected not to hide behind a professional facade but to let the client know their own thoughts and feelings. Accepting the thoughts and feelings of the client unconditionally allows the client to explore increasingly strange and novel feelings in themselves. This 'unconditional positive regard' shares some features with the theological concept of 'grace' or unmerited favour, and the similarity may be due in some small part to his early theological training. Feeling safe is essential for the therapeutic process to work. Rogers came to the view that the therapeutic process is a model of all interpersonal relationships. He formulated a general theory of interpersonal relationships which he summarised as follows. The theory assumes that if (a) two people are minimally willing to be in contact, (b) each is able and minimally willing to communicate and (c) contact continues over time, then the greater the degree of congruence of experience and communication in one person, the stronger the tendency towards reciprocal communication and mutual understanding. His client-centred (later called person-centred) therapy is distinctive in three ways. First, it is founded on a belief in the capacity and potential of the client. Second, the therapeutic relationship is seen as pivotal – everything follows from the quality of the person-therapist relationship. Third, there is a belief that the progress of therapy follows a predictable pattern based on the interpersonal characteristics of the person-therapist relationship: when certain conditions exist, a certain process will occur.

The confidentiality of therapy sessions had acted as a barrier to research and fostered the growth of a mystique about counselling and psychotherapy. In order to test and develop his ideas, it was essential for Rogers to subject the therapeutic process to systematic scrutiny. In this regard, he was a pioneer in the scientific investigation of the therapeutic process. He introduced the practice of recording therapy sessions with the client's permission and demonstrated that this neither interfered with nor jeopardised the process or outcome. He applied content analysis procedures to classify and count a client's statements in order to explore hypotheses about their personality, self-concept and growth through the therapeutic process. Having a permanent record of a therapy session made possible the systematic analysis of therapist-client dialogue and opened up ways of identifying complex relationships that could not be detected in a session itself or from the therapeutic outcome. This approach was to inform the development of widely used rating scales for the measurement of process and change during psychotherapy.

Although many of Rogers ideas are now regarded as relatively uncontentious, his early efforts to publish and lecture on his person-centred ideas attracted considerable criticism. He was promoting the systematic quantitative investigation on therapeutic processes at a time when there were no examples of comparable research in psychoanalysis. What he was proposing was regarded by some as impossible because it was thought that therapists and their patients would never let anyone listen in on and measure their sessions. Thus, criticisms were directed against his efforts to re-define the role of the 'patient', the perceived threat to the integrity of the therapy session by the use of recording apparatus, his relative neglect of unconscious processes and his efforts to de-mystify the psychotherapeutic process. Rogers argued that diagnostic measures tend to be inadequate, prejudicial, and often misused. His policy of eliminating them from the therapeutic process was regarded by some as disturbing and profoundly unwise. His championing of 'non-directive' therapy was often dismissed as conceptually muddled and impossible to attain. However, towards the end of his career, he introduced a pragmatic caveat to his position on unconditional positive regard:

> I have learned that in any significant or continuing relationship, *persistent* feelings had best be expressed. If they are expressed as *feelings*, owned by *me*, the result may be temporarily upsetting but

ultimately far more rewarding than any attempt to deny or conceal them.

(1980, p. 44)

Much of the disapproval of Rogers' ideas and work has diminished with the growth in interest in comparative analyses of different therapeutic processes, and the incorporation of person-centred sympathies in a wide range of therapies, although the somewhat naive phenomenology underlying his theory of the person continues to attract criticism. (Phenomenologists place great emphasis on examining conscious experience while trying not to be influenced by expectations or pre-conceptions.) Moreover, the successes of others, notably, Heinz Kohut, in integrating many of Roger's ideas into Kohout's own version of psychoanalysis were important in achieving a rapprochement between humanistic psychology and psychoanalysis.

Rogers' numerous contributions can be summarised as follows: (1) He developed a model of psychotherapy which is built around a growth model, rather than a medical model; this model is based on the hypothesis that the individual has within him/herself the capacity for self-understanding and self-direction; it demonstrates that these capacities are released in a relationship with certain definable qualities, and it incorporates the view that the human organism is basically constructive and trustworthy. (2) He formulated a theory of the necessary and sufficient conditions which initiate a definable process in a therapeutic relationship and the changes in personality and behaviour which occur as a result of this process. (3) He developed an approach to therapy characterised by the terms 'non-directive', 'client-centred' and 'person-centred'. (4) He lifted the veil of mystery from psychotherapy and opened it to scrutiny and study, by recording therapeutic interviews. (5) He completed a number of important studies on the process and outcome of therapy, and the connection between the qualities in the relationship and the changes that occur. (6) He encouraged the application of the dynamic principles learned in therapy to a wide variety of fields: teaching and learning, marriage relationships, family life, intensive groups, administration and management, resolution of conflict and community development.

Carl Roger's major writings

Rogers, C. R. (1942). *Counseling and psychotherapy; newer concepts in practice.* Boston: Houghton Mifflin.

Rogers, C. R. (1951). *Client-centered therapy; its current practice, implications, and theory.* Boston: Houghton Mifflin.

Rogers, C. R. (1957). The necessary and sufficient conditions of therapeutic personality change. *Journal of Consulting Psychology, 21,* 95–103.

Rogers, C. R. (1959). A theory of therapy, personality, and interpersonal relationships: As developed in the client-centered framework. In S. Koch (Ed.), *Psychology: A study of a science, formulations of the person and the social context* (Vol. 3, pp. 184–256). New York: McGraw Hill.

Rogers, C. R. (1961). *On becoming a person.* Boston: Houghton Mifflin.

Rogers, C. R. (1980). *A way of being.* Boston: Houghton Mifflin.

Further reading

Cohen, D. (1997). *Carl Rogers. A critical biography.* Constable.

Kirschenbaum, H. (1979). *On becoming Carl Rogers.* Delacorte Press.

Rogers, C. R. (1967). Autobiography. In E. G. Boring & G. Lindzey (Eds.), *A history of psychology in autobiography* (Vol. 5). Appleton-Century-Crofts.

Thorne, B. (1992). *Carl Rogers.* Sage.

44 Hermann Rorschach (November 8, 1884–April 2, 1922)

Rorschach's childhood and education in art drove the development of a set of ink-blots that were thought to be effective in the evaluation of unconscious parts of the subject's personality.

The German poet and physician Justinus Kerner was losing his sight when he invented klecksography (circa 1879); the art of dropping ink onto paper and making intriguing shapes by folding the paper in half. Because of the human tendency to see patterns in randomness, these patterns often seem to resemble concrete objects and Kerner would elaborate on these images, turning them into people and objects then using them to illustrate his poems.

These patterns caught the attention of psychologists such as Alfred Binet and Victor Henri as early as 1885. They suggested that such shapes could be used in the study of involuntary imagination, which is a cognitive methodology that uses imagination as the modus for the bridge between the conscious and unconscious. From Binet, this idea spread to the intelligence theorist's practitioners who started to explore the extent to which the patterns could form an instrument for testing. By 1910, there was an 'ink-blot' type test in the Manual of Mental and Physical tests. It was, however, the Swiss psychiatrist Hermann Rorschach who went on to create possibly the most recognisable psychological test of all time.

Hermann Rorschach was born in Wiedikon Zürich, Switzerland, to Ulrich and Philippine (nee Wiedenkeller). Ulrich was a painter and teacher. He had a minor speech impediment which he could overcome. but it could often make him appear unusually reserved; he was, however, known to be a kind-hearted gentleman. Ulrich's parents had been embroiled in constant bickering to the point that Ulrich was convinced his parents never loved one another. Creating a loving, stable family

DOI: 10.4324/9781003229179-45

home was fundamental to him, and he married Philippine who was a warm, loving, energetic mother who was full of mirth and merriment. The couple had four children: Klara (1883) who died at 6 weeks old, Hermann, Anne and Paul. Ulrich was an involved father for the times; he would make special efforts to read to the children, take them on long walks explaining the history of old buildings, take them butterfly hunting and write plays in which the children would act.

Hermann grew up on the banks of the Rhein in the Renaissance city of Schaffhausen. When Anne was born, they moved to a larger home on the Geissberg mountain, where they lived for 3 or 4 years, and Hermann grew up mesmerised by natures surprises. Hermann attended the Schaffhausen Gymnasium from 1898 to 1904. It was German tradition that fraternity students would receive nicknames. It has been said (Murphy, 2004) that so passionate was Rorschach about the pastime of klecksography that his fraternity friends called him 'Klexs' 'inkblot', however, an alternative explanation was that Hermann's was being praised for his drawing skills (Searls, 2017): *klecksen* also means to daub.

'Klexs' performed well at school, despite suffering from a much-reduced financial situation in comparison to his peers who were from prominent Swizz families. He began to show an early interest in transformational experiences, such as putting yourself in another's frame of mind, including a plea for gender equality. He created whimsical artworks and delivered lessons on Darwin, arguing that his work should be decidedly and affirmatively taught to children. By the end of his school years, he was already working as a tutor.

This period also saw the tragic death of both of his parents. In the summer of 1897, the Philippines was found to be suffering from diabetes. In an age before insulin, treatments were largely based on a starvation diet; little could be done, and his mother died after four bedridden weeks. One year later, Ulrich announced he would marry their Aunt Regina, Philippine's younger half-sister, and Hermann's godmother. The children did not receive the news well, but the marriage brought a brief period of happiness to the Rorschach family and a new baby, whom the children affectionately called Regineli. Poor Ulrich, however, was stricken by lead poisoning from his early career as a Journeyman painter. He was suffering from periods of fatigue and dizzy spells, which soon developed into depression and delusions. He died in the early hours of June 8, 1903. Hermann was also very ill with a severe lung infection. He was too ill to attend his father's funeral.

Watching his parents suffering and being unable to do much were powerful motivators that influenced Hermann's desire to become a doctor, but for now Hermann had no time for his own grief. He and his siblings were about to experience a life very different from the loving, kind family life filled with imagination and joie de vivre. Regina was widowed without a pension. Strict almost to the point of cruelty, she neither seemed to understand her step-children, nor have the courage to appreciate their different personalities and needs. The family home was restrictive and kept deliberately cold with the children's hands turning blue on occasions; there was no playtime, only constant chores. Hermann was now 18 and had to grow up fast becoming father to his siblings and an emotional crutch to his Stepmother. Hermann, however, held onto the *talent for living* inherited from his father.

A year after his father's death, the family had finally scrapped together sufficient funds for Hermann to attend University in Zurich to study medicine. Zurich was a thrilling city to live in at that time, full of multicultural influences, anarchists and revolutionaries. Vladimir Lenin was in exile and the Russian influence was prevalent. Hermann had a passion for Russian culture and life. He had mastered the language in 2 years, without tuition and held Russian women in great esteem. He was a firm friend of the head of the Ivan Mikhailovich Tregubov, who was a close friend of Leo Tolstoy and head of the pacifist group Dukhobors.

His medical school schedule was punishing, but Hermann made time for language, art, reading and conversation. He was a competent student, who loved life and still obtained the best academic results in his year. This was a dynamic time for the field of medicine and psychology. Zurich was the centre for work which transformed the understanding and treatment of mental illness with advances coming from psychiatrists such as Freud and Jung. But these transformations were not without their feuds and Hermann Rorschach developed a pragmatic sanction towards psychoanalysis; he practised it and taught it, but always clarifying what he felt it could do and it could not do. He had no interest in paranormal psychology. Freud, Jung and other leading psychiatrists at the time studied séances and other spiritual mediums to attempt to bridge the unconscious. But he did revisit techniques such as word association, which had been largely left behind by Jung. The exploration of symbols and cultural phenomenon which replaced it, the myths, religions, art and the Jungian 'energy-life' were a fascination but also a technique that he found he could apply in attempting to diagnose the causes of mental illness and interpret the mind. For Hermann Rorschach, the future of psychology would be driven by the nature of perception, and Zurich was the hub of where psychoanalysis was receptive to new developments.

In the spring of 1906, Rorschach was finally practising medicine and feeling some repugnance towards the gauche and, on occasions, discourteous behaviour of his peers to their patients, who were often of poor social standing if not, in fact, completely impoverished. '*We have to be cold*' he wrote '*but to be crude about it, to turn into moral idiots, no, physicians don't have to do that*' (p. 54). The attitude from his peers and not unsurprising distrust of his patients contributed to a general feeling that Rorschach had had enough. He wanted to move away and began to take advantage of the opportunities that advanced medical school students had for study in other institutions, alternating his time between Zurich, Berlin and other short-term posts across Switzerland. His time in Berlin was not entirely pleasant; he found it cold, the society dull and conformist and the spiralling metropolis unhealthy so in July 1906 he travelled from Berlin for the broader horizons of Moscow.

In Moscow, Rorschach attended cultural and political events, experienced the panorama from the Kremlin tower and the silence of 25,000 sledge rides. The Russians took him out of himself, and when the time came to return to Western Europe, it was a considerable comedown but his developing relationship with Olga Stempelin gave him a way to live. Olga was from Kazan, in the present-day Republic of Tatarstan, Russia, and had first met Hermann as a medical student in 1906. Their relationship had slowly developed, and they became engaged in 1909. Olga returned to her home town to work with cholera patients in 1908 and as soon as his final exams were completed, Hermann followed her for a permanent life in Russia, where he could make a better income and pay off his debts. However, the process of securing his credentials proved endlessly bureaucratic, and Hermann and Russia began to fall out of love. Hermann's disillusionment was so great that he even went to the point of expressing complete disapproval of his sister's Russian love interest based on what he called the reactionary nature of the Russian state. He stayed 5 months before finally returning to Switzerland to set up practice in the Münsterlingen Clinic while Olga remained in Russia for a further 6 months. They finally married in Geneva on April 21, 1910. They went on to have two children, Elizabeth, born in 1917, and Ulrich, born in 1919.

One year after his marriage to Olga, Rorschach started his first experiments with inkblots. His first blots were not standardised in any way; he developed them afresh at each new presentation. Then, gradually he and his friend and schoolteacher Konrad Gehring began annotating the blots, recording what had been observed. When the blots were tested on school children, the results were uninteresting. The students rarely saw much in them; however, when he showed them to psychiatric patients, they saw much more, and Rorschach began to explore their use as a bridge between what the patient was seeing and what the psychologist could explore. This work was, however, paused. Hermann had gone as far as he could with it, and he needed to complete his MD dissertation (supervised by the eminent Swiss psychiatrist Paul Bleuler who coined the term 'schizophrenia'). The topic dissertation was not entirely unrelated. 'On Reflex Hallucinations and Related Phenomena' is the study of the connections between what we see and what we feel. An exploration of the cross-sensory perceptions that occur in such conditions as Proustian memories (memories triggered by tastes, smells or sounds) and synaesthesia, which is the merging of senses which are not usually connected. In 1913, Hermann was promoted and transferred to Münsingen, near Bern. Olga remained in Münsterlingen as she had her own medical career to pursue. In Bern, the focus of his work on perception began to broaden into an examination of the interplay between psychology and culture and the recognition that people see the world in different ways.

Finally, in 1914, Hermann tackled the Russian bureaucracy and was permitted to take the Russian state medical examinations. He and Olga left Switzerland for Moscow at a time when new cultural and scientific movements were sweeping across the county. He was offered a post at a leading psychoanalytical clinic in Kryukovo which treated voluntary patients suffering from nervous conditions. In this peaceful, rural setting, patients would receive treatments such as hypnosis, suggestion, rational emotive therapy and psychoanalysis. Here, Hermann brought his exploration of synaesthesia, visual art and self-expression to the study and treatment of mental illness, but he still struggled to settle in the unpredictability of the Russian culture and Hermann left once again to settle in Switzerland, this time for good. Olga was reluctant to leave and it was almost a year before she finally joined her husband and when she finally returned, they moved again, this time to Herisau, in the northeast of Switzerland, where the family finally found somewhere that they could call home; their gypsy wanderings had come to an end.

His years of travelling gave Rorschach more breadth of experience than most of his peers. This had developed him into a creative problem solver who, had begun, through his Russian experiences, to make connections between art and science and he had developed a deep understanding of the power of visual imagery in the exploration of psychological phenomenon. For example, he had begun to make significant breakthroughs with seriously ill patients by providing them with art supplies. For most patients, however, talking about pictures was easier than making them.

The Great War and the nationalistic rivalry in Switzerland were at their height. These years brought significant financial burdens to the family and Hermann supplemented his meagre income by making furniture and toys (more often for his own children). Not all was well within the family and Hermann's late-night working would lead to repeated arguments. Olga had a fiery and violent temper who would throw crockery to the point that the kitchen wall was permanently stained with coffee. Hermann was also frustrated by his inability to serve

> now it's the Germans duty to kill as many Frenchmen as possible, and the Frenchmen's duty to kill as many Germans as possible, while it's our duty to sit here right in the middle and say, 'Good morning' to our schizophrenic patients.

As asylums began to be requisitioned for the ever-growing war casualties, Hermann and Olga were eventually able to serve for a period of 6 weeks, helping in the transportation of 2,800 psychiatric patients from the French asylums. This was distressing work. While pioneering specialist care was provided in these newly acquitted War Hospitals, the cost to the mentally ill and their families was terrible. Asylums that were not requisitioned became overcrowded spreading distress and disease.

By 1917, Rorschach had returned to his obsession with improving his tests of free association. Visual imagery could go much deeper into the human psychology, and some recent work, although inconclusive, by a Polish medical student Szymon Hens reignited his focus. He was convinced that the way forward was better images, and he started to make hundreds of images, to find patterns that made some sense – images had something 'there'; images with meaningful spaces that would trigger description and insight. But also, images that would be devoid of craftsmanship or artistry. It was also important that the blots did not look like a test or a puzzle. His patients were distrustful and agitated so the blots had to elicit attention and not encourage the patient to be attentive to what they might mean. The symmetry of the inkblots was also key. Early blots were not constrained by regularity, they were shaped blots which were simply interesting or strangely shaped. Rorschach, however, made the crucial decision to create images that were pleasing to the eye and therefore encourage participation from the patient. To achieve this, he would hand paint ink patterns, then use horizontal/bilateral symmetry, a pattern which mirrors the symmetry of faces. In a second break from previous inkblots, Rorschach used colour. He was long aware of the connection between colour and affectivity. He wanted his inkblots to confront the viewer, so he applied the colour red.

These blots were only blots, and they could claim to be nothing more, but with imagination they became interpretations. The only issue with measuring the imagination was that some answers were imaginative, and some were not and when dealing with psychotic patients; it is impossible to determine if they are using their imagination or if they believe what they are seeing is real. Therefore, as Rorschach designed and developed his inkblots, he had to similarly figure out and design what his experimental work with those blots would actually do.

We know very little about the intermediate stages of the test development process because there are no surviving correspondences between 1917 and the summer of 1918, when he finally wrote up the remaining 10 inkblots and their testing process for publication. The framework was detailed with a focus on how the patients responded with extensive data analysis. He expanded on this manual later in his career, but never changed it.

Publication provided a challenge. His presentation of his findings to the Herisau medical association was poorly received and publishers all refused it. If it were not for the intervention of the respected psychiatrist Walter Morgenthaler, the blots may never have been published. A small Swiss publishing house, the House of Bircher, agreed to print the test. The printers, however, bungled the printing process and the crisp blots were turned into shades of grey. Rorschach resilient to this setback, decided that the spoiled inkblots presented an opportunity for further interesting interpretation. Response to the test was, however, at best indifferent and at worst, hostile. Only a few copies were ever sold and during the German Society of Experimental Psychology conference, William Stern delivered a scathing review, denouncing the test as contrived and superficial.

On the April 1, 1922, Hermann Rorschach was taken suddenly ill and by 10 am the following morning he had died from peritonitis and Olga estimated that the family made only about 25 Swiss francs from Hermann's labours. It would be another 13 years before the test would finally come to life.

The inkblot test is more of a method than a theoretical approach to the study of schizophrenia, which eventually evolved into a general test of personality. The theoretical routes are found in Freud's work on object relations which suggests that the way in which people relate to situations and other people has its roots in infancy where traumatic experiences become objects in the unconscious. The test it was hoped, would provide therapists with a route into unconsciously held motivations, beliefs, perceptions and emotions by using the clustering of responses from the test takers. Those responses would cluster on responses related to needs, base motives and conflicts that could be traced to real-life situations.

Carried by the Jewish-German Psychologist Bruno Klopfer, the cards eventually crossed the Atlantic to America in 1935, where they began their superlative journey. Klopfer fled the increasingly oppressive Nazi regime in 1933. En route to America, he spent a year with Carl Jung at the Zurich Psychotechnic institute where he learned about the cards. Klopfer had an exotic, magnetic and alluring personality. Often holding the cards so close people would think he was smelling them; he was quickly surrounded by a loyal following of Rorschach disciples. Debate and conversation about the test spread. Psychology students were in love with the test, psychology professors were less excited, popularity did not necessarily equate with helpfulness.

As the Rorschach cult grew, there were offshoots in approach, differences and warring factions. In the end, there were as many as five different methods of interpretation with no possibility of unification, but the test continued to triumph as Klopfer and his colleague Gustave Gilbert explored the minds of Hitler's inner circle during the Nuremberg trials.

The most comprehensive scoring system was published in 1974 by John Exner, with a growing emphasis that the test was not a test, but a method to understanding. But Rorschach confusion continued, and, in the end, tests considered more objective were gaining ground. By the 1990s, the method was struggling for survival. The final knock out blows were delivered by James Wood in his *Psychological Science* publication. Woods attacked the reliability and validity of the test and others soon followed, some calling for a complete moratorium of its use. The test routinely generated abnormal and dysfunctional labels for its test takers, and in no way represented normal people. There was almost no independent peer-reviewed evidence to support the claims of the Rorschach community yet child custody decisions, mental illness diagnoses, and employment decisions were based on it.

By 2001, the public were listening. The inkblots, to the dismay of Rorschach devotees, were released into the public domain. The publication by Wikipedia was described as reckless and cynical but welcomed by those who argue that pseudoscience has no place in psychology. Today, Rorschach bashing is an engrained tradition in psychology in Europe and the United Kingdom, where there is a strong tradition for complex theoretical modelling (for example, Freud, Broadbent, Eysenck). The test/method remains enormously popular in countries such as Japan, where the labour-intensive nature of Rorschach mastery contributes to its popularity. Despite the visual and cultural touchstone that is the Rorschach test, the first complete biography of Hermann Rorschach was not written until 2017.

Hermann Rorschach's major writings

Rorschach, R., with Lemkau, P., & Kronenberg, B. (Trans.). (1942). Psychodiagnostics: A diagnostic test based on perception, including Rorschach's paper the application of the form interpretation test. Published posthumously by Emil Oberholzer, Verlag Hans Huber, Switzerland. *JAMA*, *120*(13), 1076. https://doi.org/10.1001/jama.1942.02830480080033. Retrieved from www.igorgrzetic.com/wp-content/uploads/2011/02/Herman-Rorschsch-Psychodiagnostics.pdf

Further reading

Murphy, K. R. (2004). Assessment in work settings. In S. N. Haynes & E. M. Heiby (Eds.), *Comprehensive handbook of psychological assessment, Vol. 3. Behavioral assessment* (pp. 346–364). John Wiley & Sons, Inc.

Searls, D. (2017). *The Inkblots: Hermann Rorschach, his iconic test, and the power of seeing*. New York: Crown.

45 Roger Wolcott Sperry (August 20, 1913–April 17, 1994)

A Nobel Prize winner, Sperry devised ingenious experiments to examine the organization of the brain and the effects of breaking the connections between the left and right hemispheres.

Born in Hertford, Connecticut, Roger Sperry's father, Francis Bushnell, was in banking and his mother, Florence Kraemer Sperry, had a business school training. His father died when he was 11, leaving his mother to care for Roger and a younger brother Russell Loomis, who went on to pursue a career in chemistry. She supported the small family unit through her work as the principal's assistant at the local high school. He completed his early education in Elmwood, Connecticut, and William Hall High School in West Hartford, and it was during his time at William Hall his athletic talent was marked through his establishing an All-State record in the javelin. Sperry graduated from Oberlin College with a degree in English literature, after which he took a decisive turn to neuroscience while completing the 2-year MA programme in psychology at Oberlin. He attended Raymond H. Stetson's lectures in psychology and it was during one of those lectures that he got the idea for a paper he published some 20 years later, *On the Neural Basis of the Conditioned Reflex*. This short paper had significant theoretical implications for those interested in understanding central nervous system pathways and conditioned learning. Although Stetson specialised in motor phonetics and the analysis of rhythm, his breadth of scholarship encouraged an interest in philosophy and the humanities, as well as in empirical research. Sperry completed an MA in experimental psychology under Stetson's supervision.

While completing his PhD at Chicago with the developmental neurobiologist Paul A. Weiss, Sperry developed surgical techniques with the stereomicroscope, which he applied and developed in much of his later

DOI: 10.4324/9781003229179-46

work. Weiss had demonstrated that movement patterns of amphibia were self-created in the embryo and were apparently independent of specific nerve connections. Sperry felt Weiss's results in amphibians might be explained by a more specific type of control in the growth of nerve circuits than the theories of the time suggested. In his doctoral research, he examined related questions in rats, testing fibre connection versus impulse specificity theory by transplanting the insertions of extensor and flexor muscles of the limbs and cutting and interchanging their nerve supply. He found that this mammalian motor system, contrary to prevailing doctrine of the time, was hardwired and highly resistant to re-education. In other words, unlike Weiss's amphibia, the wrongly connected nerves or muscles continued indefinitely to produce maladaptive reversed limb movements.

Ramon y Cajal's descriptions of developing axons had suggested that growth cones moved in an ordered and directed manner, work that was to win him a share of the 1906 Nobel Prize with Camillo Golgi. However, it was Sperry's investigations of the spectacular regenerative capacity of axons in the visual pathway of amphibians that provided the strongest evidence that the formation of neural pathways in the brain is very precise. From 1941 to 1946, Sperry worked in Karl Lashley's laboratories, first as a Fellow of the National Research Council at the Harvard Biological Laboratories and then as a Fellow of Harvard University at the Yerkes Laboratories of Primate Biology in Orange Park, Florida.

In a series of brilliant experiments involving the rotation of eyes in amphibians, the optic nerves were sectioned and the eyes rotated through 180 degrees. Would vision be normal after regeneration or would the animal forever view the world as upside down and right-left reversed? The animals saw the world as upside down and reversed from right to left. No amount of re-learning could modify those responses (despite the remarkable capacity of the amphibian nervous system to regenerate when altered) suggesting that they were not organised through a learning process. The chemoaffinity theory he developed in the early 1940s attempted to account for his findings by linking the functional interconnections of neuronal elements to developmental principles of differentiation and cytochemistry. The existence and regulative role of preferential cell-to-cell affinities which he postulated were confirmed by scores of experiments motivated by this theory. Although a number of more recent studies have challenged the chemo-affinity theory, it still stands as one of the most important insights in developmental neurobiology.

It was during this period with Lashley that Sperry developed his ideas on the use of corrective nerve and muscle surgery for motor losses in humans. At that time, it was commonplace to surgically transplant nerves to antagonistic muscle groups and then to subject the patient to an intensive programme of rehabilitation designed to re-train the transplanted nerves. During a period of military service, he persuaded surgeons that motor-nerve transplants were being carried out too liberally in the mistaken belief that the human brain could easily learn any number of new uses for motor nerves after they had been surgically connected to foreign muscles. This resulted in significant modifications to the conventional treatment protocols of the time.

Shortly after moving to the Department of Anatomy at Chicago, Sperry began to work on the function of the corpus callosum, a part of the brain connecting the two hemispheres. 1949 brought mixed fortunes: he contracted tuberculosis from a monkey he had been dissecting in order to obtain tissues for nerve transplants; more happily he married Norma Gay Deupree and they had a son, Glenn, and a daughter, Janet Hope. Sperry's studies on the corpus callosum elucidated some of its major functions in interhemispheric memory transfer and eye-hand co-ordination. Joseph Bogen suggested that the split-brain work might be extended to humans suffering from severe epilepsy – earlier studies indicated that commissurectomy appeared to have little adverse impact on general levels of intelligence and motor co-ordination. The first callosalectomy was performed in 1962 on a World War II veteran with progressively worse fits. The procedure was followed by a dramatic reduction in the number and severity of the man's seizures. Later work on humans allowed investigators to compare cognitive abilities between the two separated halves of the brain, something which had been impossible before that time. The left half of the brain appeared to be superior to the right in analytical, sequential and linguistic processing, while the right half appeared to perform better in holistic parallel and spatial processing. Thus, his findings supported the German physiologist Gustav Fechner who, nearly a century before, predicted that splitting the brain would reveal two spheres of consciousness within a single cranium.

The idea that the right hemisphere was not an unconscious and minor part of the brain, subservient to the elaborate control of the left, was first articulated by Hughlings Jackson. However, the idea was largely ignored, except in the work of Russell Brain, Oliver Zangwill and some others, until Sperry demonstrated that the right hemisphere has its own consciousness and that it can be conscious and intelligent (e.g. in non-verbal and visual-spatial tasks) in a way different from the left. His work on human split-brain studies stimulated additional research by many of his prominent collaborators, such as Jerry Levy, who has suggested the reason the brain has two halves is that the cognitive processes for language and for spatial-perceptual functions are incompatible and need to be kept apart. Sperry's ground-breaking studies on the functional specialisation of the cerebral hemispheres won him a share of the 1981 Nobel Prize for Physiology or Medicine. Sperry's first published paper begins

> the objective psychologist hoping to get at the physiological side of behaviour is apt to plunge immediately into neurology trying to correlate brain activity with modes of experience . . . the result in many cases only accentuates the gap between the total experience as studied by the psychologist and neural activity as analysed by the neurologist.
>
> (Sperry, 1939)

Although this theme runs throughout Sperry's work, he returned to it very explicitly some 30 years later in his explorations of the emergence of consciousness from the unified brain. He proposed that subjective experience plays a principal role in brain function and in pursuing this argument, he contended that behaviourism and other reductionistic perspectives need to be replaced by a new approach to the concept of consciousness. In formulating this new approach, he placed considerable emphasis on the concept of 'emergence'. Emergence occurs whenever the interaction between two or more entities (e.g. atoms or molecules) creates a new entity with new laws and properties that did not previously exist. Consciousness in Sperry's view is a product of, and dependent on, neural activity but is nevertheless separate from it. It is generated by the activity of cerebral networks as an interacting entity. This newly emerged property – consciousness – continuously feeds back to the central nervous system, resulting in a dynamic process of emergence, feedback, newly emergent states further feedback and so forth. Thus, in Sperry's view, reducing consciousness to its separate neural components eliminates the emergent phenomenon of consciousness.

One might imagine that the original questions posed by Sperry would have long been settled. For example, how is it that neurons become so precisely interconnected in development? Is neural activity important for development of patterned connections? These and other questions have yet to be fully answered but it is testament to the significance of his work that many of his early studies are frequently cited alongside contemporary investigations. More generally Sperry was quick to recognise the wider implications of the evidence that many mental abilities are carried out, supported and coordinated predominantly in one cerebral hemisphere or the other. He was a staunch critic of the prevailing educational systems of the West, as well as science in general, for their neglect of nonverbal forms of intellect. Society, he argued, discriminates against the right hemisphere.

Roger Sperry's major writings

Gazzaniga, M. S., Bogen, J. E., & Sperry, R. W. (1962). Some functional effects of sectioning the cerebral commissures in man. *Proceedings of the National Academy of Sciences of the United States of America, 48*(10), 1765–1769.

Gazzaniga, M. S., & Sperry, R. W. (1967). Language after section of the cerebral commissures. *Brain: A Journal of Neurology, 90*(1), 131–148.

Sperry, R. W. (1939). Action current study in movement coordination. *Journal of General Psychology, 20,* 295–313.

Sperry, R. W. (1943). Effect of 180-degree rotation of the retinal field on visuomotor coordination. *Journal of Experimental Zoology, 92,* 263–279.

Sperry, R. W. (1951). Mechanisms of neural maturation. In S. S. Stevens (Ed.), *Handbook of experimental psychology* (pp. 236–280). New York: Wiley.

Sperry, R. W. (1952). Neurology and the mind-brain problem. *American Scientist, 40,* 291–312.

Sperry, R. W. (1959). Preservation of high order function in isolated somatic cortes in callosum-sectioned cats. *Journal of Neurophysiology, 22,* 78–87.

Sperry, R. W. (1969). A modified concept of consciousness. *Psychological Review, 76*(6), 532–536.

Sperry, R. W. (1981). Changing priorities. *Annual Review of Neuroscience, 4,* 1–15.

Further reading

Schmitt, F. O., & Warden, E. G. (Eds.). (1974). *The neurosciences.* Third Study Program. Cambridge, MA: MIT Press.

Voneide, T. J. (1997). Roger Wolcott Sperry. *Biographical Memoirs of Fellows of the Royal Society, 43,* 463–471.

46 Vygotsky (Vygotskii, Vygodskaya), Lev (Leon) Semeonovich (1896–1934)

Vygotsky formulated a theory of cognitive development based on the linkages between social-historical factors, as reflected in educational systems, and those of a more imminent inter-personal nature, such as parent-child interactions.

Vygotsky was born the second eldest of eight children to a middle-class Jewish family and grew up in Gomel (his father was the bank manager), near Belarus' borders with Russia and with the Ukraine. His mother, Cecilia, was fluent in several languages and although trained as a teacher never taught for any appreciable length of time. Though greatly interested in the arts and humanities, the fact that Jews were prohibited from teaching in public schools directed him to a career in medicine and he entered Moscow's medical school by dint of academic merit and good luck, the Jewish entry quota having been altered from selection to lottery. He transferred from medicine to law after about a month and took several courses on which Zinaida, one of his sisters, had also enrolled. At that time it was possible to register at more than one university, and in 1914 he also registered for a degree in humanities at Shanavsky's University – though it was not a qualification recognised by the government of the day. There he was offered an opportunity to read widely – his thesis was on Hamlet – before returning to Gomel in late 1917. Much of the time at home was spent caring for his mother, who had contracted tuberculosis, and his 13-year-old brother, who died from typhoid before the year was out. Lev was diagnosed with tuberculosis in 1919, a disease that was to kill him at the age of 37. On returning to Gomel, he also taught at various institutions, established a psychology laboratory at a teachers' college and wrote a psychology text for teachers. During this period, he read widely and familiarised himself with the works of James and Freud. He also pursued his interests in the arts and founded the literary journal *Verask*. In January 1924, he

DOI: 10.4324/9781003229179-47

presented three papers at the Second Psychoneurological Congress in Leningrad. These argued against Pavlov's 'reflexology' as a psychology of consciousness, and in support of the less mechanistic 'reactology' (the study of mental effort as reflected in peripheral motor activity such as the speed with which a person would react to a physical stimulus) favoured by K.N. Kornilov, Director of the Institute of Experimental Psychology at Moscow. Vygotsky was offered a position at the Institute and there encountered neuropsychologist Luria, who was at that time a psychoanalyst. During his time at the institute, Vygotsky wrote his doctoral thesis on the psychology of art. Like Luria he had a wide range of interests and pursued several of these including 'defectology', a term which does not have a literal English language equivalent but loosely refers to the education of children with sensory, physical and learning impairments. At this time Vygotsky was promoting applications of a version of Kornilov's reactology, as reflected in his use of reaction-time measures, to the analysis of a range of problem-solving activities. Kornilov was an advocate of a version of psychology broadly similar to Watson's behaviourism although he did not reject a consideration of psychological states to the same degree. Vygotsky's adaptation of Kornilov's position was based on less mechanistic principles, reflecting his attempt to incorporate a place for social and cultural influences in the analysis and explanation of behaviour.

Vygotsky's most influential work is his conceptualisation of the representation of knowledge and the significance of interrelationships between the macro- and micro-social influences. His analysis is directed by the importance of the linkages between social-historical factors, as reflected in the educational systems into which a child is introduced, and those of a more imminent interpersonal nature, such as parent-child interaction. For example, Vygotsky took the view that language is not simply a tool whereby the mental activity of one individual, the parent, interacts with that of another, the child. It is a contrivance that has shaped cultural change and is integral to the environment given to both adults and their children. This position on the nature and function of language partly reflects the influence of a more radical position that had been formulated much earlier by Wilhelm von Humboldt. von Humboldt formulated the Weltanschauung (world view) hypothesis: thought is impossible without language and language determines thought. How people come to think is a product of the particular language that is the prevailing medium of expression for their society. Vygotsky's constructivist framework demands a very significant role for social and cultural factors and in this regard is a good deal more sophisticated than the extreme determinism favoured by von Humboldt. It is somewhat similar to Piaget's in its claim that learning and development involve fusing new information with existing knowledge structures and adjusting prior understanding. Unlike Piaget, Vygotsky considered the development of thinking, cognitive development, as more than a progressive construction of more complex structures on simpler ones. Cognitive development is a socio-genetic process: it is carried out in the social activities of children with adults who have the potential to generate and lead development. The essence and uniqueness of human behaviour lie in the intercession of social tools and social signs, particularly language. Vygotsky's theory is based on four main tenets: (i) children construct their knowledge of the world, (ii) development cannot be isolated from its social and cultural context, (iii) learning can lead to development and (iv) language plays a crucial role in cognitive development.

Vygotsky places thinking and problem-solving in three groups: some kinds of thinking can be performed independently by the child and others cannot be performed even with help. Between these two are things a child can do with guidance. He referred to the difference between what a child can do with assistance and what she can do independently as the zone of proximal development (ZPD). With the assistance and guidance of adults, a child will develop the ability to complete tasks on their own. The ZPD is central to Vygotsky's framework and captures his belief that learning is a socially and culturally mediated activity. The ZPD can be thought of as the difference between the actual development level of a child, as determined by independent problem-solving, and their level of potential development, as determined through problem-solving under adult guidance or in collaboration with more capable peers. Development is nothing less than a dialectical process of mastering cultural tools and resources. Drawing on his knowledge and experience in the area of defectology, Vygotsky opposed the ideas of William Stern, who devised the notion of mental age and intelligence quotient (IQ), in preference for a view of intellectual disability as a process rather than a static condition with which a child is lumbered from birth. Pursuing this line of argument, and consonant with the ideas of Luria, he suggested that psychological assessment should focus on understanding mental processing and specifically the strategies employed by the child to solve a whole range of problems with which they are confronted. Like Piaget, he valued the analysis of errors for what it could reveal about a child's problem-solving strategies and inform the beneficial interventions of the teacher.

Vygotsky was strongly committed to the development of a Marxist psychology consonant with the characteristics of a natural science. Neither the founders of Marxism nor the contemporary Soviet psychologists of his time had made much progress in completing this task, though not for the want of trying. For example, Aleksei Leont'ev spent much of his career attempting to formulate a position based on the Marxist thesis and Vygotsky's psychology and in so doing developed a theoretical position not dissimilar from Gibson's ecological optics. Vygotsky's efforts were directed to formulating a psychology based on laws that establish the concepts through which human activity might be described. In his view, Watson's behaviourism was correct in its assertion that a scientific psychology is only possible as a natural science but, while recognising and defining the task, it failed to complete the Marxist task by virtue of its neglect of social, historical and cultural forces. The Gestalt proposition, as developed by Wertheimer and others, could be regarded as an improvement because, in introducing the concept of structure to the analysis of experience, it combined both descriptive (behavioural) and functional (adaptive) accounts of behaviour. Gestalt theory is a materialistic psychology that approximates behaviourism but offers more because it can accommodate internal, mental processes such as 'ideas' and 'thought'. Vygotsky took the view that contemporaneous Marxist formulations, while achieving a degree of conceptual purchase on the contribution of social forces, had failed to reach the achievements of the behaviourists in America and Gestalt psychologists in Germany. What Vygotsky was attempting imposed a requirement to identify a new unit of study for psychology, as well as a new way of thinking about method:

> The search for method becomes one of the most important problems of the entire enterprise of understanding the uniquely human forms of psychological activity. In this case, the method is simultaneously prerequisite and product, the tool and the result of the study.
> (Vygotsky, 1978, p. 65)

Vygotsky's conception of method is closely linked with that of praxis – his method is not just about the systematic application of technique, it is about something to be practised. Vygotsky could have pursued his alternative to Watson's behaviourism and the Gestaltists in its theoretical form, but his concern with method almost certainly influenced his preference to follow an empirical, evolutionist route that explored cultural differences in thinking. This work was strongly influenced by his collaboration with Luria and included a series of studies of peasant communities in Uzbekistan. Those studies showed that Uzbeks either could not or would not categorise perceptual stimuli on the basis of Gestalt laws of similarity. For example, they would not classify a triangle drawn as a series of short, dotted lines with an equivalent triangle with a solid line perimeter. Instead, they preferred to categorise on the basis of the objects they thought they could associate with the forms. For instance, the triangle with the solid line perimeter might be classified as a spearhead, whereas the triangle constructed of short, dotted lines might be classified as a kind of tree. One reading of this research contends that this was an intellectually motivated investigation of thinking as a culturally embedded activity. Another points to the absence of any discernible resistance to the politicisation of the findings (Uzbeks who had received Soviet education showed signs of the higher mental process typical of the Russians, whereas others did not) as so-called 'scientific' support for Soviet policies directed to the extermination of millions of Islamic folk living in Uzbekistan.

Vygotsky's work was slow to have an impact on European and American psychology. There were several reasons for this. First, his work was banned from publication under the Soviet regime until 1956. Kornilov's reactology, Bekhterev's reflexology and Vygotsky's constructivism were viewed as failing to adequately represent Marxist Leninist psychology and rejected in favour of Pavlov's model of brain functioning. Second, his death at the age of 37 meant that his international presence was not well established. For example, he was aware of Piaget's work and commented on it in his own writing, but Piaget was unaware of Vygotsky's until late in his own career. Third, differences between the Russian and American psychological traditions imposed a combination of ideological and terminological barriers. Bruner and others were instrumental in introducing Vygotsky's ideas to the attention of psychologists in the English-speaking world but even the timing of that entrée was a matter of coincidence: Bruner first heard of Vygotsky's ideas at a party in the home of neurologist Wilder Penfield's. Bruner was particularly struck by the parallels between his own ideas on language and thought and incorporated many of Vygotsky's positions into his cultural account of a naturalistic developmental theory.

Lev Vygotsky's major writings

Rieber, R. W. & Carton, A. S. (Eds.). (1988). *The collected works of L.S. Vygotsky*. New York: Springer.
Vygotsky, L. S. (1978). *Mind in society: The development of higher psychological processes*. Massachusetts: Harvard University Press.

Further reading

Luria, A. R. (1935). Professor Leon Semenovich Vygotskii. *Journal of Genetic Psychology*, 46, 224–226.
Van der Veer, R., & Valsiner, J. (1991). *Understanding Vygotsky's: A quest for synthesis*. New Jersey: Blackwell.

47 Wilhelm Maximilian Wundt (1832–1920)

Wundt is generallt credited with founding the discipline of psychology as a separate science and established the first experimental psychology.

Wundt was born at Neckarau, a suburb of Mannheim. The son of a Lutheran minister, Maximilian Wundt, and Marie Frederike, he was the youngest of four children; only he and a brother 8 years his elder survived infancy. At the age of 4, the family moved to Heidelsheim. Wundt was shy and timid, his only childhood friend being a mentally handicapped boy with severe communication difficulties. For a time, his liberal education was supervised by a young vicar who worked in his father's church. At 13 he enrolled at the Bruchsal Gymnasium, and it was perhaps not too surprising that this introduction to a formal education environment proved to be something of a personal and academic disaster. He found it very difficult to make friends, endured a regime of corporal punishment and was regarded by his teachers as an academic failure whose time might be better spent planning for a career in the postal service. A move to the Heidelberg Lyceum, where his older brother and a cousin were both pupils, brought some improvement both personally and academically. His father died during his first year at the Lyceum. After graduating, he enrolled on the pre-medical degree at Tubingen University and after a year transferred to the University of Heidelberg, where he was an outstanding medical student. After graduating, he studied physiology at Berlin with Johannes Müller and Émil du Bois-Reymond with the intention of pursuing a career in experimental physiology. However, he returned to Heidelberg, where he completed a Docent in Physiology shortly before Helmholtz's arrival as Professor and Head of the Physiology Department. He was for a short time a laboratory assistant to Helmholtz and shared space with the Russian physiologist Ivan Sechenov, though Sechenov recalled that Wundt

DOI: 10.4324/9781003229179-48

was so withdrawn he never actually heard him speak (Thorne and Henley, 2001). The American psychologist G. Stanley Hall maintained that Helmholtz had dismissed Wundt for mathematical ineptitude, although Wundt disputed that claim and pointed out that Helmholtz was always supportive.

After leaving Heidelberg, Wundt had a brief career in politics that included election to the Baden Parliament in 1867 before returning there to a teaching position in 1871. He married Sophie Mau the same year. A brief period at Heidelberg, during which his most influential book *Principles of Physiological Psychology* (1873–1874) was published, was followed by an even shorter one as Professor of Philosophy at the University of Zurich. In 1874, Leipzig offered the Chair in Philosophy to Kuno Fischer, who declined because he was at the time Rector at Heidelberg. The Chair and the salary were split and offers made to Max Heinze to fill a new professorship in the history of philosophy and to Wundt who took up the position of Professor of Physiology in 1875. He remained there for the rest of his career, completing his autobiography at the age of 85 – 8 days before his death. In the same year, he took up the chair at Leipzig, Wundt established a laboratory dedicated to experimental psychology located in the Konvikt, a building which once stood in the court of the university building at Augustusplatz. Seven years later, it was officially designated the Institute for Experimental Psychology. All subsequent psychological laboratories were closely modelled in their early years on Wundt's Institute. In 1882, the neuropsychiatrist Paul Flechsig established a laboratory for cerebral-anatomical investigations of a range of psychiatric disorders. The presence of both laboratories attracted some of the best minds to Leipzig, including Pavlov, Spearman, Titchener James McKeen Cattell, Granville Stanley Hall and Hugo Münsterberg. The consensus view is that Wundt established the first experimental psychology laboratory although this has been contested and the position one takes on this depends on the kind of facility one is prepared to count as a lab. That in turn depends on what one counts as experimental psychology. By 1875, James had a small room containing various pieces of equipment for demonstration purposes. However, if a 'small room' criterion is applied, then Wundt had use of such space from 1865 – he used it to store various pieces of physiological and psychophysical equipment. If a 'significant laboratory' criterion is applied – as claimed by G. Stanley Hall – then the facility Hall founded in 1881 counts as the first. (Cambridge University might have had the first laboratory had they not rejected a proposal first mooted around 1875.) The chronological detail in this debate is relatively unimportant – its interest lies in the way it throws light on the spirited scientific forces and competitive personalities of the period.

Wundt supervised 166 doctoral dissertations in psychology over his career, and his efforts to establish and propagate the new experimental psychology are reflected in the fact that he was one of the most prolific writers in the history of psychology. Boring (1957) estimated that between 1853 and 1920 he wrote about 54,000 pages – an average of one word every 2 minutes, 24 hours per day for 68 years. The list of principal publications given later represents the tip of an iceberg. Although the hugely influential *Principles of Physiological Psychology* went through several revisions, Wundt felt he needed a more effective method of disseminating the findings emanating from his laboratory and in 1881 established *Philosophische Studien* to achieve that purpose. He originally intended to name the journal *Psychologische Studien* (*Psychological Studies*) but that name was taken by a different publication specialising in spiritualism and psychical investigations.

In *Principles of Physiological Psychology*, Wundt set out the case for an alliance between physiology and psychology, the product being a new science he called 'physiological psychology' or 'experimental psychology', as it would be called today. For Wundt the goal of psychology was to study all aspects of human experience, and he made a basic distinction between the methodological requirements for the investigation of lower mental processes, such as seeing and hearing, and higher mental processes such as language and thought. While it is very clear that he considered experimental methods to be perfectly suited to the investigation of lower level processes, his position on their suitability for the examination of higher mental functions, such as language, and social processes, such the behaviour of social groups, is less clear. Some historians take the view that Wundt considered non-experimental methods, such as comparative analysis and historical analysis, to be more appropriate to the study of higher mental functions and social processes. To support their position, they refer to the fact that he developed a Völkerpsychologie (social psychology) that is somewhat different from his physiological psychology. Other historians take a different view and suggest that some of Wundt's arguments have been taken out of context and that he regarded experimental methods to be suitable to the analysis of social processes but he didn't apply them himself because he was not personally interested in that field of psychology.

A core idea in Wundt's thinking is the distinction between immediate and mediate experience. He argued that other sciences, such as the physical sciences, were based on mediate experience: the development and use of special instruments to measure reality as it is. For example, spectrometers could be used to measure the wavelengths of light and thereby provide an experience of the world mediated by this apparatus. The mediated experience does not resemble light as it is usually experienced – the 'immediate' experience of light. Thus, for Wundt the science of psychology is concerned with investigating the world as it is experienced and specifically with using experimental techniques to examine consciousness – immediate experience as it occurs. This position contrasts with that promoted by others, such as Oswald Külpe, who rejected the distinction between immediate and mediate experience and promoted the use of systematic experimental introspection to study complex thinking – something which Wundt regarded as an impossible venture because thought cannot be observed while one is thinking. Using a model taken from the physical sciences, Wundt pursued a lifelong programme of enquiry with the goals of (i) detecting and describing the basic elements of immediate experience and (ii) discovering the universal laws that govern the way in which the basic elements are combined into more complex mental experiences. The majority of the studies conducted in his laboratory focused on the analysis of sensation, perception, reaction times and attention. The kind of experiment he designed is illustrated by his 'thought meter'. This is a relatively simple device comprising a clock with a bell and a pendulum that swings across a calibrated scale. He noticed it was possible to attend to the sound of the bell or to the precise position of the pendulum against the scale, but not both experiences simultaneously. There was a gap of about one-tenth of a second in shifting the focus of attention from one to the other. His studies on attention led him to distinguish between perception (a term he used to refer to all of those automatic, involuntary processes involved in responding to a physical stimulus) and apperception (the part of the perceptual field a person attends to – apperception and attention are synonyms and refer to active processes under voluntary control). His concept of apperception was intended to capture the creative synthesis of all of the elements of immediate experience and, therefore, has sometimes been referred to as the law of psychic resultants. The philosopher Gottfried Leibniz originally used 'apperception' to refer to that part of perception concerned with the interpretation and recognition of what is perceived, while Immanuel Kant and Johann Herbart also used it to refer to the processes of assimilating and interpreting new sensory impressions. Wundt used the term still more selectively to refer to the active mental process by which individuals voluntarily select and structure internal experience and focus consciousness. Focusing of attention involves a deliberate, voluntary, purposeful act of will – this is a core feature of Wundt's system of psychology and indicates why it is usually referred to as *voluntarism*. The implication of Wundt's distinction can be illustrated as follows. Imagine a situation where one knows a person's complete biography in every detail. In theory one could use that knowledge to accurately predict how they would react when presented with a particular stimulus. Apperceived stimuli are subject to quite different forces, such as inner motives, emotions and free will and are subject to laws of psychic rather than physical causality. Wundt concluded that reactions to apperceived stimuli cannot be predicted with any accuracy because psychology, as he understood it, could not gain sufficient conceptual or experimental purchase on the conscious experience of 'voluntary effort'.

Some of Wundt's students attempted to measure the span of apperception and the psychiatrist Emil Kraepelin extended Wundt's idea on the control of attention to the study of 'dementia praecox' ('insanity of the young' – an early name for schizophrenia). Wundt's training in physiology led him to think that the neuroanatomical locus of the process of apperception was situated in the frontal lobes of the cerebral cortex, a position consistent with the view of a number of eminent physiologists who took the view that this part of the brain was connected with intelligence. He also thought that the physiological substrate of the apperception process was necessarily an inhibitory one because one of its primary functions was to restrain the unwanted interference of other neural excitations not directly involved with the process.

Introspection was an important tool of experimental psychology, but it is important to make a distinction between the way Wundt used the term and how it is conventionally understood. Wundt was adamant that introspection – the process of analytic self-reflection – had no place in experimental psychology. This may surprise those readers who will be familiar with the way Wundt is profiled in some introductory texts as a leading exponent of introspective methods of enquiry; he was, but most definitely not in the way often implied by the term. His approach was based on the development and systematic application of techniques that were intended to uncover the content and structure of internal perceptions. His 'introspection' is founded on the systematic investigation of internal perceptions. This kind of introspection was only possible with appropriate training, and he insisted that everyone in his laboratory should be trained to the required standard. The analysis of internal perceptions was based on rigorous adherence to specific rules: (i) immediate rather than mediate experiences must be reported, (ii) the observer needed to be aware when a stimulus was about to be introduced and not taken by surprise, (iii) they should be at a heightened state of attention, (iv) their reports of their internal perceptions needed to be repeated many times and (v) the conditions under which internal perceptions were reported needed to be varied systematically in order to ensure the results could be generalised across a wide range of situations. Using this approach, he developed a three-dimensional theory of feelings: pleasurable-unpleasurable, strain-relaxation and arousing-subduing. Using the 'method of expression', some of Wundt's students tried to relate the dimensions back to specific physiological changes in pulse, breathing and so on. These were mostly unsuccessful although later attempts to map the structure of basic emotional experiences have identified dimensions that are somewhat similar to Wundt's.

Although Wundt is the acknowledged founding father of experimental psychology and a prolific author, he has often been misunderstood. He founded two psychologies – experimental psychology and Völkerpsychologie. He is principally remembered for the former, and his Völkerpsychologie is hardly ever referenced in introductory textbooks on psychology. However, he devoted a great deal of time to philosophical and sociological analyses of higher mental functions as expressed in language, myth, art forms and social customs. For example, he published studies on the psychological interpretation of language, with a particular emphasis on the interrelation of psychical and physiological factors in the development of language structure. His approach to the analysis of social groups, which he pursued through an examination of language, was based on his belief that the language and vocabulary of people could provide insights into their psychology. There is a great deal of later research interest in the relationship between a person's language and their identity. It was left to the philosopher and historian of culture Wilhelm Dilthey to take up the challenge as it was posed by Wundt, namely that higher level mental processes could be studied using experimental techniques. Dilthey argued that whereas the physical world could be understood using systematic observation and the identification of laws, the social world could only be understood with reference to the meanings generated by its inhabitants. He took the view that psychology should be the preferred method of the 'cultural sciences', just as mathematics is the gold standard of the natural sciences. It was a big idea for psychology – too big to be embraced with any degree of confidence by a young discipline still carving its own identity as a natural science.

Many of Wundt's students developed and modified his approach, and this in part may account for his characterisation as an experimental psychologist with a commitment to reductive explanations for human behaviour. For example, Titchener was one of Wundt's most eminent pupils but the school of structuralism that he established in North

America is in many respects a far cry from the philosophical positions underpinning Wundt's two psychologies, his voluntarism and his view that higher mental processes could not be fractionated using experimental methods. Wundt's work did not 'lead' to structuralism in any simple or direct way because he did not set out to explain human consciousness as a structured aggregate of basic elements. Thus, many of the stock criticisms levelled against Wundt – his reliance on introspection, his commitment to reductionism and the idea that his framework presaged the emergence of Titchener's structuralism – are simply wrong and much of the work of contemporary historians of psychology has concentrated on correcting the numerous misunderstandings that have crept into historical profiles of his ideas and methods.

Wilhelm Wundt's major writings

Greenwood, J. D. (2003). Wundt, Völkerpsychologie, and experimental social psychology. *History of Psychology*, 6(1), 70–88.

Wundt, W. (1894). *Lectures on human and animal psychology*. New York: Macmillan.

Wundt, W. (1911). *Einführung in die Psychologie* [Introduction to psychology]. Leipzig: Voigtländer.

Wundt, W. (1920). *Erlebtes und Erkanntes (What I have experienced and discovered)*. Stuttgart: Alfred Kröne.

Wundt, W. (1948). Principles of physiological psychology, 1873. In W. Dennis (Ed.), *Readings in the history of psychology* (pp. 248–250). New York: Appleton-Century-Crofts.

Further reading

Blumenthal, A. L. (1975). A re-appraisal of Wilhelm Wundt. *American Psychologist*, 1081–1088.

Bringmann, W. G., Balance, W. D. G., & Evans, R. B. (1975). Wilhelm Wundt 1832–1920: A brief biographical sketch. *Journal of the History of the Behavioral Sciences*, 11, 287–297.

Kirschmann, A. (1895). Review of Lectures on human and animal psychology [Review of the book *Lectures on human and animal psychology*, by W. Wundt]. *Psychological Review*, 2(2), 179.

Rieber, R. W. (Ed.). (1980). *Wilhelm Wundt and the making of a scientific psychology*. New York: Plenum.

Thorne, B. M., & Henley, T. B. (2001). *Connections in the history and systems of psychology*. Boston: Houghton Mifflin.

Titchener, E. B. (1921). Wilhelm Wundt. *American Journal of Psychology*, 32, 161–178.

48 Philip George Zimbardo (March 23, 1933) – at the time of writing aged 90

Zimbardo designed the Stanford Prison Experiment, a study of iconic status that it alerts us to the consequences of deindividuation and of the need to mitigate its pernicious effects.

The son of George and Margaret (Bisicchia), Philip Zimbardo spend his childhood and adolescence in the South Bronx ghetto of New York. At the age of five and a half, he contracted double pneumonia and whooping cough and spent 6 months in a grim hospital ward for children with life-threatening contagious diseases. He and Stanley Milgram were in the 12th grade at James Munroe High School and lost contact with one another but met up again in 1960. By then Milgram had been appointed Assistant Professor at Yale and Zimbardo was holding down a position at New York University while moonlighting at Yale in order to make enough money to live in the Big Apple. While completing a master's at Yale, Zimbardo was influenced by Carl Hovland, who had published work on persuasive communication and attitude change, including the effects of propaganda films on military personnel during wartime. Zimbardo's doctoral thesis explored the determinants of opinion conformity.

The starting point for Zimbardo's most influential contribution to psychology is his observation that Milgram's investigations of obedience to authority were limited to situations where a potent authority figure, such as someone masquerading as a laboratory scientist, had direct control of research participants and constantly monitored their behaviour. However, in many real-world circumstances where people comply with unreasonable demands, the authority figure is usually not present. Instead, the authority figure must create the psychological conditions under which others can be trusted to comply with their odious demands. In a replication and extension to Milgram's work he ensured

DOI: 10.4324/9781003229179-49

that, during the period where participants were required to shock a person they believed to be a hapless victim, there was no authority figure present. In an extended program of work, he identified the conditions under which people will comply in the absence of authority. These include removing a person's sense of uniqueness by placing them in a group environment and creating a sense of anonymity and disguise by requiring them to wear uniforms. Under these circumstances, people endure diminished cognitive functioning – their problem-solving skills and level of critical awareness appear to be reduced – and the effect can be enhanced by offering alcohol and other intoxicants. Bandura extended this line of work by considering the minimal conditions necessary to create a degree of dehumanisation.

Zimbardo argues that being in the presence of others can cause deindividuation, a feeling of anonymity and a reduced sense of ourselves as individuals. Under these circumstances, people appear to experience a sense of reduced accountability – a perceived reduction in the likelihood that they will be held responsible for their actions. Zimbardo's ideas were influenced by several well-established theories of collective behaviour. For example, the ideas of the French physician and social psychologist Gustav Le Bon were influential in early theories of crowd behaviour. Le Bon's ideas were not well organised and largely based on anecdotal studies conducted during the French Revolutions and observations of mob behaviour on the streets of Paris. Le Bon concluded that crowds are inherently irrational and ostensibly governed by a collective, primitive mind. However, crowd behaviour can be purposeful because the crowd provides opportunities for people with similar attributes to find a collective of like-minded individuals through which similar needs and personal characteristics can find expression. Le Bon implicated three processes in the governance of crown behaviour: anonymity, which reduces a sense of responsibility and increases a sense of power; contagion: which causes shared feelings to propagate very quickly through the crowd; and suggestibility: which facilitates a less critical acceptance of instructions from others about how one should behave. An alternative position contends that aggressive behaviour is a product of the kind of people who turn up as part of a crowd and who, through a process of convergence, alter the norms regarding the acceptability of violent behaviour. Zimbardo's deindividuation theory draws on parts of both positions to explain the diminution of personal constraints that sometimes occurs in groups. This process can be structured into three components: inputs, internal changes and behavioural outcomes. Inputs, or the causes of deindividuation, include feelings of anonymity, diffusion of responsibility and a heightened state of physiological arousal. Internal changes associated with the deindividuated state involve, first, a reduced sense of self-awareness favourable to the uninhibited performance of a range of tasks and, second, altered experiences such as disturbances in concentration and judgment and a sense of unreality. The destructive consequences of deindividuation can include callous acts of omission (e.g. failing to notice and respond to the plight of those in distress) and acts of commission leading to violence towards others. Paradoxically, one of the consequences of this process of deindividuation is that, given appropriate pro-social cues, people may sometimes behave altruistically and in so doing re-establish a sense of individuality and personal responsibility.

Zimbardo is credited with a series of ingenious experiments, conducted with his graduate students Craig Haney and Curt Banks, that examined the anatomy of social accountability and deindividuation. For example, in one study participants were invited to put on lab coats and hoods as soon as they arrived. Names were not used and the room was darkened to preserve anonymity. In a comparison condition, the participants wore their normal clothes, had large name tags and sat in a well-light room. All of the participants were then instructed to deliver (supposed) electric shocks to another person. Those in the anonymous condition behaved considerably more aggressively towards the person, delivering more and longer shocks. Zimbardo extended his research beyond highly contrived laboratory contexts in a famous, but controversial, study known as the Stanford Prison Experiment. Students who had volunteered for a psychological study of prison life were 'arrested' and confined to a simulated prison in the basement of the Stanford University psychology building. The 'guards' were also paid volunteers. In time, the participants started to behave according to their role: they behaved more and more like actual prisoners or actual guards in real prisons. The scheduled 2-week study had to be terminated after only 6 days because of the fairly brutal ways the student-guards were treating the so-called prisoners. In effect, Zimbardo and his colleagues had demonstrated that people would use implicit and explicit social norms concerning the roles they were occupying and allow those to shape their behaviour. It has been argued that people who participated in the study were merely behaving as they thought they were expected to behave, but Zimbardo and others have countered that even if they were simply 'playing the roles' they were in effect no different from others occupying those roles for the first time in real prisons. The study was published the same year he married Christina Maslach, and they had a son and a daughter. (He had another son by an earlier marriage.)

The timing of the Stanford Prison Experiment coincided with prison riots at San Quentin and Attica. Politicians, clamouring for an explanation while trying to assuage moral panic in the media, wanted to hear about Zimbardo's work. Thus, an oral report was presented to the Congressional Subcommittee on Prison Reform and the Stanford Prison Experiment was set to become one the best-known psychological studies. Some of its strongest critics contend that while it has a veneer of validity that accolade is unjustified. For example, the psychoanalyst Erich Fromm argued: 'The difference between the mock prisoners and real prisoners is so great that it is virtually impossible to draw analogies from observation of the former' (Fromm, 1973, p. 90). Fromm went on to argue that, apart from a general lack of precision in the presentation of the findings, the study lacked convergent validity: no attempt was made to check the results against the experiences of inmates in prisons of the same type. Consonant with that criticism is the fact that the study is usually not cited in mainstream texts on prison psychology and criminology. Zimbardo has replied that studies of real-world conflicts show that, in the great majority of cases, nations and societies make conspicuous changes to their appearance in a manner consistent with his deindividuation and dehumanisation hypothesis.

An unexpected outcome of the Stanford prison experiment led Zimbardo to initiate a ground-breaking line of research into shyness. Zimbardo was particularly struck by the degree to which many 'prisoners' would adapt to the bullying and arbitrary tactics imposed by the 'guards'. Some prisoners appeared to trade their autonomy for the role of the 'good prisoner' and in so doing internalised negative self-images. Zimbardo inferred that these 'prisoners' appeared to despise themselves and noted that they were reviled by their 'guards' as weak and ineffectual. Zimbardo extended the prisoner-guard metaphor to a conceptualisation of shyness as a self-imposed prison of silence and social confinement. However, at that time there was almost no research on shyness and what little there was related almost exclusively to children. Thus, he set about conducting a number of large-sample surveys which showed that 40% of respondents reported being chronically shy while only about 5% believed they were never shy. He followed this with a multi-method program using case studies, in-depth interviews as well as experimental and observational techniques, and the findings have informed the development of a hugely successful intervention program for shy adults based on a combination of individual and group cognitive behaviour therapy. His early survey studies also inspired others to explore the relationships between shyness and disorders such as social phobia and social anxiety.

Why did Zimbardo and Milgram conduct their studies on authority and compliance when they did? Awareness of what went on in Auschwitz, Treblinka and Nazi prisoner of war camps was probably at least partly responsible. Their investigations could also be regarded as just another manifestation of a prevailing anxiety in American mood of the period. For example, in 1950 the sociologist David Riesman published an enormously popular paperback, *The Lonely Crowd*, that focused on understanding how the increasing power of corporate and government institutions influenced national character. That book, a best-seller throughout the 1950s, explored basic questions about conformity and individuality in post-war America and its ideas and arguments figured in a great deal of social and political commentary of the period. More specifically, the Stanford Prison Experiment can be regarded as a logical extension of the highly influential studies of conformity and obedience reported by Asch and Milgram. Like Milgram, Zimbardo demonstrated that people are capable of odious behaviour under circumstances which common sense predicts they will rebel. Like Milgram's work, it is almost certain that replication of his prison experiment would not receive ethical approval. Everett Dean Martin, a political theorist and analyst of crowd behaviour, once remarked that the real value in studying crowds lies in the insight one gains into the destructive potential of crowd-mindedness and the need to guard against its tyranny. Similarly, the almost iconic status of the Stanford Prison Experiment may be due to the fact that it alerts us to the consequences of deindividuation and of the need to mitigate its pernicious effects.

Philip Zimbardo's major writings

Haney, C., Banks, W. C., & Zimbardo, P. G. (1973). A study of prisoners and guards in a simulated prison. *Naval Research Review, 30*, 4–17.

Zimbardo, P. G. (1970). The human choice: Individuation, reason, and order versus deindividuation, impulse, and chaos. In W. J. Arnold & D. Levine (Eds.), *1969 Nebraska symposium on motivation* (pp. 237–307). Lincoln, NE: University of Nebraska Press.

Zimbardo, P. G. (1971). The power and pathology of imprisonment. *Congressional Record*. (Serial No. 15, October 25, 1971). Hearings before Subcommittee No. 3, of the Committee on the Judiciary, House of Representatives, Ninety-Second Congress, First Session on Corrections, Part II, Prisons, Prison Reform and Prisoner's Rights: California. Washington, DC: U.S. Government Printing Office.

Zimbardo, P. G. (1972). Pathology of imprisonment. *Society, 6*(4), 6–8.

Zimbardo, P. G., & Leippe, M. R. (1991). *The psychology of attitude change and social influence*. New York: McGraw-Hill Book Company.

Zimbardo, P. G., & Radl, S. L. (1981). *The shy child*. New York: McGraw Hill.

Further reading

Banuazizi, A., & Movahedi, S. (1975). Interpersonal dynamics in a simulated prison: A methodological analysis. *American Psychologist, 30*, 152–160.

Crozier, W. R. (2001). *Understanding shyness: Psychological perspectives.* Palgrave.

Fromm, E. (1973). *The anatomy of human destructiveness.* New York: Holt, Rineheart and Winston.

Drury, S., Hutchens, S. A., Shuttlesworth, D. E., & White, C. L. (2012). Philip G. Zimbardo on his career and the Stanford Prison Experiment's 40th anniversary. *History of Psychology, 15*(2), 161–170.

Index

312   *Index*

Printed in Great Britain
by Amazon